THREE TREATISES ON MAN

CISTERCIAN FATHERS SERIES: NUMBER TWENTY-FOUR

THREE TREATISES ON MAN

A Cistercian Anthropology

Edited by
Bernard McGinn

CISTERCIAN PUBLICATIONS
Kalamazoo, Michigan
1977

Ecclesiastical permission to publish this volume was received from Bernard J. Flanagan, Bishop of Worcester, 5 September 1972.

© 1977, Cistercian Publications, Inc.
1749 West Michigan Avenue—WMU
Kalamazoo, MI 49008

Cistercian Studies Series   ISBN 0 87907 000 5

Three Treatises on Man:
A Cistercian Anthropolgy   ISBN 0 87907 024 2

Library of Congress Catalogue Card Number: 77-184906

Available in Europe and the Commonwealth from
A. R. Mowbray & Co Ltd
Osney Mead
Oxford OX2 0EG

Title Page design by Gale Akins at Humble Hills Graphics; Kalamazoo
Printed in the United States of America

CONTENTS

ABBREVIATIONS

Note: For references to Sacred Scripture the abbreviations found in the Revised Standard Version are employed.

AHDL	*Archives d'histoire doctrinale et littéraire du moyen âge*
BGPM	*Beiträge zur Geschichte der Philosophie und Theologie des Mittelalters*
CC	*Corpus Christianorum*
CF	*Cistercian Fathers Series*
CS	*Cistercian Studies Series*
CSEL	*Corpus scriptorum ecclesiasticorum latinorum*
De hom	Gregory of Nyssa, *De hominis opificio;* PG 44:125-256
De statu	Claudianus Mamertus, *De statu animae;* CSEL 11:3-197
DQA	Augustine of Hippo, *De quantitate animae;* PL 32:1033-80
DS	*Dictionnaire de spiritualité*
DUCS	Hugh of St Victor, *De unione corporis et spiritus;* PL 177: 285-94
Ep an	Isaac of Stella, *Epistola de anima;* PL 194:1875-90
LDE	Gennadius of Marseilles, *Liber de dogmatibus ecclesiasticis;* PL 58: 979-1000
Nat corp	William of St Thierry, *De natura corporis et animae;* PL 180: 695-726 1. *Phys corp Physica corporis;* 695-708 2. *Phys an Physica animae;* 707-26
PG	*Patrologiae cursus completus: series Graeca,* ed. J. P. Migne
PL	*Patrologiae cursus completus: series Latina,* ed. J. P. Migne
RAM	*Revue d'ascétique et de la mystique*
RSPT	*Revue des sciences philosophiques et théologiques*
RTAM	*Recherches de théologie ancienne et médiévale*

FOREWORD

WE PRESENT HERE THREE rather particular and not well known treatises of early Cistercians. Two of the authors are known and well-known, William of St Thierry and Isaac of Stella; the identity of the third we do not know though his treatise has had perhaps more influence than the other two. Aelred's better known *De anima* will appear in a separate volume of the Cistercian Fathers Series. Bernard's anthropology is everywhere evident in his writings but it was never drawn together by him into a single treatise.

We are grateful to the various translators who have worked hard to produce a faithful but readable English version of these texts which are quite technical in their content and concise in their expressions. And we want to say a special word of thanks to Professor Bernard McGinn for his fine introduction and extensive editing.

What perhaps most strikes the reader of these treatises is the fact that these Cistercian scholars, even while drawing heavily on pagan sources, were not able to speak of man without constantly relating him to his God and maker. Man is made in the image of God, this is the key to their anthropology. And this is the significant contribution they can make to present-day thinking—reminding us that man is an image. To understand him we must see him in the light of his Exemplar. Perhaps much of the failure of modern behavioral sciences to truly comprehend man lies in the fact that the men who are

vii

trying to lead the search do not possess this essential key. May these texts invite them and every reader to look within and experience the profound joy of discovering themselves as fascinating images of a good and creative God.

M. Basil Pennington ocso

INTRODUCTION

THE THREE TREATISES ON THE SOUL contained in this volume—none of them previously available in English—may seem bizarre to the modern reader. It would be nonetheless a mistake to dismiss them summarily as the naive products of underdeveloped theology and primitive science. Read on a superficial level they may seem nothing more; but in reality they have valuable insights to offer not only about the nature of medieval thought but also concerning some perennial theological problems.

Even more than many other products of Cistercian thought in the twelfth century, these treatises can only be understood and appreciated in the light of their appropriation and transformation of a rich and varied theological tradition. Without a grasp of their antecedents and context, William of St Thierry, Isaac of Stella, and the anonymous compiler of *The Spirit and the Soul* will make little sense to us. One way to approach the background of these treatises is through the question: "Why did the Cistercian writers compose treatises on the soul (*de anima*) rather than on man (*de homine*)?" Granted the interest that they take in the whole man, why is their anthropology expressed through the medium of a discussion of the soul? How did the soul come to occupy the center of the stage in the medieval theory of man?

THE CONTEXT

SOME BACKGROUND TO THE CISTERCIAN DE ANIMA

The answer to these questions leads us back into the history of the effect of classical understandings of man upon the interpretation of the Christian faith. When the implicit and unthematized anthropology of the Scriptures encountered the complex variations of classical thought upon man, the stage was set for the creation of the patristic anthropologies which provided the *terminus a quo* for medieval theories of man. A few general remarks on the nature of this patristic speculation are necessary to set the context for the Cistercian treatises of the twelfth century.

The Greek creation of the idea of the soul, that which is both the principle of life and the true self, was made possible by the development of the *philosophical* understanding of God, man, and the world.[1] The thought of Plato was a decisive step in this evolution.[2] While it cannot be denied that sections of the Old Testament, especially the Book of Wisdom, and parts of the New Testament as well, were influenced by Greek anthropological thought, the fundamental differences between the Greek and Hebraic views of man have frequently been pointed out by many modern authors.[3] One of the most important of these differences concerns the unity of man. The Scriptural texts usually treat man as a unified being active in history—one to whom the alienation incipient in the distinction of soul and body is unknown. The

1. On the development of the concept of the soul in Greek thought, cf. E. Rohde, *Psyche: the Cult of Souls and Belief in Immortality among the Greeks* (N.Y., 1966). (N.B. Works cited will be referred to in the most recent editions throughout these notes.) Also cf., B. Snell, *The Discovery of Mind: The Greek Origins of European Thought* (N.Y., 1960); E. Dodds, *The Greeks and the Irrational* (Berkeley and Los Angeles, 1963); W. Jaeger, *The Theology of the Early Greek Philosophers* (Oxford, 1967); G. S. Kirk and J. E. Raven, *The Presocratic Philosophers* (N.Y., 1965); and P. Ricoeur, *The Symbolism of Evil* (N.Y. 1967).

2. For Plato on the soul, besides the above, cf. W. K. C. Guthrie, "Plato's Views on the Nature of the Soul," *Recherches sur la tradition platonicienne (Entretiens Hardt* III, Geneva, 1955), pp. 3-22; and T. M. Robinson, *Plato's Psychology* (Toronto, 1970).

3. For the Old Testament doctrine of man, cf. W. Eichrodt, *Man in the Old Testament* (London, 1951); and his *Theology of the Old Testament* (London, 1961), Vol. I, *passim*. For the New Testament some idea of the general doctrine and the difficulties of interpretation can be had by comparing R. Bultmann, *The Theology of the New Testament* (N.Y., 1955), and J. A. Robinson, *The Body: A*

unity of man in Platonic thought (to choose the most influential classical system) is the unity of the soul as the intelligible principle of order behind the appearances of the body.

Despite the many differences, however, there were some profound affinities between Greek and Hebraic anthropology, not least of all in the consciousness present in each tradition of man as a responsible agent. The responsible character of man, as we tend to find it expressed in Greek thought, is conditioned by an intellectualism that equates the right with the rational, while the Biblical sense of responsibility is seen in terms of unquestioning obedience to the will of God. For both, however, man takes individual responsibility and by that very fact achieves a certain unity of consciousness. Man's unity is in a sense the unity of a pilgrim—for the one, he is the pilgrim in the world of history, moving forward and becoming himself by responding to the situations in which he hears the call of God; for the other, he is the pilgrim as observer, ultimately indifferent to the multiplicity of situations in his search for the ideal principles above and beyond history which give meaning to his journey.

Despite the evidence for the influence of Greek ideas in the Scriptures themselves, it was only in the post-testamentary period that the major confrontation between the two systems developed. In two essential areas the writers of early Christianity maintained basic continuity with Biblical anthropology: first, in the conception of man as a responsible agent in history; and second, in the idea that eternal life is the free gift of God, and not something belonging to man by nature.[4] In a third essential area of anthropology, however, there is a marked shift of perspective. Prompted by a collapsing civilization's intense guilt feelings,[5] abetted by the presence of dualistic theories of man in the cultural mileau, the tendency

---

Study in Pauline Theology (London, 1952). For a perceptive treatment of the way in which the Greek and Hebraic views of man condition literary expression, cf. E. Auerbach, *Mimesis* (N.Y., 1957), Chap. I.

4. H. A. Wolfson, "Immortality and Resurrection in the Philosophy of the Church Fathers," *Immortality and Resurrection*, ed. K. Stendahl (N.Y., 1965), pp. 54-96, esp. pp. 57-60.

5. E. R. Dodds, *Pagan and Christian in an Age of Anxiety* (Cambridge, 1965), Chap. I.

became more and more evident to speak of man in terms of his inner, more noble, more enduring part, to overlook the historical concreteness of Biblical man and concentrate attention upon the soul alone. This movement of thought had many ramifications: the shift of interest from the resurrection of the body to the immortality of the soul;[6] the frequently found misunderstanding of the Biblical opposition of flesh and spirit in terms of the Greek opposition of body and soul; the bent that the Christian authors shared with their contemporaries towards the vilification of the body and bodily processes, and the adoption of sometimes excessive ascetical programs.[7]

This process of interaction also had important positive effects upon the growth of Christian theology. Theoretically speaking, i.e., insofar as it contributed to the creation of a systematic Christian understanding of man, the most important effect of Greek thought on early Christian anthropology was the adoption of the Platonic understanding of "image" (*eikon*) as the central anthropological concept. The thought that man in his intellectual nature was in some way the image of God had long been traditional among the Greeks. For Plato, the term "image," used of the relationship of the sensible and intelligible worlds, not only implied the inferiority of the sensible, but also stressed the imitation and participation of the sensible in the intelligible.[8] This note of participation was to prove decisive for Christian thought. The famous verse of the Book of Genesis (1:26) describing the creation of man: "Let us make man in our image and likeness;" and Paul's use of the term seemed to give Scriptural warrant for making "image" a central category in Christian speculation on man.[9]

For the Christian Fathers, "image theology" became a pri-

6. O. Cullmann, "Immortality of the Soul or Resurrection of the Dead? ," *Immortality and Resurrection*, pp. 9-53.

7. Dodds, *op. cit.*, Chaps. II-IV.

8. For Plato on the image, cf. *Rep.* 501b; *Laws* 716d; *Phaed.* 248a; *Theaet.* 176b sqq; etc.

9. On Paul's use of image, cf. Rom. 1:19; 8:29; 1 Cor. 15:49; 2 Cor. 3:18; 4:4; Col 1:15; etc.

mary way to describe man's relation to God. Frequently, the relation was expressed in terms of the exemplary causality of the *Logos*, the Second Person of the Trinity, in the work of creation: man was the image of the Image, or made according to the Image. Despite many variations, especially on the differences between image and likeness, it may in general be said that in the patristic writers known to the medievals the use of the image theme heightened the body-soul dichotomy—the image of God was generally said to reside in the soul, and not in the whole man. Image and likeness, indeed, became a hallmark of Platonizing theology, not only in anthropology, but in the Trinitarian and Christological areas as well.[10] While its adoption aided in the spiritualization of the more concrete Biblical anthropology, it also allowed for a theological expression of the relation of the divine to the human and the creation of theories of the reformation of the image lost through sin which were to have immense repercussions on the form of Christian life and the structure of Christian society. All these tendencies remained in force in the twelfth century. They form an important part of the background of these three treatises.

The channels through which the anthropological speculation of the ancient world reached the Middle Ages were many and varied. Augustine of Hippo (354-430) was the most important single patristic source available to the twelfth-century authors. He was both the ancestor of many of the profound insights found in this literature and the cause of some of its tensions and ambiguities. The African bishop's thought on man and the soul underwent a considerable evolution during his long intellectual pilgrimage, an evolution that must be understood against the background of the strong influence of Neoplatonism on his early works.[11]

10. For an introduction to image theology in the Christian tradition, cf. T. Camelot, "La théologie de l'image de Dieu," *RSPT*, 40 (1956), pp. 433-71; G. B. Ladner, *The Idea of Reform* (Cambridge, 1949); R. Javelet, *Image et ressemblance au douzième siècle* (Paris, 1967), 2 vols; and S. Otto, *Die Funktion des Bildbegriffes in der Theologie des 12. Jahrhunderts*, BGPM 40, 1 (Münster, 1963).
11. For the theory of man in Augustine, cf. E. Gilson, *The Christian Philosophy of St. Augustine* (N.Y. 1967); A. C. Pegis, *At the Origins of the Thomistic Notion*

Plotinus, a late third-century philosopher and the father of Neoplatonism, pushed the inherent oppositions of the soul-body dichotomy in Greek thought to an extreme point, but without succumbing to a dualistic position similar to the Gnostics or the Manichaeans. It is clear that for Plotinus man was the soul, nothing more, nothing less;[12] but the soul itself was not unitary. Picking up a clue from the seemingly separate souls of the later Plato (e.g., *Timaeus* 69cd, and 90 ac, where only the rational part is really immortal and can be separated from the lower parts), and in line with his profound conception of the omnipresence and immanence of the higher stages of reality in the lower, Plotinus said that there are really two souls for each individual, an upper soul, the real man, which never departs from the intelligible realm of *Nous* or Mind, and the lower soul, or shadow man, fallen into the dregs of the material world.[13] Man, i.e., the soul, is at the same time "fallen" and "still there." At times, Plotinus even admits a triple view of the soul in having reason mediate between the upper and lower souls.[14]

---

of man (N. Y. 1963); R. A. Markus, "Augustine–Man: Body and Soul," in *The Cambridge History of Later Greek and Early Medieval Philosophy* (Cambridge, 1967), pp. 354-61; M. D. J Chenu, "Situation Humaine: Corporalité et Temporalité," *L'Homme et son destin d'après les penseurs du moyen âge* (Paris, 1960), pp. 23-49; C. Coutourier, "La structure metaphysique de l'homme d'après S. Augustin," *Augustinus Magister* (Paris, 1954), Vol. I, pp. 543-50. With regard to the extent of the influence of Plotinus on Augustine, R. J. O'Connell, *St. Augustine's Early Theory of Man, A. D. 386-91* (Harvard, 1968), and *St. Augustine's Confessions* (Harvard, 1969), holds for a strong influence, as did P. Henry, *Plotin et l'Occident* (Louvain, 1934). Other scholars think that Plotinus's pupil Porphyry was the major source of Augustine's Neoplatonism, e. g., W. Theiler, *Porphyrios und Augustin* (Halle, 1933; reprinted in his *Forschungen zum Neuplatonismus,* Berlin, 1966, pp. 160-251); and J. J. O'Meara, *The Young Augustine* (London, 1954).

12. E.g., *Enn.* IV, 7, 1: "If this body, then, is really a part of us, we are not wholly immortal; if it is an instrument of ours, then, as a thing put at our service for a certain time, it must be in its nature passing. The sovran principle, the authentic man, will be as Form to this Matter or as agent to this instrument, and thus, whatever that relation be, *the Soul is the man.*" (trans. S. MacKenna)

13. E.g., *Enn.* I,1,7; I,4,14; II,1,5; II,3,9; III,8,5,; IV,1,1; IV,8,4; IV,8,5; IV,8,8; VI,7,5. For an introduction to Plotinus's theory of the soul, cf. A.H. Armstrong, *The Architecture of the Intelligible Universe in the Philosophy of Plotinus* (Amsterdam, 1967), pp. 83-109; and his "Plotinus: Man and Reality," in *The Cambridge History of Later Greek and Early Medieval Philosophy,* pp. 222-35.

14. E.g., *Enn.* II,9,2; V,3,3; V,9,1-2.

Plotinus's theory of the double soul effectively removed man from the sphere of history. Looked at from one point of view, it could even be said to destroy the responsible character of moral action: salvation, union with the One, the return home, could be viewed as a process of awakening the soul to the fact that it had never really left its true home.[15] Augustine seems not to have been aware of the conflict between Plotinian thought and the Christian theory of man at the earliest stages of his career;[16] but his continuing reflection on anthropological problems in the light of the doctrines of creation and of the resurrection of the body eventually led to a reaction against these early views.[17]

Augustine's thought on the nature of man and of the soul was to be a rich mine for the twelfth-century theorists. In questions of the origin of the soul, its immateriality and immortality, the manner of its presence in the body, and the nature of the soul as the image of God, his authority was of central weight. Some of these concerns will appear in our analysis of the Cistercian treatises. One area of his thought, however, may be singled out for inspection as symptomatic of the difficulties of mixing Scriptural and Greek anthropologies, viz., Augustine's problem in giving systematic expression to the unity of man.[18]

The two-soul theory of Plotinus was never clearly advanced by the African bishop;[19] other Plotinian themes, such as the fall of the soul, accepted in the earlier works, were criticized in more mature ones.[20] But if the soul itself is one for Augustine, what can we say of man? Is man just the soul, or is he soul and body? If the latter, how is the union of soul and

15. Armstrong, "Plotinus: Man and Reality," pp. 226-27.
16. This is the conclusion of O'Connell's well-argued work, *St. Augustine's Early Theory of Man*; e.g., p. 278.
17. O'Connell, *op. cit.*, p. 284. The Origenist controversy in the late fourth century was important in this reaction; cf. *op. cit.*, pp. 147-48.
18. The best studies of this significant problem are to be found in Chenu, *op. cit.*, pp. 38-49; and Pegis, *op. cit.*, pp. 33-59.
19. Despite O'Connell's hesitations about the early Augustine, *op. cit.*, pp. 166-68. Cf. also Markus, *op. cit.*, p. 360.
20. E.g., *Epistula 166 (De origine animae)*, IX, 27 (*CSEL* 44, pp. 582-84), written c. 415 A.D.; *De natura et origine animae*, I, 4-6 (*CSEL* 60, pp. 305-07), c. 419; and the *De civitate Dei*, XI, 23 (*CC* 48, pp. 341-42), c. 413-26.

body to be understood? Augustine was concerned with this problem from the beginning of his career, as a famous passage in his work *On the Morals of the Catholic Church* (388 A.D.) indicates;[21] but the difficulty that he had in defining man is evidence of the ambiguity of his position. The traditional definition, "man is a mortal rational animal," is, of course, present in Augustine;[22] but what was the understanding he had of this intellectual coin? The frequent appearance of the Platonic definition that man is "a soul using a body" (*I Alcibiades* 129e),[23] both in earlier and later works,[24] gives us a clue to his mind in the matter. His occasional use of the Platonic category of the body as the "prison of the soul" confirms this.[25] The systematic side of Augustine's thought, largely Neoplatonic, pushed him towards an equation of man with the soul which his sense of the historical materiality of man in the Bible made it impossible for him to accept upon more careful consideration. He therefore separates himself from Plato and Plotinus in always accepting man as in some way a composite of body and soul;[26] but he never solved the problem of how the soul, a spiritual substance, unites with the substance of the body to produce the third substance— man.[27] Even his manner of conceiving this union varied: he

21. *De mor. ecc.* XIV, 6 (*PL* 32, 1313). Compare with *De civ. Dei* XIX, 3 (*CC* 48,p.662), where virtually the same formulation is said to be taken from Varro.
22. *De ordine* II, 11, 31 (*PL* 32, 1009); *DQA*. I, 25, 47 (*PL* 32, 1062); *De orig. an.* VI (16) (*CSEL* 44, p. 569); *De civ. Dei* IV, 13 (*CC* 47, p. 261).
23. The definition is found in Plotinus, e.g., *Enn.* I, 1, 3; VI, 7, 5.
24. *DQA* XIII, 22 (*PL.* 32, 1048), c. 388A.D.; *De mor. ecc. cath.* I,4,6,; I,27,52 (*PL* 32,1313,1332), c. 388 A.D.; *In Joan. Evang.* XIX,5,15 (*CC* 36, p. 199), 416-17 A.D. Similar texts may be found in the *De civ. Dei* IX, 9-10 (*CC* 47, pp. 257-58) and X, 6 (*CC* 47, pp. 278-79). The soul also appears to be the true man in *De natura et origine animae* IV, 2 (*CSEL* 60, p. 380), c. 419 A.D.
25. *Contra Acad.* I,3,9 (*PL* 32,910), c. 386; *Epist.* 166,#27 (*CSEL* 44,p.583), c. 415. On this question, cf. P. Courcelle, "Tradition platonicienne et traditions chrétiennes du corps-prison," *Revue des études latines,* 43 (1966), pp. 430-33.
26. *De Gen. ad litt.* VII,27,38 (*PL* 34,369); *De nat. et orig. an.* IV,2,3, (*CSEL* 60, p. 381); *DQA* I, 2 (*PL* 32,1036); *De civ. Dei* I, 13; X, 29; XIII, 24 (*CC* 47, pp. 14-15, 304-6; *CC* 48, pp. 408 sqq.).
27. His final and most un-Platonic statements are from the *De Trin.,* I, 10,20: "*sicut caro animae meae, alia substantia est ad animan meam, quamvis in uno homine*" (*Bibliothéque Augustinienne* ed., I, p. 144); and XV, 7,11: "*Homo est substantia rationalis constans ex anima et corpore*" (ed. cit., II, p.446).

toyed with the Neoplatonic "union without confusion" explanation,[28] but eventually declared the union to incomprehensible.[29] While it is correct to note with E. Gilson and R. A. Markus that Augustine is not really interested in metaphysical definitions, but in the moral life of man, which his emphasis on the spirituality and substantiality of the soul allows him to highlight,[30] what this variation of treatment shows is that on one level at least Augustine failed to systematize the two understandings of man to which he was heir.[31]

Other areas of his thought served as a partial remedy for this failure. First of all, the difficulty he had in showing how man is a being whose nature it is to be material was circumvented to some degree by the stress he placed on the human soul as mediator between the spiritual and material levels on the chain of being. E. Gilson perceptively notes, ". . .the metaphysical reason for the union of soul and body in Augustine is simply that soul is to serve as an intermediary between the *body* it animates and the *Ideas of God* which animate the soul."[32] Thus it is the Neoplatonic hierarchical viewpoint with all its possibilities expressive of man as dynamic midpoint between the divine and earthly spheres,[33] bringing the spiritual to the material and the material to the spiritual, which, when stressed by Augustine, allowed for an at least

28. Markus, *op. cit.*, pp. 357-59. The theory comes from Porphyry, and is found in *Ep.* 137,3,11 (*CSEL* 40, pp. 109-11), and *De civ. Dei* X, 29 (*CC* 47, pp. 304-06).

29. *In Joan. Evang.* XIX, 15 (*CC* 36, p. 199); *De civ. Dei* X, 29; XXI, 10 (*CC* 47, 304-6; CC 48, 775-76); *Epist.* 137, 3,11-12 (*CSEL* 40, pp.109-11).

30. Gilson, *op. cit.*, p. 45; Markus, *op. cit.*, p. 359.

31. On the question of definitions of man in Augustine, Gilson (pp. 44-49) and Markus (pp. 355-57) tend to stress Augustine's attempt at unifying body and soul, while O'Connell (pp. 185-87, 256, 274-75) stresses the Platonic theme of the soul as man.

32. *Op. cit.*, p. 49; cf. also Markus, *op. cit.*, p. 359 (on *moderatio* as a cognate theme).

33. On man as the midpoint of the chain of being in Augustine, cf., e.g., *De beata vita* IV, 23-32 (*PL* 32, 970-75); *De gen. ad litt.* VI, 12,22 (*PL* 34, 348); *De civ. Dei* IX, 13,3 (*CC* 47, p. 260); *In Joan. Evang.* XX, 11; XXIII, 5 (*CC* 36, pp. 209, 235); *De Trin.* XII, 11,16 (ed. cit. II, 240). This is the *mese taxis* description of soul, originating in *Timaeus* 35a, found in Plotinus, *Enn.* III, 2,8-9, and IV, 8,7; and according to Theiler also in Porphyry. Cf. O'Connell, *St. Augustine's Early Theory. . .*, pp. 155-56, 193-97.

symbolic solution to the problem of putting a biblical understanding of man in Platonic terms. It is possible to assert that
Augustine's consciousness of failure in handling what M.-D.
Chenu terms the *corporalité* of biblical man was part of the
motivation behind his development of a theology stressing
the temporal dimension of human existence. The one serves
to correct the deficiencies of the other: Augustine, creator of
perhaps the most impressive theology of history in the Christian tradition, preserved the substantial unity of man by creating a theology of the temporal subject without a corresponding theology of man as corporeal nature. In Plotinus
man escapes time by recognizing that his true self has always
been above, united with *Nous*. In Augustine, man creates his
history by a conversion which mirrors the decision of God in
Christ to save the world, but it is a history that mutes the
essential involvement of the material elements in the process
of salvation.

The harmful effects of Augustine's theology of man in the
medieval period have been well discussed by M.-D. Chenu
among others.[34] The repetition of the sterile aspects of the
African doctor's thought was always a temptation to a
medieval theologian; courage to confront the key problems
and central insights of his work was often the most significant source of new theological vitality. In the twelfth century, when the problem of the meaning of man confronted
theology with a renewed immediacy, the major themes of
Augustine's thought were taken up and developed in a truly
remarkable fashion.

Augustine was not the only influence on twelfth-century
anthropology; there were other channels through which older
theories of man reached the medieval authors. For purposes
of clarification, these channels can be reduced to two: the
Eclectic Tradition, and the Greek Patristic Tradition.

The term Eclectic Tradition is here used to describe a body
of texts, stretching from the early fourth to the late sixth

34. *Op. cit.,* pp. 34-38.

century, of diverse literary genera and intellectual value, containing both pagan and Christian anthropological material. The religious allegiance of the authors of these texts is frequently difficult to determine, so intermingled had Christian and pagan elements become. While rarely of original value in themselves, they were of great importance to the medieval world as transmitters of the wisdom of the past.[35]

To adopt a roughly chronological order (insofar as this can be determined), the list would include the lost treatise of Porphyry (c. 232-305), *The Return of the Soul*,[36] the extent of whose influence on the Fathers, especially Augustine, was probably considerable.[37] In the case of texts that actually survived into the twelfth century, major importance must be given to the partial translation and long commentary of Chalcidius on the *Timaeus* of Plato. It dates from the early fourth century.[38] It is worthy of note that Chalcidius's *Commentary* witnesses to an earlier stage of the history of the Platonic tradition than that described under the rubric of Neoplatonism, as does the Hermetic tract *Asclepius* (c. 300),

35. Many of these texts are generally ignored in the history of philosophy. The best introduction to them is P. Courcelle, *Les lettres grecques en occidente de Macrobe à Cassiodore* (2nd ed.; Paris, 1948). This is now available in an English translation by H.Wedeck, *Late Latin Writers and their Greek Sources* (Cambridge, Mass., 1969). For a brief introduction to some of the more obscure, cf. E. Gilson, *History of Christian Philosophy in the Middle Ages* (N.Y., 1955), pp. 585-87, 601-3. For a spirited, if incautious, discussion of their influence on the medieval world view, cf. C. S. Lewis, *The Discarded Image* (Cambridge, 1967), pp. 45-91.

36. The fragments collected in J. Bidez, *Vie de Porphyre le Philosophe néo-Platonicienne* (Gand, 1913), pp. 29*-44*, are not complete, according to Courcelle, *op. cit.*, pp. 394-97.

37. Besides the works mentioned above, cf. H. Dörrie, "Das fünffach gestufte Mysterium: Der Aufstieg der Seele bei Porphyrios und Ambrosius," *Mullus: Festschrift Theodor Klauser* (Münster, 1964), pp. 79-93. Porphyry's presentation of the myth of the Fall and Return of the Soul, as well as the problems his dictum *corpus est omne fugiendum* caused the Fathers, are major elements in his influence.

38. Edited by J. H. Waszink, *Timaeus a Calcidio translatus Commentarioque Instructus* (*Plato Latinus IV*) (London and Leiden, 1962). Cf. J. F. Sulowski, "Studies on Chalcidius. Anthropology, Influence and Importance," in *L'Homme et son destin*, pp. 153-61.

whose translation into Latin was known to Lactantius and Augustine and avidly read in some twelfth-century circles.[39] Thus it is an oversimplification to treat the philosophical basis of twelfth-century anthropology as if it were purely Neoplatonic.[40] At a somewhat later date *The Marriage of Mercury and Philology* of Martianus Capella (c. 400),[41] and the approximately contemporary *Commentary on the Dream of Scipio* of Macrobius[42] stand in a curious shadow-world between Christianity and paganism. Along with Chalcidius and Boethius, Macrobius was the most influential of the writers of the Eclectic Tradition on the medieval period. Widely, if unsystematically, acquainted with the Neoplatonists, Macrobius was a chief source of the transmission of knowledge of the three Neoplatonic hypostases,[43] as well as information on man as microcosm[44] and the myth of the fall of the soul, to the Middle Ages.[45]

Towards the end of the fifth century, *The State of the Soul* of Claudianus Mamertus (d. 474),[46] and the *Book on the Dogmas of the Church* of Gennadius of Marseilles (d. 505)

39. Edited A. D. Nock and A. J. Festugière, *Corpus Hermeticum,* II (2nd ed.; Paris, 1960 [Budé]), pp. 296-401. On Hermetic influence on the twelfth century, cf. T. Silverstein, "Liber Hermeticus Mercurii triplicis de VI rerum principiis," *AHDL,* 22, (1956), 217-301; and R. B. Woolsey, "Bernard Silvester and the Hermetic *Asclepius,*" *Traditio,* 6 (1948), 340-44.

40. Cf. R. Klibansky, *The Continuity of the Platonic Tradition during the Middle Ages* (London, 1939), pp. 27,36.

41. Ed. A. Dick, *De nuptiis Mercurii et Philologiae* (Leipzig, 1925), Cf. Courcelle, *op. cit.,* pp. 198-205.

42. Ed. I. Willis, *Macrobii Comentarii in Somnium Scipionis* (Leipzig, 1963). Translated with Introduction and notes by W. H. Stahl, *Macrobius: Commentary on the Dream of Scipio* (New York, 1952).

43. *Comment.* I, 14 (ed. Willis, pp. 55-60).

44. *Comment.* II, 12 (9-11) (ed. Willis, pp. 131-32). On the soul in general, cf. I, 9-14.

45. On the influence of Macrobius, P. Courcelle, *op. cit.,* pp. 3-36; and "La posterité chrétienne du 'Songe de Scipion,' " *Revue des études latines,* 34 (1958), pp. 205-34. Also, P. M. Schedler, *Die Philosophie des Macrobius und ihr Einfluss auf die Wissenschaft des christlichen Mittelalters, BGPM,* 13,1 (Münster, 1916); E. Jeauneau, "Macrobe, source du platonisme chartrain," *Studi Medievali,* 3rd Series, 1 (1960), 3-24; M. A. Elferink, *La Descente de l'âme d'après Macrobe* (Leiden, 1968).

46. Ed. A. Engelbrecht, *Claudiani Mamerti Opera* (Vienna, 1885), pp. 3-197 (*CSEL* 11). Cf. Courcelle, *op. cit.,* pp. 223-35; and E. L. Fortin, *Christianisme et culture philosophique au cinquième siècle: La querelle de l'âme en Occident* (Paris, 1959).

should be included in this tradition.[47] In the sixth century, the imposing figure of Boethius (c. 480-524), the "last of the Romans," also contributed to it. Second only to Augustine in influence on the twelfth century, the thought of Boethius, especially in his *The Consolation of Philosophy*,[48] deserves a more extensive treatment than can be accorded here. He was much more unabashedly Neoplatonic, less aware of the inherent tensions between biblical and classical views of man than was Augustine, especially in his undeviating acceptance of the myth of the fall of the soul;[49] but his solution to the problem of the compatibility of the freedom of man with the providence of God in the last book of *The Consolation* was an important defense of one of the key analogies which facilitated the fusion of the two anthropologies, the idea of man as a responsible agent.[50] Towards the end of the sixth century, the *Book on the Soul* of Cassiodorus (c. 477-570) provided another grab bag of psychological and anthropological data for a later era.[51]

Besides Augustine, many of the Latin Fathers had directed attention to problems of anthropology and attempted to come to grips with their double heritage. Tertullian (d. c. 220) had written a treatise entitled *The Soul*,[52] and the pro-

47. *PL* 58, 979-1000. Cf. Courcelle, *op. cit.*, pp. 221-23.
48. The edition used here will be H. F. Stewart and E. K. Rand, *Boethius: The Theological Tractates and the Consolation of Philosophy* (London-Cambridge, 1962; Loeb Library).
49. *In Porphyrium ed.* I, 3 (*CSEL* 48, pp. 8-9); *De Consol. Phil.* III, metrum 12 and prosa 12 (ed. Rand, pp. 286-97).
50. The *Consolation* has been described as a Neoplatonic mystical apocalypse whose aim, according to H. Liebeschütz, is ". . . to discover the motives of the human soul's alienation from its genuine self and to point the way back from shadow to truth." (*Cambridge History*, p. 547; compare with Courcelle, *op. cit.*, p. 280). On the psychology of Boethius and its influence, cf. Courcelle, *op. cit.*, pp. 278-300; and now his monumental, *La Consolation de la Philosophie dans la tradition littéraire: antécédents et posterité* (Paris, 1967). Also, K. Bruder, *Die philosophischen Elemente in den Opuscula Sacra des Boethius* (Leipzig, 1928); V. Schurr, *Die Trinitätslehre des Boethius im Lichte der 'skythischen Kontroversen'* (Paderborn, 1935); and V. Schmidt-Kohl, *Die Neuplatonische Seelenlehre in der Consolatio Philosophiae des Boethius* (Meisenheim, 1965).
51. Ed. J. W. Halporn, "Magni Aurelii Cassiodori Senatoris Liber de Anima," *Traditio*, 16 (1960), pp. 39-109; cf. Courcelle, *op. cit.*, pp. 316-41.
52. Ed. J. H. Waszink, *Opera Tertulliani* (*CC*, Turnhout, 1954), Vol. II, 781-869.

nounced Neoplatonism of Ambrose of Milan (d. 397) had
been influential on the young Augustine.[53] Jerome (d. 420)
and Gregory the Great (d. 604) were also sources of information,[54] less organized and extensive than Augustine, though
scarcely less pessimistic in their evaluations of the corporeal
aspects of man.

The other major tradition that influenced the medieval
theories of man came not from the West, but from the East—
the Greek Patristic Tradition.[55] The first notable figure here
is Origen (d. 253), the great Alexandrian theologian whose
influence on the twelfth century has begun to be uncovered
only recently.[56] In terms of the Cistercian treatises, this influence is particularly evident in the case of William of St.
Thierry, as will be seen below. Origen also had an extensive
secondary influence through the writings of his followers.
The most important of these, Gregory, Bishop of Nyssa in
Cappadocia (d. 394), was a major theological thinker in his
own right. Gregory's understanding of man, though affected
by his reading of Origen, is a highly original attempt to col-
late Biblical and Platonic elements.[57] His *The Image or the
Creation of Man*, translated into Latin by Denis the Little in
the sixth century and John the Scot in the ninth,[58] was

53. Especially in his *In Hexaemeron* (ed. C. Schenkl, *CSEL* 32,1), Vienna,
1896), and *De Isaac* (*ibid.*).

54. E.g., Jerome, *In Ezech.* I (*PL* 25, 22-23), and *In Matt.* II (*PL* 26, 91-94).
Gregory, *Homeliae in Ezech.* II, 5 (*PL* 76, 984-98), and *In Evang. Hom.* II, 39 (*PL*
76, 1293-1301).

55. For an introduction to this tradition, cf. I. P. Sheldon-Williams, "The Greek
Christian Platonist Tradition from the Cappadocians to Maximus and Eriugena,"
Cambridge History, pp. 421-533; and E. von Ivánka, *Plato Christianus* (Einsiedeln,
1964), especially Sections III, IV, VI, VII.

56. Cf. H. Crouzel, "L'anthropologie d'Origène," *RAM*, 32 (1955), pp.
354-85; and *La théologie de l'image de Dieu chez Origène* (Paris, 1956). On
Origen's influence in the Middle Ages, cf. H. de Lubac *Exégèse Médiévale* (Paris,
1959), Vol, I, chap. 4, pp. 221-304.

57. J. Danièlou, *Platonisme et théologie mystique* (Paris, 1953[2]), pp. 46-83; E.
von Ivánka, *op. cit.*, pp. 151-85; Sheldon-Williams, *op.cit.*, pp. 447-56; A. H.
Armstrong, "Platonic Elements in Gregory of Nyssa's Doctrine of Man,," *Domini-
can Studies* 1 (1948), pp. 113-26.

58. Greek original in *PG* 44, 123-256. The translation of Dionysius is in *PL* 67,
347-408; that of John the Scot in M. Cappuyns, "Le *De Imagine* de Gregoire de
Nyssa, traduit par Jean Scot Erigène," *RTAM*, 32 (1965), pp. 205-62.

". . .a Christian version of the Neoplatonic theory of the descent and return of the soul."[59] Put as simply as possible, the significance of the influence of Origen and Gregory of Nyssa (besides its value as an indirect source for many classical philosophical themes) was to heighten what might be called the static problems of patristic anthropology, especially the narrowing of anthropology to a more restricted concentration on psychology. This can be seen in the strong division between body and soul emphasized by Gregory's account of the two creations of man,[60] and the descent of the soul.[61] But the dynamics of the late classical worldview allowed for a systematically extrinsic, but symbolically useful, mitigation of these tendencies. Man as the midpoint of the universe, linking the spiritual and the material,[62] man as he who not only descends, but as the ascending one who restores all things to God through Christ[63]—these attempts at expressing the unity of the material and the spiritual are also strong in this tradition, especially in the writings of the great Cappadocian.

Circulating in the twelfth century under the name of Gregory was a treatise containing many Gregorian themes, but actually written by Nemesius, Bishop of Emesa (c. 400), *The Nature of Man* or *Premnon physicon*. Translated by Bishop Alfanus of Salerno in the late eleventh century and again by Burgundio of Pisa in the mid-twelfth,[64] this somewhat disorganized survey served as a handy epitome of

59. Sheldon-Williams, *op. cit.*, p. 449.

60. *De hom.* II; XVI (*PG* 44, 131-33; 178-88, esp. 181B).

61. Cf. Armstrong, *op. cit.*, pp. 120-23; Sheldon-Williams, *op. cit.*, pp. 449-52; Daniélou, *op. cit.*, pp. 56-60.

62. *Passim* in the *De hom.* II and XVI, e.g., in its intellectual expression as the two faces of knowledge in 132D-33A.

63. Sheldon-Williams, *op. cit.*, pp. 452-56.

64. Greek original in *PG* 40, 503-818. Translation of Alfanus: *Nemesii Episcopi Premnon Physicon*, ed. C. Burkhard (Teubner; Leipzig, 1917). Burgundio translation: *Gregorii Nysseni (Nemesii Emesini) Peri Physeos Anthropou, liber a Burgundio in latinam translatus*, ed. C. Burkhard (Vienna, 1891). An English translation with helpful notes may be found in *Cyril of Jerusalem and Nemesius of Emesa*, trans. W. Telfer (Library of Christian Classics IV, Philadelphia, 1955), pp. 203-453.

psychological data for the men of the twelfth century, as John of Salisbury noted in his *Metalogicon*.[65] The *Premnon physicon* was important for another reason, too. Already in *The Creation of Man* of Gregory one can note a curiosity and concern with physiological and medical material[66] that to some extent was mirrored in contemporary works of Augustine, such as the *Literal Commentary on Genesis*. This tendency reached its climax in Nemesius, whose fourth Book is an extensive summary of ancient medical knowledge. Such physiological and medical interest cautions us against an overly rigid view of the Platonic tradition as eschewing concern for the body. P. Ricoeur's demonstration that Plato's projection of the Socratic analysis of the unjust soul onto the body allowed for a mutual transfer of symbols of "health," "disease," and "medicine" between body and soul suggests one root for the concern;[67] and the Pythagorean interest of the *Timaeus* with physiology suggests another. It seems that at times of particularly strong interaction between Platonic thought and biblical anthropology, the growth of psychological theory was frequently accompanied by an intense interest in medicine and physiology. The period roughly 370-400 A.D. appears to have been such a time, and the treatises produced then, along with much Judeo-Arabic material, were an important stimulus for a comparable period in the twelfth century (c. 1120-70).

The Pseudo-Dionysius (c. 500), the anonymous Syrian monk who pretended to be St. Paul's Athenian convert and disciple, was the most influential of the Greek Platonic theologians in the twelfth century. His explicit treatment of the

65. *Metal.* IV, 20 (ed. C. Webb, Oxford, 1929, pp. 182-83). Among the important pieces of information which Nemesius passed on to the Middle Ages were: (1) a succinct analysis of the divergent views of Plato, Aristotle, and Plotinus on the nature of man (I, 107); (2) a combining of the ideas of man as the midpoint of creation with a hierarchical picture of the universe which K. Reinhardt claimed went back to the Stoic Poseidonius (I, 8-13); (3) a clear expression of the microcosm theme (I, 90); (4) a discussion of the ancient theories of the soul in Book II; and (5) a treatment of the difficulties of explaining the union of soul and body (Book III).

66. *De Hom.* XXX (*PG* 44, 239-56).

67. *The Symbolism of Evil*, p. 337.

soul is not extensive (e.g., a passage on the three motions of the soul,[68] and remarks on its unity[69]); his real importance lies rather in transmitting to the Middle Ages a carefully organized hierarchical picture of the world, an overriding interest in anagogy, or the ascension of all things to God, and a concern with symbols that stressed the place of the material world in this process of ascension. The Janus-like figure of the Pseudo-Dionysius confronts any historian of medieval thought with a problem of perspective: from one point of view, in his thought, Neoplatonic man as intellectual being and immortal soul seems to have triumphed over any historical dimension of biblical man; from another, the dimension of engagement with the material world, attenuated in Augustine's theory of man, bursts unexpectedly into prominence through the categories of hierarchy and symbolism.[70]

From the sixth to the ninth centuries A.D., the confusion and collapse that descended upon the political and cultural world of Western Europe are all too evident in its intellectual life as well. Early medieval concern with the problem of man—now largely restricted to the problem of the soul—took the form of highly jejune surveys of material gathered from what little was available of the philosophical and theological tradition.[71] The relevant sections of Isidore of Seville's (d. 636) *Two Books of Differences* and *Etymologies* are excellent examples of this genre.[72] There was a revival of interest in the Carolingian period, as Alcuin's (d. 804) *The Explanation of the Soul*,[73] the *Treatise on the Soul* and *The Universe* of Rabanus Maurus (d. 856),[74] and the writings of Ratramnus

68. *De divinis nominibus* IV, 9 (*Dionysiaca*, ed. P. Chevallier, 2 vols, Paris, 1937), I, 190-94.
69. *De div. nom.* V, 7 (*Dionysiaca* I, p. 346).
70. The point is made by M.-D. Chenu, *op. cit.*, p. 38.
71. Neglect of early medieval psychology is indicated by the fact that the last general survey published was that of K. Werner, *Der Entwicklungsgang der mittelalterlichen Psychologie* (Vienna, 1876). The thesis of G. Mathon, *L'anthropologie chrétienne en Occident, de saint Augustin à Jean Scot Erigène* (Lille, 1964), has not yet appeared in print.
72. *Differentiarum libri duo*, II, 13-30 (*PL* 83, 75-85); *Etymologiae* XI (*PL* 82, 397-424).
73. *PL* 101, 639-47.
74. *Tractatus de anima* (*PL* 110, 1109-20); *De universo* VI (*PL* 111, 137-78).

of Corbie (c. 870) indicate.[75] The real contribution of the Carolingian period to the twelfth century (its decisive influence rests not only on the speculative power of the thinker, but also on the function he served in melding the Greek Patristic Tradition and the Augustinianism of the West) is John Scotus Eriugena's (d. c. 877) *The Division of Nature*, or *Periphyseon*.[76] In this work, Platonic exemplarism as an explanation for man as the image of God has triumphed to the extent that man is not defined even as the soul, but as the idea of man in the divine mind.[77] The deeply Platonic sides of some of Augustine's views are considerably strengthened by the presence of the Greek Fathers, especially Gregory of Nyssa[78] and the Pseudo-Dionysius. A double stance is again evident, however, for John the Scot's work was also a major channel for complexes of ideas, especially those of the theory of man as the microcosm,[79] which were part of the machinery that allowed twelfth-century studies of the cosmic mystery of man to avoid explicit dualism and to reaffirm in symbolic manner at least the unity and materiality of the human person.

That concern for the problem of the soul which was briefly enkindled at the court of Charles the Bald,[80] and is evidenced

75. *De natura animae*, ed. A. Wilmart, "L'opuscule inédit de Ratramne sur la nature de l'âme," *Revue Bénédictine* 43 (1931), pp. 207-33; and the *De diversa et multiplici animae ratione (PL* 125, 933-52).

76. *PL* 122, 441-1022. Cf. now the critical edition of Book I, *Iohannis Scotti Eriugenae Periphyseon (De Divisione Naturae). Liber Primus*, ed. I.P. Sheldon-William (Dublin, 1968). On the psychology of John the Scot, cf. B. Stock, "The Philosophical Anthropology of Johannes Scottus Eriugena," *Studi medievali*, third series, 8 (1967), pp. 1-57.

77. *De div. nat.* IV, 7 (*PL* 122, 768B): "Imo vero intelligo, non aliam esse substantiam totius hominis, nisi suam notionem in mente artificis. . . ."

78. E.g., two kinds of bodies (*PL* 122, 583; 800-06); and existence of sex only after the Fall (*PL* 122, 309; 377B; 799B).

79. E.g., *De div. nat.* IV, 7 (*PL* 122, 763). Cf. M. Cappuyns, *Jean Scot Erigène: sa vie, son oeuvre, sa pensée* (Paris, 1933), pp. 353-60, especially p. 357, note, for other texts.

80. This included an interesting controversy on the World Soul (almost axiomatic in times of Platonic revival), cf. P. Delhaye, *Une controverse sur l'âme universelle au IXe siècle* (Lille, 1950); and G. Mathon, "Jean Scot Érigène, Chalcidius et le problême de l'âme universelle," *L'Homme et son destin*, pp. 361-75. Cf. *De mundi coelestis terristrisque constitutione (PL* 90, 881-910). On the part of Ratramnus of Corbie, Hincmar of Reims, and John the Scot in this controversy, cf. Cappuyns, *op. cit..*, pp. 91-94.

in the works of Rabanus, Ratramnus, and John the Scot, bore little fruit in the difficult centuries ahead. It is impossible to believe that men were reduced to such a brutish level of existence that the mystery of human existence ceased to be of central concern; but the leisure, the intellectual curiosity, and the level of society necessary for such concern to produce original insights and leave any permanent record were lacking.

THE TWELFTH-CENTURY CONTEXT

The physical expansion of western society in the eleventh and twelfth centuries that has continued to attract the attention of modern historians was accompanied by an equally remarkable renewal of theology.[81] Speculation on man played an important role in many of the intellectual currents of the day, both scientific and theological. Our three treatises, William of St. Thierry's *The Nature of the Body and the Soul*, Isaac of Stella's *Letter on the Soul*, and *The Spirit and the Soul*, were an important part of the Cistercian participation in this movement of thought.

Anthropological speculation took a number of different directions in the twelfth century. Some of the most hotly debated questions among the masters of the schools were basically anthropological in intent: e.g., the question of the origin of the human soul, that of the transmission of original sin, questions on the nature of human freedom, etc. Our authors, however, by their lack of interest in such questions demonstrate a connection with other traditions in the anthropology and psychology of the period. Their concentration on classifying the powers of the soul, on the nature of the soul's ascent to God, and on medicine and physiology are clues to this connection and the community of thought which it demonstrates.

Among the most distinctive notes of the three treatises is a concern for systematizing the nature and powers of the soul,

81. For an introduction to 12th century Europe, cf. R. W. Southern, *The Making of the Middle Ages* (New Haven, 1963).

and, to a lesser extent, of the body as well.[82] This systematizing effort is found in a wide variety of twelfth-century thought on man. It is present among some of the natural scientists, such as Adelhard of Bath (active c. 1105-45),[83] and William of Conches (d. c. 1154),[84] a famous master whose name was associated with the Cathedral School at Chartres. John of Salisbury (d. 1180), who studied at Chartres as a youth, also discussed such classifications in his *Metalogicon*.[85] The most important later scholastic author who shows similar concerns was Alan of Lille (d. 1202),[86] who also appears to have been influenced by the Chartrain tradition. Finally, there are anonymous treatises like the interesting *The Seven Sevens* which seem to be connected with the interests of the Chartrains and are also involved with the systematization of the powers of the soul.[87]

While the classifying and systematizing movement was thus evident in the Chartrain tradition, the same concern was present in a number of other schools of twelfth-century thought. For two major groups of theologians, the Victorines and the Cistercians, discussion of the nature of the soul, classification of its powers, and the manner of its union with the body, was important, as a foundation for a theory of the destiny of man as the image and likeness of God. Technical questions of psychology were thus directly related to a wider anthropological and spiritual program designed to provide a theoretical

82. The best introductions to the systematizing concern of 12th century anthropology are L. Reypens, "Ame (son fond, ses puissances, et sa structure d'après les mystiques)," *DS* (Paris, 1937-), Vol. I, 441-46; and P. Michaud-Quantain, "La classification des puissances de l'âme au XIIe siècle," *Revue du moyen âge latin*, 5 (1949), pp. 15-34.

83. Especially in his *Quaestiones Naturales*, ed. M. Müller, *Die Quaestiones Naturales des Adelardus von Bath*, BGPM 31, 2 (1934). On Adelhard, cf. C. H. Haskins, *Studies in the History of Mediaeval Science* (N.Y., 1967[2]), pp. 20-42.

84. Especially in his *De philosophia mundi* (PL 172, 39-102); and *Dragmaticon* (Strasbourg edition, 1567).

85. IV, 8-20 ed. C. Webb., pp. 172-187).

86. Especially in his *Distinctiones dictionum theologicalium* (PL 210, 685-1012; e.g., 819D, 922AB); and his *Sermo de sphaera intelligibili* and *Sermo in die Epiphaniae*, ed. M.-T. d'Alverny, *Alain de Lille. Textes inédits* (Paris, 1965), pp. 163-80; 241-45.

87. *De septem septennis* (PL 199, 945-64). Cf. M.-D. Chenu, "Une definition phythagorienne de la verité," *AHDL* 36 (1961), pp. 7-13.

basis for man's return to God.[88] The Victorine School, as represented in the great Hugh,[89] in Richard,[90] possibly in Achard,[91] and to a lesser extent in Godfrey,[92] was primarily interested in determining the various stages in the soul's ascent to God; but in order to do this these scholastics turned their attention to questions of classification and the problem of the union of the body and the soul. Given the‚importance of the Victorine influence on the evolution of twelfth-century theology, the appearance of this type of theological anthropology among these authors was an important sign of its prominence and significance. In terms of the combination of a concern for classification and a theory of the ascent of man to God, the Cistercian writers were to show them-

88. What E. Gilson called "speculative mysticism" in his *History of Christian Philosophy in the Middle Ages*, (N.Y., 1955), pp. 164-71.

89. The most important of Hugh's works are the *De unione corporis et spiritus (PL* 177, 285-94); *Soliloquium de arrha animae (PL* 176, 951-70); and the *De sacramentis (PL* 176, 173-618). Of the numerous works about Hugh the following are of particular use for his psychological theory: H. Ostler, *Die Psychologie des Hugo von St. Viktor, BGPM* 6, 1 (Münster, 1906); J. Kleinz, *The Theory of Knowledge of Hugh of St. Victor* (Washington, 1944); R. Baron, "La situation de l'homme d'après Hugues de St. Victor," *L'Homme et son destin,* pp. 431-36; and the same author's "Spirituelle médiévale: le traité de la contemplation et ses espèces," *RAM* 39 (1963), pp. 137-51. On the influence of Hugh, cf. E. Bertola, "Di alcuni trattati psicologici attributi ad Ugo di San Vittore," *Rivista di Filosofia Neoscolastica* 51 (1959), pp. 436-55.

90. Many of Richard's works deal with the problem of the soul and the manner of its ascent to God. Cf. *Benjamin minor (PL* 196, 1-64); *Benjamin Maior (PL* 196, 63-192); *De eruditione hominis interioris libri tres (PL* 196, 1229-1366); and the *De statu hominis interioris,* ed. J. Ribaillier, *AHDL,* 34 (1967), pp. 7-128. For studies of Richard, cf. J. Ebner, *Die Erkenntnislehre Richards von St. Viktor, BGPM* 19, 4 (Münster, 1917); E. Ottaviano, *Riccardo di San Vittore, la vita, le opere, il pensiero* (Rome, 1933), pp. 453-66; G. Dumeige, *Richard de St. Victor et l'idée chrétienne de l'amour* (Paris, 1952); R. Javelet, *Psychologie des auteurs spirituels du XIIe siècle* (Strasbourg, 1959); and J. Robilliard, "Les six genres de contemplation chez Richard de Saint Victor et leur origine platonicienne," *RSPT* 28 (1939), pp. 229-33.

91. The ascription of the *De discretione animae, spiritus et mentis* to Achard has been challenged by N. Haring, "Gilbert of Poitiers, Author of the *De discretione animae, spiritus et mentis* commonly attributed to Achard of St. Victor," *Mediaeval Studies,* 22 (1960), pp. 148-91; and defended by J. Chatillon, "Achard de St. Victor et le *De discretione animae, spiritus et mentis,"ADHL,* 31 (1964), pp. 7-35.

92. Godfrey's *Microcosmos* has been edited and discussed by P. Delhaye, *Le Microcosmos de Godefroy de St. Victor. Etude théologique. Texte* (Lille, 1951), 2 vols.

selves closely allied to the Victorines, despite differences in particulars.

The systematic thinkers of the Chartrain, Victorine, and Cistercian traditions demonstrated their intellectual openness in the use that they made of two of the more novel components of twelfth-century thought, the Judaeo-Arabic medical and philosophical material,[93] and the *Orientale lumen*, the writings of the Greek Fathers.[94] The expansion of thought in the eleventh and twelfth centuries cannot be understood apart from the activity of translation for which the age is so justly famous.[95] New translations of classical Greek texts were important; so also were versions of Greek patristic works previously unavailable to the theologians of the West. Not the least important side of the translating efforts of the time, however, were the versions of Arabic texts, many of which were at least partially dependent on classical sources unknown to the Latin-speaking world.[96] Two waves of new material are evident here, although the former is the more important for our three Cistercian treatises.

An interest in medicine, largely dependent on the late Latin translations of Greek works, had been traditional among the monks of the early Middle Ages.[97] Nevertheless, it is evident that in the eleventh century, the Arabic world, with its wider access to classical texts, especially those of Galen, and its own valuable medical traditions was far in advance of Western Europe. One of the first ways in which Western theolo-

93. While the term Judaeo-Arabic is more correct, because the Jewish authors involved were Arabic-speaking (e.g., Isaac Israeli and Ibn Gabirol to name but two), for the sake of simplicity the term Arabic will be used hereafter.

94. On the *Orientale lumen* (the term is taken from William of St. Thierry), cf. M.-D. Chenu, *La théologie au douzième siècle* (Paris,1957), Chaps. XII and XIII.

95. For an up-to-date survey of the extent of the medieval translating activities, cf. P. Thillet, M.R.P. McGuire and J. Wippel, "Translation Literature, Greek and Arabic," *New Catholic Encyclopedia* (Washington, 1967), Vol. 14, pp. 248-56.

96. The most complete survey of the translations from the Arabic is still the work of M. Steinschneider, *Die Europäischen Übersetzungen aus dem Arabischen bis Mitte des 17. Jahrhunderts* (Graz, 1904; photomechanical reprint 1956). On Arabic medicine in general, cf. D. Campbell, *Arabian Medicine and its Influence in the Middle Ages* (London, 1926), 2 vols.

97. Cf. L. C. MacKinney, *Early Medieval Medicine with Special Reference to France and Chartres* (Baltimore,1937); and H. Schipperges, *Die Benediktiner in der Medizin des frühen Mittelalters* (Leipzig, 1964).

gians demonstrated a willingness to expand their intellectual frontiers was in turning towards the Arabic medical and physiological material for their program of systematizing the nature and powers of the soul and its relation to the body.

Mention has already been made of Alfanus of Salerno (d. 1087), the first translator of Nemesius's *Premnon physicon*.[98] While the connections of Alfanus with the traditions of Salerno as a medical center are by no means clear (as is the case with so much of the early history of this famous school), it is important to note that the literature emanating from Salerno was the first strong infusion of Arabism into Western thought.[99] The most important figure in this effort of transmission was Constantine the African (d.1087), a native of Tunisia who after many wanderings ended his life as a monk at Monte Cassino.[100] Constantine was the first to make available a wide range of Arabic medical knowledge to the Latin world; indeed, many of the works that appeared under his name are little more than paraphrases of his Eastern sources.[101] The turn towards Arabic medicine should not be

---

98. On Alfanus, cf. P. O. Kristeller, "The School of Salerno: Its Development and its Contribution to the History of Learning," *Studies in Renaissance Thought and Letters* (Rome, 1956), pp. 506-07.

99. On the School of Salerno, the best survey is that of Kristeller in *Studies in Renaissance Thought and Letters,* pp. 495-551. In terms of the use of School of Salerno," Kristeller notes that it is important to distinguish between "... medieval practice, practical instruction in medicine, medical literature, organized teaching of medicine, and finally a corporation or college of physicians organized under a president, conferring degrees and issuing diplomas." (p. 499). As used here, the term will be restricted to the provenance of medical literature. Cf. also the same author's "Beitrag der Schule von Salermo . . .," *Artes Liberales. Von der antiken Bildung zur Wissenschaft des Mittelalters* (Leiden, 1959), pp. 84-90.

100. On Constantine the African, cf. Kristeller, "The School of Salerno," pp. 508-10; L. Thorndike, *A History of Magic and Experimental Science* (N.Y., 1923), Vol. I, pp. 743-59; and G. Sarton, *Introduction to the History of Science* (Baltimore, 1927), Vol. I, p. 769.

101. The most important of the works of Constantine are: (1) the *Pantegni*, a version in twenty books (ten theoretical and ten practical) of the *Royal Art of Medicine* of the famous Arab doctor, Ali ibn Abbas (second half of 10th century); (2) the *Viaticus*, a briefer introduction to the medical art, dependent on Ibn al Jezzar; (3) treatises on diets, urines, and fevers of the Jewish author, Isaac Israeli; (4) various treatises of Hippocrates and Galen, especially the *Aphorisms* of the former; (5) the *Liber graduum*, whose exact provenance is unknown; and (6) shorter works probably of his own composition, such as the *De stomachi affectionibus, De melancholia,* and *De oculo.*

restricted to the School of Salerno. One of the most influential Arabic works was the tract *The Difference of the Spirit
and the Soul* composed by Constabulinus (Costa-ben-Luca, d.
935), a Syrian from Baalbek; it was translated by John of
Spain at Toledo before the middle of the twelfth century.[102]
Much of the speculation on the various forms of *spiritus* had
its origin in this work.[103]

The influence of the Arabic sources upon the Latin writers
in the first half of the twelfth century is evident in the texts
of the natural philosophers and in some of the spiritual
writers; its effect upon the three Cistercian treatises will be
discussed below. The medical Arabism of the first half of the
century, however, was only the first wave of what was to
become a flood towards its end. The second wave of translations was of far greater philosophical import, although they
did not lack an interest in medical and scientific questions.
The center of the translating effort shifted too, much of the
work being done in association with the famous "School" of
Toledo. Avicenna was the great philosopher who overshadow-
ed this second wave, but the writings of Ibn Gabirol and the
Book of Causes (an Arabic reworking of the *Elements of
Theology* of the Neoplatonic philosopher Proclus [d. 490])
were also of importance. This new input of material affected
a number of the Latin works of the second half of the century which displayed an interest in naming and classifying the
powers of the soul. The Toledo translator of Avicenna and
Gabirol, Dominicus Gundissalinus (active c. 1160), in his *The
Soul* and *The Immortality of the Soul*, shows this influence,[104] as do the anonymous works, *The States of the Interior*

---

102. Edited by S. Barach, *Excerpta ex libro Alfredi* (Innsbruck, 1878), 120-39.

103. On the importance of *spiritus* in the 12th century, cf. M.-D. Chenu,,
"*Spiritus,* le vocabulaire de l'âme au XIIe siècle," *RSPT,* 41 (1957), pp. 209-32;
E. Bertola, "Le Fonti Medico-Filosofiche della Dottrina dello 'Spirito'," *Sophia,*
26 (1958), pp. 48-61; and H. Schipperges, "Die Schulen von Chartres unter dem
Einfluss des Arabismus," *Sudhoffs Archiv für der Geschichte der Medizin und der
Naturwissenschaften,* 40 (1956), pp. 193-210.

104. *De anima,* ed. J. T. Muckle, "The Treatise 'De anima' of Dominicus Gundissalinus." *Mediaeval Studies,* 2 (1940), pp. 23-103; and the *De immortalitate
animae,* ed. by G. Bülow in *BGPM,* 2, 3 (Münster, 1897), pp. 1-38.

Man,[105] and *The Flux of Being.*[106] In terms of the three Cistercian treatises which we are considering, although it seems that there is no question of direct dependence of any of the treatises on this material,[107] the popularity of *The Spirit and the Soul* is at least partially explained by its association with currents of thought introduced by the second wave.

Many scholars have directed their attention to the effects of Greek patristic thought on the theology of the twelfth century, effects that are by no means to be restricted to the interests of systematizing anthropology. The natural scientists and early masters of Chartres, while deeply influenced by what we have called the eclectic tradition, were not remarkable for their knowledge of the Greek Fathers. Some of the masters, however, did show an acquaintance with John the Scot. The later traditions of Chartres, especially those connected with Gilbert of Poitiers and his followers, were very strongly affected by the new Greek material made available by the twelfth-century translators.[108] The situation is even more revealing in the case of the Victorine and Cistercian authors. Although other early twelfth-century Schools, most notably that of Laon,[109] seem to have taken an interest in the writings of the Pseudo-Dionysius and John the Scot, Hugh of St. Victor (d. 1141) was a key figure in popularizing Dionysian theology in his *Commentary on the Celestial Hierarchy.*[110] The same influence is found in his pupil,

105. Edited by M.-T. D'Alverny, "Les pérégrinations de l'âme dans l'autre monde d'après un anonyme de la fin du XIIe siècle," *AHDL,* 15-17 (1940-42), pp. 239-99.

106. Known as the *Liber Avicennae in primis et secundis substantiis et de fluxu entis* and edited by R. de Vaux, *Notes et textes sur l'Avicennisme latin aux confins des XIIe-XIIIe siècles* (Paris, 1934), pp. 88-140.

107. As de Vaux has noted, *op. cit.,* p. 145; cf. also E. Gilson, "Les sources greco-arabes de l'augustinisme avicénnisant," *AHDL,* 4 (1930) p. 86, note 1.

108. N. Haring, "The Porretans and the Greek Fathers," *Mediaeval Studies,* 24 (1962), pp. 181-209.

109. S. Otto, *Die Funktion des Bildbegriffes. . .,* pp. 51-52.

110. *PL* 175, 923-1154. On the importance of this work, cf. R. Javelet, *Image et ressemblance,* I, pp. 331-33; R. Roques, "Connaissance de Dieu et théologie symbolique d'après l'*In Hierarchiam Caelestem Sancti Dionysii* de Hugues de St. Victor," *Structures théologiques de la Gnose à Richard de St. Victor* (Paris,

Richard, the Prior of St. Victor.[111] Bernard of Clairvaux, however much he may deserve the epithet of theological conservative in some areas, was deeply conversant with Greek theology and made much use of it in his theory of mysticism.[112] Bernard's friend and confidant, William of St. Thierry, is an even more striking witness to the import of Greek theology on the anthropology of the twelfth century. J.-M. Déchanet has demonstrated the significance of the thought of Origen and Gregory of Nyssa on the abbot of St Thierry.[113] Isaac of Stella was no less influenced by the *Orientale lumen*; it shows as clearly in his doctrine of the divine nature as in his *Letter on the Soul.*[114]

In short, it is evident that the systematizing aspect of twelfth-century speculation on man, whether of the more naturalistic variety evident in the scientists and the masters of Chartres, or of the spiritualistic tendency found in the Victorines and Cistercians, stood at the crossroads where past anthropological traditions met and were appropriated and transformed by the genius of twelfth-century theology. In terms of this general background, a more precise analysis of the sources of William, Isaac, and *The Spirit and the Soul* will

---

1962), pp. 294-364; H. Weisweiler, "Die Ps.-Dionysiuskommentare des Skotus Eriugena und Hugos von St. Viktor," *RTAM,* 19 (1952), pp. 26-47; and S. Otto, *op. cit.,* pp. 127-36.

111. Cf. G. Dumeige, "Influence du pseudo-Denys en Occident: Richard de St. Victor," *DS* (Paris, 1937-), Vol. III, 324-29.

112. E. Gilson emphasized Bernard's dependence on Maximus the Confessor in his *The Mystical Theology of St. Bernard* (N.Y., 1940), pp. 25-28; and J. Leclercq showed his acquaintance with Origen in a number of articles, especially "Origène au XIIe siècle," *Irenikon,* 24 (1951), pp. 425-39. For a summary article, cf. J. Daniélou, "S. Bernard et les Pères grecs," *St. Bernard théologien (Analecta Sacri Ordinis Cisterciensis* 9, 1953), pp. 46-55. Bernard's debt to the Pseudo-Dionysius does not appear to be large; cf. E. Boissard, "S.Bernard et le Pseudo-Aréopagite," *RTAM,* 26(1959),pp. 214-63.

113. J. M. Déchanet, *Aux sources de la spiritualité de Guillaume de St.-Thierry* (Bruges, 1940), especially Chap. III; and *Guillaume de St.Thierry. L'homme et son oeuvre* (Bruges, 1942).

114. A. Frachebound, "Le Pseudo-Denys l'Aréopagite parmi les sources du cistercien Isaac de l'Etoile," *Collectanea ordinis cisterciensium reformatorum,* 9 (1947), pp. 328-41; and 10 (1948), pp. 19-34; and B. McGinn, "*Theologia* in Isaac of Stella, " *Cîteaux,* 21 (1970), pp. 219-35.

disclose their place in these various currents of anthropological speculation. Then we can turn to the question of their significance for the Cistercian movement as a whole.

THE THREE TREATISES

WILLIAM OF ST THIERRY

William of St Thierry is the writer who has deservedly profited the most from the renewal of interest in Cistercian theology in the past generation. The importance of Bernard of Clairvaux has, in one way or another, always been realized; the theological stature of William has begun to receive its due only recently. Those in any way acquainted with the literature on William will be aware of how difficult it is to summarize the thought of such a rich thinker in a brief compass. Indeed, it would be out of place to attempt a full summary here, especially when in this series a number of distinguished scholars of William's writings have already had their say.[115] There is, however, a need for a study of the treatise *The Nature of the Body and the Soul,* or *The Physics of the Body and Soul* as it was also known.[116] This study will concentrate on determining the way in which William made use of a variety of sources in his theological anthropology, and in making some suggestions about the significance of this anthropology for his better-known mystical treatises like *The Mirror of Faith, The Enigma of Faith,* and *The Golden Epistle.*

Born at Liège about 1085, William may have studied at Laon before becoming a Benedictine at the Abbey of St

---

115. J. Hourlier and J.M.Déchanet in their respective Introductions to volumes I and II of *The Works of William of St Thierry.*

116. The only other study devoted to this treatise is that of J.-M. Déchanet in his *Aux sources de spiritualité de Guillaume de Saint-Thierry* (Bruges,1940), especially pp. 26-59. The extent of my dependence on Déchanet's work will be obvious throughout, but the research of the past thirty years could not fail to widen knowledge of the sources used by William (e.g., his dependence on Claudianus Mamertus and his use of the *Pantegni* of Constantine) and call into question some of Déchanet's interpretations (e.g., on the extent of the Augustinianism shown in the text).

Nicasius at Reims. Elected abbot of nearby St Thierry in 1119, he had alrady met St Bernard and come under his influence. By 1124 he was begging Bernard's permission to join the Cistercians, but it was not until 1135 that he could lay down his abbatial charge and retire in bad health to the Cistercian abbey of Signy where he remained until his death in 1148.

The first question that confronts a student of *The Nature of the Body and the Soul* is that of its time and place of composition. Although some of the works of William come from his period as the abbot of St Thierry,[117] the bulk of his writings are from his time at Signy. Modern authorities are in general agreement that   *The Nature of the Body and the Soul* dates from then, though any more precise determination is hypothetical.[118] A date around 1140 may be as close as we can reasonably come.[119]

The second problem that confronts an investigator of the treatise is that of its originality. William announces in his Prologue ". . .that what you read is not my own; rather have I gathered here in one place what I have taken from the books, partly of the philosophers and physicians,[120] partly from ecclesiastical teachers, and not merely their sense, but

117. Notably the *De contemplando Deo, De natura et dignitate amoris, De sacramento altaris,* and the *Meditationes.* Cf. A. Wilmart, "La série et la date des ouvrages de Guillaume de Saint-Thierry," *Revue Mabillon,* 14 (1924), pp. 157-67, especially the chart on p. 156.

118. Wilmart, *op. cit.,* p. 166; J.-M. Déchanet, *Aux sources. . .,* pp. 57-58, note 1; and in his Introduction to *The Works of William of St. Thierry. Vol.2. The Exposition of the Song of Songs* (Spencer, 1970), p. viii; and C. H. Talbot, *Ailred of Rievaulx: De Anima. Mediaeval and Renaissance Studies: Supplement I* (London,1952), pp. 47-48, all affirm that it dates from the Signy period. L. Bouyer in his *The Cistercian Heritage* (Westminster, 1958), p. 85, suggests an earlier date, perhaps basing himself on some hesitation shown by Déchanet in his early works.

119. We do know that William was working on the *Speculum fidei, Aenigma fidei,* and the *Epistola aurea,* for which the *De natura corporis et animae* might be seen as a preparation, c.1144-45, cf. Wilmart, *op. cit.,* 166 sqq.

120. The term *physicus* used here originally meant "a student of natural philosophy *(physica),*" but by the early part of the 12th century had come to mean "physician" due to the new stress on the necessity for a theoretical grounding and close alliance of philosophy and medicine. Cf. P. O. Kristeller, "The School of Salerno," pp. 515-17.

their spoken or written words." This confession is strengthened by the great dependence on past sources even to the point of frequent and extensive verbatim quotations. Nevertheless, J.—M. Déchanet and others have made a strong case not only for the originality of the work, but also for its fundamental importance in a general evaluation of William's theology.[121] It is to be hoped that the present examination of the treatise will help to confirm this judgment.

William's Prologue situates the work squarely in the main line of twelfth-century anthropological speculation by embodying two of its major themes: that of self-knowledge and that of man as the microcosm, the image of the world. The advice of the Delphic maxim that true wisdom was to know oneself was the cornerstone of Cistercian speculation on man;[122] the microcosm theme was even more widespread, especially among authors with an interest in natural philosophy and medicine.[123] What is most significant about the way in which William utilizes these twelfth-century commonplaces, however, is seen in the division of his treatise into a natural science or "physics" of the body and a natural science of the soul (*Physica corporis, Physica animae*). Among the theologians of the era, the Abbot of St Thierry is distinctive in giving such a separate and important role to the necessity of the knowledge of the material component of man for an adequate anthropology. While other Cistercian authors, especially Isaac of Stella, display an interest in the new wave of Arabic medicine, none of them give it the same systematic place that William does in the creation of a total anthropology.[124] William's attempts at constructing lines of communica-

121. *Aux sources . . .*, pp. 58-59; and the same author's *William of Saint Thierry: The Man and his Work.* CS 10 (Spencer, Mass.: Cistercian Publications, (1972), pp. 35, 138-139, 151-152. Cf. also L. Bouyer, *op. cit.,* p. 94.

122. On self-knowledge in William, cf. J.-M. Déchanet, "La connaissance de soi d'après Guillaume de Saint-Thierry," *La vie spirituelle: Supplement,* 56 (1958), pp. 102-22.

123. For an introduction to the history of the theme of the microcosm, cf. R. Allers, "Microcosmos from Anaximandros to Paracelsus," *Traditio,* 2 (1944), pp. 319-409.

124. P. Michaud-Quantain, "La classification des puissances de l'âme au XIIe siècle," pp. 20-21, speaks of the Galenic inspiration of William's medical knowl-

tion between his physics of the body and physics of the soul
may be tenuous analogies at best, but that should not blind
us to their fundamental message, viz., that any theory of
man's ability to experience God which abstracts from the
best contemporary insight into the nature of man's physical
situation in the world does so at its own peril.

The first part of the treatise, *The Physics of the Body*, is
notable for its strong adherence to the new medicine as
known through the writings of Constantine the African and
possibly *The Difference of the Spirit and the Soul* of Constabulinus.[125] Ancient medicine was based upon the theory of
the four elements (fire, air, water, and earth) which create
the four humors whose balance is the key to the health of the
body. It is no surprise then that William begins his *The
Physics of the Body* with a brief discussion of the elements
and humors.[126] He goes on to make his close dependence on
Salernitan medicine more explicit in the second section, not
only by citing *The Book of Degrees*,[127] but also by his classification of the four natural powers; i.e., the appetitive, the

edge, though he does admit direct contact with Oriental sources. While many of
the particulars of William's doctrine might be ultimately traced back to Galen,
both in terms of total organization and the channels of transmission, it is more
correct to describe it as Arabic. Michaud-Quantain is mistaken in claiming
Boethius as a source for William's classifications of the powers of the soul.

125. We cannot be sure if William really knew the work of the Syrian author,
since the dating of the translations emanating from Toledo is so uncertain. John
of Spain dedicated his translation of the *De differentia spiritus et animae* to
Raymond the archbishop of Toledo from 1126 to 1151. Thus it is possible that
William, writing around 1140, might have had access to the work; indeed, several
particulars cited below point in this direction. Against this, however, it must be
noted that most of the medical material available in the *De differentia* was also to
be found in Constantine's works and that there seem to be no verbatim quotations of the *De differentia* in William's treatise. On John of Spain, cf. Steinschneider, *op. cit.*, pp. 40-50; L. Thorndike, *A History of Magic and Experimental
Science* (N.Y., 1923), Vol. 2, pp. 73-78; and C. H. Haskins, *op. cit.*, pp. 13-14.

126. Despite the traditional and general character of the doctrine here, para-
graphs 1, 2, and 3 of William's treatise show strong resemblance to the treatment
of the four humors in Constantine's *De communibus medico cognitu necessariis
locis (Pantegni)*, Book I, 25 (Basle, 1539), pp. 20-23.

127. On this work cf. L. Thorndike, *op. cit.*, Vol. 1, pp. 750-51. The work is
printed in the 1536 Basle edition of the works of Constantine, pp. 342-87.

retentive, the digestive, and the expulsive.[128] The first three sections of the work are, indeed, very much of an amalgam resulting from the revision of traditional monastic medical knowledge in the light of the more systematic Arabic wave of the first part of the twelfth century, as is demonstrated by the more extensive description of the four humors (reddish bile or choler, blood, phlegm, and black bile or melancholia) appearing at the end of section two and throughout section three.[129] Many of the particulars of the description of the operation of the humors suggest a source in the *Pantegni* translated by the monk of Monte Cassino.[130]

The fourth section introduces one of the most characteristic notes of William's physiology, and one which again displays his direct dependence on the text of Constantine, the doctrine of the powers or spirits by means of which the body is controlled: the natural power in the liver which man has in common with vegetative and animal life, the spiritual power (the power of breath) in the heart which he shares with all animals, and the animal power in the brain some of whose operations are peculiar to him alone.[131] These three powers provide a motif for the remainder of the first part of the treatise, although William's discussion of them tends to be

128. On the four powers (*appetitiva,contentiva,digestiva,expulsiva*) in the writings of Constantine, cf. *Pantegni* IV, 11, p. 82; *De stomachi naturalibus et non naturalibus affectionibus* (Basle, 1536, pp. 219-23) ; and *De melancholia* II (Basle, 1536, p. 286). The *De differentia spiritus et animae* III (ed. Barach, p. 137) also knows these four powers, but uses a slightly different terminology (*attractiva, retentiva, digestiva, expulsiva*).

129. The humors appear in the *Premnon physicon* IV, 1 (*ed. Burkhard*, p. 59). The doctrine of the four humors being formed in the liver is also present in William of Conches, *De philosophia mundi* IV, 19 (*PL* 172, 92B-93A). Constantine wrote a separate treatise entitled *De melancholia* (Basle, 1536, pp. 280-98).

130. E.g., the harmfulness of red bile's dominance (cf. I, 25, p. 23); and the operation of the *vena cava*, portal vein, and the pancreas (II, 12-13, pp. 38-39).

131. On the three powers in Constantine, cf. IV, 1, p. 79. Constabulinus mentions a *spiritus vitalis* in the heart and a *spiritus animalis* in the head, but has no third spirit for the liver (*ed. cit.,* p. 124). Isaac of Stella is closer to Constabulinus in his *Sermon 35* (*PL* 194, 1808A), as is William of Conches *De philosophia mundi* IV, 22 (*PL* 172, 94B).

digressive. The division of the natural power into generative, supportive, and nutritive functions is also from Constantine.[132]

The fifth, sixth, and seventh sections, in discussing the animal power or spirit, distinguish three sections or lobes in the brain: the forward lobe responsible for sensation and imaginative power, the middle lobe for reason and discernment, and rear lobe for memory and movement. This threefold division of the brain goes back to Galen. There are a number of variations in ascribing powers to the three lobes; but Nemesius's *Premnon physicon*,[133] *The Difference of Spirit and Soul* of Constabulinus,[134] and Constantine's *Pantegni*[135] all have a division where the front lobe is associated with imagination, the middle with reason, and the rear with memory. This division was also popular with Chartrain authors.[136] William emphasizes that the spirits of which he speaks are corporeal, instruments of the soul, not to be identified with the spiritual soul itself.[137] Thus, in the first part of this treatise he is chiefly being influenced by the medical senses of the term *spiritus* that were common in the twelfth century,[138] though it must be remembered in other treatises he sometimes uses *spiritus* for the highest dimension of the soul itself.

132. *Pantegni* IV, 11, p. 81.

133. XIII, 6-7 (ed. Burkhard, p. 89).

134. II (*ed. Barach*, p. 130). This passage is quite close to William and is an argument for his acquaintance with the text.

135. IV, 9 (*ed. cit.*, p. 91).

136. E.g., William of Conches, *De phil. mundi* IV, 24 (*PL* 172, 95B); John of Salisbury, *Metalogicon* IV, 17 (ed. Webb, pp. 182-83). It is also found in Adelhard of Bath, *Quaestiones naturales*, chap. 18 (*ed. cit.*, p. 22), and *De eodem et diverso* (ed. H. Willner, *BGPM* 4, 1, pp. 32-33). Consideration of only the forward lobe as the seat of imagination and the middle lobe as that of reason is found in Thierry of Chartres' *Librum hunc*, in the *De septem septennis*, and Clarenbald's *Tractatus super librum Boethii de Trinitate*.

137. The cooling action of this corporeal spirit on the heat of the heart described in sections 5-6 appears to be reminiscent of Constabulinus, *De diff. spir. et an.* II (*ed. cit.*, pp. 122-23).

138. Cf. M.-D. Chenu, "Spiritus . . .," pp. 224-25; and E. Bertola, "Le Fonti medico-filosofiche della Dottrina dello Spirito."

The description of how spiritual power,[139] acting in the posterior lobe of the brain, effects motion through the nerves also shows William's dependence on Arabic material. The seven pairs of nerves which leaving the brain communicate motion to the body,[140] the description of the spinal cord, or the *nucha* as the Arabs call it,[141] and the knowledge of the two membranes protecting the brain,[142] are all found in the familiar texts that have been so frequently cited already.

Section eight returns to the action of the animal spirit in the proper sense (i.e., apart from its connection with the inferior operations of the body) to begin the discussion of sensation which will conclude the first part of the treatise. The fullest attention is given to the faculty of sight, the noblest faculty and one of exceptional importance to Christian anthropology influenced by classical thought. As J. Malevez and J.-M. Déchanet have pointed out, William uses sensation as a basic analogy for his interpretation of that faculty of the soul by which man can reach union with God.[143] The metaphysics behind his theory of sensation is part of the whole Hellenic tradition based upon the principles of like being known by like and the active function of the soul in all forms of knowledge in Platonic thought.[144] In analyzing the

139. William's sliding terminology can be a bit confusing. He uses "spiritual power or spirit" both for the original spiritual power connected with the heart (sections 4-5), and also for that power as it ascends to the head, is purified there, and in turn gives movement to the body (sections 6-7). This more general use of "spiritual power" is defined as: "Virtus ergo spiritualis est quae vivificat omnia, et a qua vivit quidquid vivit in corpore. Et hic est *spiritus spiritalis.*" Is is also called "vital spirit."

140. *Pantegni* II, 9, p. 35; *De diff. spir. et an.* II (*ed. cit.,* pp. 127-28).

141. *Pantegni* II, 10, pp. 35-7; III, 12, p. 59; *De diff. spir. et an.* II (*ed. cit.,* p. 128).

142. Found in William of Conches, *De phil. mundi* IV, 24 (*PL* 172, 95A) with a specific reference to Constantine; cf. *Pantegni* II, 9, "De nervis," pp. 34-7.

143. J.Malevez, "La doctrine de l'image et de la connaissance mystique chez Guillaume de Saint-Thierry," *Recherches des sciences religieuses,* 22 (1932), pp. 270-77; J.-M. Déchanet, "Amor Ipse Intellectus est: La doctrine de l'amour-intellection chez Guillaume de Saint-Thierry," *Revue du moyen âge latin,* 1 (1946), pp. 350-54.

144. Malevez suggests Augustine's *De Trinitate* XI (especially chap. 2) as the source for William's doctrine of sensation. This may well be so, but it might also be added that similar doctrines of sensation are general among many patristic and medieval theologians.

doctrine of this section of the work, Déchanet has pointed
out that William's account of sensation involves three mo-
ments: (1) the presence in the sense organ of something of
the same nature as the object sensed; (2) the encounter of the
active interior element and the element emanating from the
object (e.g., in the case of sight, the light emanating from the
eyes and the light from the object); and (3) the transformation of the one who senses into the object sensed.[145] While
William does not make the application between this theory of
sensation and his theory of mystical union explicit here, the
long discussion of sensation in *The Physics of the Body*
shows how basic this treatise was to his later work. In this he
was only following a standard Cistercian pattern: a *De anima*
was the necessary foundation for an adequate theory of
mysticism.

The physiology of sensation described in these final sections is also dependent upon Constantine. This is especially
true of the long section on sight,[146] but in a general sense it
may also be said to apply to the other senses as well.[147] The
first part of the treatise closes in section ten with a return to
the theory of the four humors. William is anxious to empha-
size that the physicians and philosophers who have spoken
well of the exterior man have failed to reach the true dignity
of the inner man made in the image of God. The exterior
man, nonetheless, shows at least a vestige of God in the unity
and harmony which he displays.[148] The author is now anxious to press on to ". . .what the Catholic Fathers have learned from God and taught to men."

145. *Ibid.*
146. *Pantegni* III, 13, pp. 59-61. Déchanet in his *Aux sourcess . . .* , p. 204,
asserts that Constantine's *De oculis* is also a source for this section. William of
Conches discusses the function of the three humors and seven sheaths of the eye
in a manner similar to William in *De phil. mundi* IV, 25 (*PL* 172, 95D).
147. Smell, hearing and taste (section 9) are treated in *Pantegni* III, 14-16, pp.
61-2. For the notion of the two *ubera* of the brain which make the sense of smell
possible, cf. *Pantegni* II, 10, p. 35.
148. Of the curious information at the end of section 10, the idea of the
geometrically circular figure of man is classical in origin, while the two hundred
and forty-one bones in the human body and the thirty-two even and one uneven
pairs of nerves connected with the *nucha* are from Constantine's *Pantegni*, II, 8,
p. 34, and II, 9, p. 37, respectively.

If the first part of William's treatise is an example of the entry of Arabic medicine into the intellectual world of twelfth-century monasticism, the second part, *The Physics of the Soul*, is no less eloquent of the influence of Greek theology.[149] Constantine the African was the dominant influence on the first part; the Cappadocian Father, Gregory of Nyssa, through his work *The Image, or the Creation of Man*, is at the center of the second part. Gregory's ideas, frequently in word-for-word citation, are interwoven with more traditional western psychology drawn particularly from Augustine and his disciple Claudianus Mamertus. It is worthy of note that William makes use of Gregory's work through the little-known translation of John the Scot (composed c.862-64) rather than the popular version of Denis the Little.[150]

William begins the first section of his *The Physics of the Soul* by adverting to the opposition between the philosophers of this world and the doctors of the Church on the question of the definition of the soul. The definitions are taken verbatim from Cassiodorus's list in his *The Soul*.[151] This theme of opposition, announced in the Prologue, mentioned at the end of the first part, and now reinforced at the beginning of the second, was of great importance to William, for despite his willingness to make use of non-Christian medical and philosophical material in the creation of a theological anthropology, the sense of theology as *sapientia* rather than *scientia* which led to his attacks on Abelard is clearly present in this treatise.

Because the treatise of Gregory upon which he depends so heavily was itself infused with medical material (as one of the prime witnesses to the first age of the mingling of Platonic psychology and medicine in Christian thought), the first few

---

149. Concerning the influence of Greek theology, the *Orientale Lumen* as William himself called it, on 12th century psychology, cf. the remarks of M.-D. Chenu, *La théologie au douzième siècle*, pp. 297-99.

150. Déchanet was the first to demonstrate this in his *Aux sources . . .*, especially pp. 26-59. He also argued for an influence of John the Scot's *Periphyseon* on the *De natura corporis et animae*; but the texts he adduced (e.g., p. 205) tend to convey very generalized notions which argue more for common patristic sources rather than direct dependence on this treatise.

151. *De anima* IV (ed. Halporn, pp. 72-73).

sections of William's *The Physics of the Soul* are quite heavily weighted in a medical direction, thus causing some overlapping with the first part. The eclectic nature of early medieval psychology facilitated the juxtaposition of diverse systems, whether in terms of the classification of the powers of the soul or of the description of the organs of the body. The threefold classification of organs with which this first section is concerned is from the thirtieth chapter of the Cappodocian's work.[152] The second section continues the medical material with a paraphrase of Gregory's treatment of the three basic organs, the brain, the heart, and the liver; it also incorporates the Cappadocians analogy between the work of a sculptor and the gradual perfection of the image of God in man.[153] Somewhat eclectically, this leads into a long section taken verbatim from Claudianus Mamertus on the microcosmic dimensions of man.[154]

The third section relates more properly to the soul as such. There are two general areas discussed, the superiority of the human soul to the senses, and the incorporeality and ubiquity of the soul. The statement that only man can truly be said

---

152. *De hom.* XXX (*PG* 44, 240D-41A). This passage provides a convincing illustration of William's use of the translation of John the Scot. Compare:

1. William (*PL* 180 709A):	2. John the Scot (*ed. cit.*, p. 257):	3. Dionysius Exiguus (*PL* 67, 400C):
Tria enim circa corporis naturam esse intelligimus	Tria circa corporis naturam intelleximus,	Tria quadam de natura corporis intelligenda percepimus,
quorum causa singula quae in nobis sunt constituuntur.	quorum causa singula quae in nobis sunt constituuntur.	quorum gratia singula quae in nobis sunt constituta esse cernuntur.
Nam quaedam propter [omit *bene*] vivere	Nam quaedam propter vivere,	Quaedam namque propter vitam,
quaedam vero propter bene vivere,	quaedam propter bene vivere	quaedam vero propter bonam vitam,
quaedam ad successionem futurorum bonorum opportunitatem habent.	alia vero ad successionem futurorum opportunitatem habent.	quaedam ad successionem posteritatis opportune formata sunt.

153. *De hom.* XXX (*ed. cit.*, pp. 257-62).
154. *De statu* I, 21 (*ed. cit.*, pp. 71, 1. 20 - 73, 1. 12).

to have a soul,[155] and the comparison of reason to a queen and the senses to her servants[156] are both dependent on Gregory, though perhaps not through the translation of John the Scot. It is in the course of this discussion that the Abbot first introduces the distinction between the soul in general (*anima*) and the intellectual soul (*animus*). While William does not make use here of the trichotomy of *anima-animus-spiritus* which was to be of importance in such later works as *The Golden Letter*[157] it might be said that this distinction between *anima* and *animus* when coupled with the *unitas spiritus* mentioned in section thirteen already hints in that direction.[158] The term *animus* is of great importance for William.[159] As O. Brooke has demonstrated, the mature mystical theology of the Abbot's last works sketches out two roads back to God, a spiritual ascent, the *credo ut experiar*, and an intellectual ascent, the *credo ut intelligam*—roads which William attempts to synthesize in his concept of *ratio fidei*.[160] The *animus* fits within the pattern of the intellectual ascent which will dominate in *The Enigma of Faith*. As Brooke says: "The 'animus,' the principle of rational, discursive reflection will be seen elsewhere to emerge as a rational speculative discipline distinct though never wholly separated from spiritual experience."[161] The remainder of the third

155. *De hom.* XXX (*PG* 44, 256B). The translation of John the Scot has an abbreviated ending (*ed. cit.*, p. 262), so William could not have gotten his material from it. The version of Dionysius contains the longer ending, but his vocabulary does not show any similarities to William's text (*PL* 67, 408A). Could William have made use of an emended version of the Irishman's translation?

156. *De hom.* X (*ed. cit.*, pp. 219-20). Contrary to William's usual manner, there is a general similarity, but no direct verbal parallels to the version of John the Scot.

157. This division, which founds the distinction of the stages of the spiritual life into *animalis-rationalis-spiritualis*, is discussed by O. Brooke, "The Trinitarian Aspect of the Ascent of the Soul to God in the Theology of William of St. Thierry," *RTAM*, 26 (1959), pp. 99-105; and J.-M. Déchanet, *Exposition on the Song of Songs*, pp. xxxiii-iv.

158. M.-D. Chenu, "Spiritus...," p. 213, shows that that *anima-animus* dichotomy was known to John the Scot, cf. *Periphyseon* IV, 16 (*PL* 122, 825).

159. Cf. Déchanet, "La connaissance de soi...." pp. 115-17.

160. Cf. O. Brooke, "William of St. Thierry's Doctrine of the Ascent to God by Faith," *RTAM,* 30 (1963), pp. 181-204; and 33 (1966), pp. 282-318.

161. *Op. cit.*, p. 288; cf. also pp. 310-13.

section is a mosaic of quotations from the *Image of Man* in the version of John the Scot, e.g., that the soul is separate from the senses;[162]that the soul is not located in any particular organ of the body;[163] the manner of the intellectual soul's presence in the body.[164] The comparison between the soul's use of the body and the musician's use of an instrument with which the section closes is also dependent on Gregory and has a general parallel in Isaac of Stella's *Letter on the Soul*.[165]

The fourth section returns to physiology, but from another point of view, that of the argument from design which affirms that ". . .nature prepares and adapts the instrument of the body to the use of reason in everything." Thus, the provision of hands frees the mouth for the delicate task of speaking what the soul wishes to say, and the hands are also the instrument of conveying the dictates of reason in writing.[166]

In section five the author emphasizes a treatment of what J.-M. Déchanet has termed the similitudes or analogies of the soul to the divine nature.[167] The third section had discussed the first of these, that of the ubiquity of the soul;[168] here, again in dependence on the work of Gregory, this analogy is further pursued. Like God, the soul is one stable power making use of all the senses, though the Abbot is quick to point out the distance of the soul from the divine nature—it is only an image.[169] The remainder of the section is an extended

162. *De hom.* XI (*ed. cit.*, p. 221).

163. *De hom.* XII (*ed. cit.*, pp. 221-23).

164. *De hom.* XV (*ed. cit.*, p. 231).

165. *De hom.* XII (*ed. cit.*, pp. 223-24). Cf. Isaac of Stella, *Ep an* 13 (*PL* 194, 1882D-83A); below, p. .

166. Based on *De hom.* VIII-IX (*ed. cit.*, pp. 218-19). There also seems to be some influence of XVI (XVII in the translation of John the Scot).

167. Déchanet, *Aux sources* . . . , pp. 39-46, who distinguishes between: (1) the image of God (*memoria, ratio, voluntas*) which is the capacity of the soul to know and love God; (2) the resemblance which is the actualization of that capacity; and (3) the similitudes or analogies which are the witnesses to that resemblance (cf. p. 38, note 1).

168. Also important for Isaac of Stella, *Ep an* 14 (1883B-84A), although his treatment depends more on Augustine and Claudianus Mamertus than on Gregory of Nyssa.

169. *De hom.* XI (*ed. cit.*, p. 221). What Déchanet calls the natural unlikeness of the soul to God, cf. *Aux sources* . . . , p. 47.

treatment of the second major analogy of the soul to God—
that of its royal nature. The erect stature of man shows his
superiority over the other animals,[170] but man's real kingly
nature consists in the rule of reason over the desires of nature.[171] Those men who allow this relation to be reversed lose
the divine image and put on an earthy one; indeed, they
become worse than brute beasts, insofar as man's thinking
capacity begets a far greater variety of vices from the passions
than can be found in beasts.[172] Man's royal prerogative consists in using the things of earth so that he may enjoy the
vision of God.[173] The same theme is pursued in the following
section in terms of a contrast—the weakness and misery of
the exterior man in comparison with all the other animals
show that his true royal power must reside in reason.[174] (Concentration on the misery of man was, of course, one of the
directions in which the self-knowledge imperative of twelfth-
century anthropology frequently proceeded.)[175] The first
part of this section also introduces the third of the analogies
between the soul and the divine nature, that of the freedom
of the will.[176]

The force of all these analogies reaches its culmination in
the seventh section. Man's power of reason is what enables
him to dominate other creatures and to make use of them.[177]
He is the image of the king of all things, but in the interior,
not the exterior man, having power instead of a purple robe,
immortality in place of a sceptre, and justice rather than a
royal diadem.[178] Man is the image of God in his capacity to

170. *De hom.* VIII (*ed. cit.,* p. 216).

171. *De hom.* XIV (XV in the version of John the Scot, p. 230).

172. *De hom.* XVIII (XIX in the version of John the Scot, p. 238). On the
various ways in which the soul can lose its likeness to God through sin, cf.
Déchanet, *Aux sources . . . ,* pp. 47-53.

173. *De hom.* II (*ed. cit.,* p. 212). The distinction of use and enjoyment is, of
course, a common one in Augustine; but William's text cites word for word from
Gregory.

174. *De hom.* VII (*ed. cit.,* p. 215).

175. Déchanet, "La connaissance de soi . . . ," p. 104; E. Gilson, *The Spirit of
Mediaeval Philosophy,* p. 217.

176. *De hom.* IV (*ed. cit.,* p. 213).

177. *De hom.* VII (*ed. cit.,* pp. 215-16).

178. The comparison is taken verbatim from *De hom.* IV (*ed. cit.,* p. 213).

share in every good; and this dignity of man as the image shows itself most directly in his freedom.[179] It may appear from the extensive quotations from Gregory of Nyssa in these last few sections that William is merely copying past doctrine without making any contribution of his own. Several points indicate, however, that with some originality he is effecting a rapprochement between traditional Greek theological anthropology and some of the new trends of twelfth-century thought. The role given to nature as the force overseeing the order of the world in the sixth section, for instance, may hint at that concern for the operations of *natura* which were so important to many early twelfth century theologians;[180] and the final passage on free will, while dependent on Gregory, by its significant introduction of the Bernardine term *liberum arbitrium* indicates an attempt to interpret Gregory in the light of one of the important themes of Cistercian anthropology.[181]

The eighth section of *The Physics of the Soul* finally brings the reader to the question of the classification of its powers. In one sense it is the central section of the entire treatise because in it William sets up the general analogies and parallels between the classification and operations of the organs

---

179. *De hom.* XVI (*ed. cit.*, p. 234).

180. Cf. M.-D. Chenu, *La théologie au douzième siècle*, chap. 1 (translated by J. Taylor and L. K. Little, *Nature, Man, and Society in the Twelfth-Century*, Chicago, 1968).

181. Compare the following:

1. William (717CD):	2. The version of John the Scot (*ed. cit.*, p. 234,11.30-33):
. . . in eo item quod sit liber omni necessitate animus, nullique naturali potentiae subjugatur, sed per se potentem ad id quod desiderat habet voluntatem,	. . . in eo item quod sit omnium necessitate liberum nullique naturali hoc est materiali potentiae subjugatur. Sed per se potentem ad id quod desiderat habet voluntatem
virtutem scilicet liberi arbitrii suam exprimit dignitatem. Res enim est dominatu carens ac voluntaria virtus, quod autem cogitur, violentiamque patitur, virtus non est. For *liberum arbitrium* in Bernard, cf. *De gra*, 2; (*Opera omnia*, ed. J. Leclercq 3 168).	res enim est dominatu carens ac voluntaria virtus, quod autem cogitur violentiamque patitur virtus esse non potest.

of the body and those of the powers of the soul which were implicit in the double structure which he gave to his work. The classifications that he uses here are not dependent on Gregory of Nyssa, but are generalized divisions present in a wide variety of patristic sources and frequently found among his fellow Cistercians. All of them are also discussed in Isaac of Stella's *Letter on the Soul.*

William begins from the traditional classification of the sciences into physics (natural science), reason or logic, and morality or ethics.[182] We cannot know what the soul is because of its spiritual nature; but we must know why it is, i.e., the reason for its existence, since we are reasonable creatures. In true monastic fashion, the goal of this knowledge is that we may live according to reason. The moral rationality of the soul is made up of the four cardinal virtues, just as the body is made up of the four elements; the four natural powers of the body (the appetitive, retentive, digestive, and expulsive) are compared to the four passions (hope, joy, fear, and sadness) by means of which the soul conducts the rational life. The threefold Platonic division of the powers of the soul into rationality, positive appetite, and negative appetite[183] is in turn compared to the division of the chief powers of the body, the natural, the spiritual, and the animal. Just as each of the powers of the body has its own proper effect, rationality is the foundation of faith, the positive appetite of hope, and the negative appetite of charity. William concludes with a discussion of the implications of this doctrine.

The ninth section continues the parallel between the body and the soul by extending it to a brief treatment of sensation. Sensation as something invisible and yet corporeal (because using the sense organs), is seen as that which mediates between the soul which is invisible and incorporeal and the visible corporeal body. Once again the fundamental Platonic law of median terms (*Timaeus* 31bc) is at work.

182. On the history of this division and its appearance in Isaac of Stella, cf. my article "*Theologia* in Isaac of Stella," pp. 220-21.
183. Cf. *Rep.* IV (439c-41d); *Tim.* 69d; etc. It is found among many of the Fathers; e.g., Tertullian, Origen, Ambrose, Jerome, Gregory the Great, and Isidore of Seville. Bernard of Clairvaux uses it, as do Isaac of Stella and Aelred of Rievaulx.

The tenth section turns to another of the themes common to Platonizing anthropology, viz., threefold comparisons of God, the soul, and the body. Like the Cistercians Isaac of Stella[184] and Nicholas of Clairvaux,[185] William's source for these comparisons is to be found in Claudianus Mamertus; the abbot of St Thierry may well be at least partially responsible for the popularity of *The State of the Soul* among later Cistercians. Beginning from a comparison between the soul and God in terms of the category of location, the general question about the relation of God, the soul, and the body to all the Aristotelian categories is then pursued, though not in a systematic fashion. William's comparison of the soul's presence in the body to the presence of God in the world was an important theme in the thought of Augustine and Claudianus, one which they inherited from Aristotle by way of Plotinus.[186] Both in this question and that of the relation of the soul to the categories of quantity and quality, Isaac of Stella seems to follow William at least through their common source in Claudianus.[187] After several verbatim quotations

184. *Ep An* 2-3 (1875C-77A), below, pp. .

185. In the late 1150's or early 1160's Nicholas of Clairvaux and Peter of Celle quarreled over the correct interpretation of a passage on the threefold comparison in *De statu* III, 7 (*ed. cit.*, p. 166). Cf. *Epistolae* 63 to 66 in *PL* 202, 491-513. M.-D. Chenu discusses this in "Platon à Cîteaux," *AHDL*, 30 (1954), pp. 99-106.

186. Aristotle, *De generatione animalium* I, 19; II, 1 (726b; 734b); and Plotinus, e.g., *Enn.* IV, 2, 1. For its presence in the Latin Fathers, cf. e.g., Augustine, *De immortalitate animae* 16 (*PL* 32, 1034); *De Trinitate* VI, 6, 8 (*ed. cit.*, I, p. 488); and Claudianus Mamertus, *De statu* I, 17; III, 2-3 (*ed. cit.*, pp. 62-64; 155-58).

187. Compare the following:

1. William:	2. Isaac:
(a) 719D:	(a) *Ep an* 3 (1876C):
Humana autem anima quia non habet molem, non habet quantitatem, qui affectuum mutabilitati subjacet, non effugit qualitatem.	Anima vero nec quantitatem habet, quia non est corpus, nec qualitate caret quia non est Deus.
(b) 719D:	(b) *Ep an* 14 (1883D):
Cum enim sicut Deus in mundo, sic quodammodo ipsa sit in corpore suo, ubique scilicet, et ubique; tota, tota in singulis sensibus, ut in singulis tota sentiat ...	Sicut vero Deus in toto, et in singulis totus, sed in semetipso; sic et anima in toto suo corpore, et in singulis membris in semetipsa tota.

from *The State of the Soul* concerning the manner of the soul's relation to sensation, William concludes from these truths, like Isaac, that the essence of the soul is identical with its powers.[188]

To know oneself for the Cistercian authors meant to know in what sense one is the image of God. The following three sections of William's treatise are those in which he gives his answer to this question.[189] The very first sentence of section eleven indicates one of the most profound insights of the Abbot's doctrine of man as the image of God, for, as J. Malevez has pointed out, William views the soul's image character not only in a static sense as something given to human nature, but also in a dynamic sense as something into which man must grow.[190] Much like Augustine in his work on *The Trinity*, William does not give a single answer to the question of the nature of man's image character; but rather circles this deep mystery with a series of ever more direct approximations and insights. In line with the conclusion of the last section that the soul is to be identified with its powers, he begins from the affirmation that if the soul is to be identified with its will, it is thus its love. God too is identified with love. Nevertheless, the love that is the soul differs from the love that is God in being variable; God is the unmoved love that causes the existence of all things. The soul's ubiquity through its power of knowledge—it can see corporeal things like its own interior parts[191] and faraway places too—suggests another way in which it may be said to be the image of the creator. Finally, the author turns to the

---

188. This is given great emphasis in Isaac, *Ep An* 3, below, p. x and in the *De Spiritu et anima*, 4 and 13, below, p. .

189. Cf. J.-M. Déchanet, "La connaissance de soi . . . ," p. 122: " . . . le *nosce teipsum* chrétien, c'est l'actualisation par l'âme — sous la action de grâce du Christ — de sa ressemblance naturelle, originelle, avec Dieu."

190. These two senses of image are related to the two directions of William's thought on the relationship of the image and the knowledge of God. Cf. J. Malevez, *op. cit.*, pp. 190-91; 196; 258-59; 262-63. J.-M. Déchanet, "Amor Ipse Intellectus est . . . ," p. 352; and O. Brooke, "The Trinitarian Aspect of the Ascent of the Soul . . . ," pp. 102-03, also stress the dynamic aspect of the soul's ascent to God.

191. The brief physiological section on the interior organs is dependent on Claudianus Mamertus, *De statu* III, 11 (*ed. cit.*, p. 174, ll. 20-24).

deepest image, the specifically Trinitarian one, where, largely quoting from a text of Claudianus which is really Augustine simplified, he finds the image of the Trinity in mind (*mens*), thought (*cogitatio*), and will (*voluntas*).[192] Discussion of this Trinitarian image emphasizes its dynamic character—the closer that man approaches to the "form that gives form" the more he becomes the image of the God who is love.[193] This is the source of man's true dignity. Self-knowledge, as we are told in section twelve, is not only knowledge of man's misery, but even more a knowledge of his equality with the angels, especially in the person of the head of man, Christ.

The thirteenth section is both the culminating point of the treatise and the best indication of how *The Physics of the Body and the Soul* was intended by the author to be the foundation for the profound theory of the mystical union outlined in his later works: The reader is referred to the studies of J. Malevez, J. M. Déchanet, and O. Brooke for a more detailed study of the way in which the doctrines sketched here are used in the Abbot's later works. In true Augustinian fashion,[194] he reminds us that all things show their origin in the threefold God in some way—every soul consists of memory, deliberation, and will;[195] and every bodily thing besides being one, is capable of being measured,

---

192. *De statu* I 26 (*ed. cit.*, p. 95, 1.18-p.97, 1.5). The triads in Augustine that are closest to this are: (1) *memoria, intelligentia, voluntas* in *De Trin.* X, 11; and (2) *Memoria, cogitatio, voluntas* in XII, 15. Cf. also XIV, 8.

193. The Trinitarian structure of William's theory of mysticism is perhaps his most original contribution as O. Brooke has pointed out in his "The Trinitarian Aspect of the Ascent of the Soul to God in the Theology of William of St. Thierry," *RTAM*, 26 (1959), pp. 85-127. Despite his dependence on Augustine, Brooke considers William closer to Bernard in his emphasis on finding the image in the history of the soul rather than in a purely psychological analysis, *op. cit.*, pp. 94-99.

194. J.-M. Déchanet minimized the Augustinian character of William's Trinitarian doctrine in his *Aux sources. . . .*, p. 35; and was followed by L. Bouyer, *op. cit.*, p. 123. O. Brooke's articles have vindicated the deeply Augustinian nature of the abbot of St Thierry's doctrine of the Trinity, as Déchanet admits in his recent *Exposition of the Song of Songs*, pp. xl-xlvi.

195. *De Trin.* XIV, 7 (*ed. cit.*, p. 370). William uses *consilium* for the middle term rather than Augustine's *intelligentia*.

numbered, and weighed.[196] The knowledge of the traces of the Trinity in all things is another means by which the soul is drawn to the "form that gives form." As the Abbot says in a passage that might be taken as the keystone of his doctrine of the divine transformation of man: "For to study it is to be formed. Whatever is drawn toward God is not its own, but his by whom it is drawn." It is according to this principle that the soul is joined to the Holy Spirit in that unity of spirit which is the heart of his mystical doctrine and which has been well exposed by the scholars mentioned above.[197] With great clarity and power William emphasizes the unique role of the Holy Spirit in the divinization of man; and although he does not pursue other major themes of his mystical theology here, such as the doctrine that love itself is understanding (*amor ipse intellectus est*), there can be no doubt concerning the consistency of doctrine between this treatise and the later mystical works.

Instead of pursuing an analysis of his own mystical themes, William closes his treatise with a symbolic presentation of the stages in which this union is realized. Symbols of ascension have been a favored way from the earliest times of bringing to speech those human experiences which are perceived as in some way going beyond the realm of the every-day. The history of the use of symbolic presentation of the ascension of the soul in Christian literature is a long one. Augustine, though normally preferring the use of the images of interiorization to portray the way in which the soul encounters God, also made some use of symbols of ascension. Perhaps the most developed of these, that appearing in the early treatise, *The Greatness of the Soul,*[198] is utilized by William as the basis for section fourteen.

---

196. Taken from a text in Wisdom 11:21, this theme was popularized by Augustine as a description of the essential characteristics of things, cf. *De gen. ad litt.* IV,3-6 (*PL* 34,299-301). Among the Cistercians, we find it frequently used by Isaac of Stella, e.g., *Sermon* 19 (1753D), *Ep an* 21 (1887A).

197. On the *unitas spiritus,* cf. Malavez, *op. cit.,* pp. 202-05; 259-60; J.-M. Déchanet, "Amor Ipse Intellectus est . . . ," pp. 361-64; and O. Brooke, "The Trinitarian Aspect of the Ascent of the Soul . . . ," pp. 107-09.

198. *DQA* 33 (*PL* 32, 1073-77), dating from c.388.

Once again, the quotation is verbatim. The first step by means of which the soul gives life to and administers the body is common to all living things, the second step, that of the senses, is possessed by men and animals. The third level, that of memory, as the foundation of arts, sciences, etc., is the specifically human. With the fourth step, that of purgation through obedience to the commandments, the ascent of the soul beyond the material begins. The fifth step, the soul's recognition of its own greatness leads to a leap toward God, that is into the contemplation of truth. In the sixth step this gaze at truth becomes peaceful and direct, and this leads to the seventh step, the vision of God. As can be seen from this analysis, Augustine's schema of ascent is more highly intellectualistic than William's own later theories about the nature of the mystical union.

The Abbot of St Thierry concludes in the fifteenth section with a description of the dynamism operative in the ascent or descent of the soul. The entry of themes from Greek theology is evident by the description of the process of ascent and descent under the rubric of *anabathmon* and *katabathmon*.[199] After the description of the joy awaiting the soul at the end of the process of *anabathmon*, there is an extended treatment of the opposing dynamism of the descending path. In its departure from the face of God the soul finds itself in the "region of unlikeness," a term used to describe the effect of original sin among some of the Fathers that was revived in the twelfth century and was very popular among Cistercian

---

199. *Anabathmon* signifying an ascent is found in Augustine, *In Psalmum* 38, 2 (*PL* 36, 413), and Ambrose, *Epist.* 26, 10 (*PL* 16, 1088C). *Catabathmon (-mus)* to the best of my knowledge is not found among the Latin Fathers, but Rufinus's translation of Origen's *De principiis* III, 5 (4) speaks of a descent as a *catabole* (*PG* 11, 329C). J.-M. Déchanet has argued for the direct dependence of much of this section on the *Enneads* of Plotinus, cf. "Guillaume et Plotin," *Revue du moyen âge latin*, 2 (1946), pp. 243-46. The absence of any known translation of the *Enneads* surviving into the 12th century and William's ignorance of Greek create a strong *a priori* argument against such direct dependence. To this investigator, at least, the parallels adduced are so general as to be common to any number of authors in the Neoplatonic tradition.

authors.[200] The region of unlikeness is equated with the land of Naid, or "commotion," according to the exegesis of Origen.[201]

The negative note upon which William of St Thierry ends his treatise serves to highlight the insight that Cistercian speculation on the nature of man, no matter how profound and learned it might be, was always meant to serve a direct moral purpose, the reformation of life as the first step in the ascent to union with God. Although this conclusion contains some of the most negative and anti-corporeal comments of the entire treatise, the final sentences do summarize William's intent and point the way towards the great works of his last years—"Only the difference of love makes this difference between the blessed soul and the damned."

ISAAC OF STELLA

The second Cistercian anthropological text translated here is Isaac of Stella's *Letter on the Soul.* Isaac was English in origin, born probably sometime around the year 1100.[202] As a young man he went to France where he absorbed some of the best theology of the day. In the absence of direct evidence we cannot be sure where he studied, but his writings show great familiarity with the theology of Hugh of St Victor and with the thought of some of the masters of Chartres, as well as a more distant connection with the School of Peter Abelard. It was probably around 1140 that he became a monk at Stella near Poitiers, where he was abbot from 1147

200. The literature on this theme is vast. For a recent summary of its use in the 12th century, cf. R. Javelet, *Image et ressemblance,* Vol. 1, pp. 266-85. On the implications of William's doctrine of sin as the *regio dissimilitudinis,* cf. Déchanet, *Aux sources . . . ,* pp. 47-53.

201. *In Jerem* XXI,10 (*PG* 13,540B), though the transmission may be indirect since this commentary does not appear to have been available in Latin.

202. For the most recent biographical studies of Isaac, cf. G. Raciti, "Isaac de l'Étoile et son siècle," *Cîteaux* 12(1961), 281-306; and 13(1962), 18-34, 133-45,205-26; G. Salet, "L'Homme," *Isaac de l'Etoile: Sermons I* (Paris, 1967), *Sources Chrétiennes* 130, 7-25; Raciti, "Isaac de l'Etoile," *DS* Vol 7,2011-16 (considerably different from his earlier treatment); and B. McGinn, *The Golden Chain (CS15),*1-23.

until approximately 1167. Under circumstances that are still somewhat unclear,[203] toward the end of his life he retired to the new foundation of Notre Dame de Chatêliers on the island of Ré off La Rochelle. We do not know when he died, but it does not seem that he survived this change of locale for any lengthy period.[203 bis]

On the basis of the famine and the heavenly signs mentioned in the epilogue of the *Letter,* J. Debray-Mulatier, has dated the work to 1162.[204] Since I have already had occasion to discuss the sources, themes, and organization of Isaac's *Letter* at length in my work *The Golden Chain: A Study in the Theological Anthropology of Isaac of Stella,*[205] the present treatment will be largely a summary of what was said there accompanied by further comments on the relation of Isaac's work to the other two treatises contained in this volume.

In contrast to William's treatise and *The Spirit and the Soul,* there is very little direct quotation in the Abbot of Stella's work. William uses extensive verbatim citation to give his own highly original thought a base in the best available medical and psychological insights. *The Spirit and the Soul* quotes even more extensively from a wide variety of sources for the purpose of collating diverse material into a handy epitome. Isaac, however, while making use of a very full spectrum of past and contemporary anthropological thought, puts his own stamp on everything he uses. With its compact and closely-argued development, this text may be said to be the most systematic of all the Cistercian treatises on the soul.

The Arabic medicine and Greek theology that we have seen to be so important in William's *The Nature of the Body and*

203. Raciti's earlier thesis connecting this retirement with Isaac's activities on behalf of Thomas Becket is suggestive, though many of the particulars of his case are unprovable given the state of the evidence, *op. cit.* 13,210-12. Salet stresses Isaac's desire for a more perfect realization of the monastic life, *op. cit.* 17-20, as does Raciti in his later work, *DS,*2013.

203. bis. Though Raciti now thinks that he lived until c.1178, cf. *DS, ibid.*

204. Cf. "Biographie d'Isaac de Stella," *Cîteaux* 10(1959),188, note 65. Other scholars have challenged this, e.g.,C.Talbot, *Ailred of Rievaulx:De Anima,* 49, assests that since a copy of the *De spiritu et anima* is listed in the library of the abbey of Prüfening in 1158 (cf.G.Becker, *Catalogi bibliothecarum antiqui,* 212, #60), the text of Isaac, on which this work depends, must be prior to this date.

205. *CS* 15. References to the earlier literature will be found here.

the Soul, is also evident in Isaac's *Letter,* though in a rather different manner. While a "physics of the body" does not become a separate organizing principle for the Abbot of Stella, as it does for the Abbot of St. Thierry, it is obvious both from the *Letter* itself as well as from Isaac's other writings that he had a great interest in and no small knowledge of medical literature. The writings of Constantine the African do not seem to have been known to him, however, for what he has of Arabic material is closer to *The Difference of the Spirit and the Soul* of Constabulinus than to the translations of the monk of Monte Cassino. He was also apparently conversant with the *Premnon physicon* of Nemesius in the version of Alfanus of Salerno. A similar situation is found in Isaac's use of the Greek Fathers. He may have known *The Creation of Man* of Gregory of Nyssa;[206] but it is the influence of the Pseudo-Dionysius, very evident in the treatise on God contained in his *Sermons for Sexagesima Sunday* and not lacking in the *Letter on the Soul* which marks him out as a participant in the twelfth-century renewal of Greek theology. Furthermore, he also displays evidence of the direct influence of John the Scot, the translator of Dionysius. Interestingly enough, there seems to be no acquaintance with Origen, though the Alexandrian theologian was known to Bernard and William.

In terms of the use of Latin patristic sources, the popularity of Claudianus Mamertus with both William and Isaac has already been noted. Naturally, Augustine also plays a large part in both treatises, though the areas of the African doctor's thought utilized by the two Cistercians show some significant differences. While William, for instance, makes use of Augustine's psychological analogies for the Trinity (though interpreting them in a more historical sense),[207] Isaac tends to use what might be called the more ontological and cosmological analogies. Isaac parts company with William

206. For Isaac's possible affinities with Gregory, compare *Ep an* 19 (1886A) on man as the likeness of all things with *De hom* XVII (*ed.,* 234); and *Ep an* 5 (1878B) with *De hom* XVII (*ed.,* 233-4). The similarities are too general to tell whether he was familiar with the translation of John the Scot or not.

207. For William's use of the Augustinian Trinitarian analogies, cf.Brooke, "The Trinitarian Aspect of the Ascent of the Soul to God . . . ," 87-99,122-3.

more dramatically in his utilization of such Latin sources as Macrobius, Chalcidius, and Boethius, as known and made popular in the twelfth century by the Chartrains and by Hugh of St Victor. Isaac's use of sources is thus both wider than that of William and less tied to the citation of texts. William's treatise, however, is directly related to later works where a full-blown and profound theory of mystical union is expounded; Isaac's *Letter* lacks such a complement. Although the broad lines for a profound theory of mysticism are suggested in the *Letter on the Soul,* the promise was never fulfilled so far as we know. The fragmentary and occasional character of the writings that remain to us suggests that the Abbot of Stella never spelled out in written form the doctrine he sketches in the last sections of the *Letter.* Be that as it may, as I have tried to demonstrate in *The Golden Chain,* Isaac's *Letter on the Soul* remains one of the most important witnesses to what might be called the symbolic understanding of the mystery of man in the twelfth century.

The term "symbolic understanding" is used here to indicate a general outlook rather than a particular approach capable of some easy definition. As has already been mentioned, the fusion of Hellenic and Hebraic understandings of man created problems for any anthropology that would attempt to do systematic justice to both sides of the heritage. Particularly in relation to problems such as the union of the body and the soul and the relation of the material world to the return to God, tensions between these two components existed which seemed to forestall any stable and fully logical solution. Insofar as both components remained indispensable, i.e., insofar as both were found to be meaningful expressions of the situation of man in the world as it was experienced by the thinkers of the time, various attempts were made to deal with, to outflank in a sense, the problems created by these logical inconsistencies. We have seen that William of St. Thierry in the eighth section of the second part of his work attempted to draw together his physics of the body and of the soul by means of analogies and parallels between various classifications and functions. Isaac of Stella approaches the same problem in a somewhat different manner. Since a conceptual and discursive solution to these implicit contradictions was impossible, he attempted to resolve the inconsistencies through the presentation of a master symbol, an image presenting a grasp of the world, man, and God which could fuse contradictions and tensions insofar as it embraced a mode of thought which attempted to go beyond considerations of pure logic. The symbol is that of the golden chain of being, that which ties together all the levels of the universe and explains their relations. It demonstrates the way in which man summarizes the universe and through it can find his way back to God. The polyvalent symbol of the golden chain is the organizing principle of Isaac's *Letter on the Soul.*

A brief analysis of Isaac's work will demonstrate this more effectively. The Abbot of Stella addressed his *Letter* to Alcher, a monk of Clairvaux, one apparently gifted in medicine and avidly interested in the anthropological speculation of the day.[208] Alcher's request for a treatise on the nature and powers of the soul (what might be termed a philosophical anthropology) will be belied in Isaac's response—as was true throughout Cistercian treatises on man, there can be no independent philosophical anthropology. To discuss the nature and powers of the soul necessarily implied the history of the soul's relation to God.

The second section summarizes in direct fashion the implications of the three fold comparison of God, the soul, and the body which the Cistercians adopted from Claudianus Mamertus and which we have already seen in William of St Thierry.[209] After a similar discussion, William had concluded to the identity of the soul with its powers, a familiar theme of what was to become the Augustinian tradition of psychological theory in the thirteenth century. It is significant that Isaac makes much more of this than does William, devoting

208. Isaac refers to Alcher's medical expertise in section 12. Peter of Celle (d.1183) addressed his *Liber de conscientia* to Alcher (*PL* 202,1083-98).

209. *De statu* III,7 (*ed.*, 166). Among contemporary non-Cistercian authors the threefold comparison was also popular with Hugh of St Victor, e.g., *De sacramentis* I,10,2 (*PL* 176,329C).

his whole third section to it, and that he does so on the basis of an appeal to some of the root principles of the Bishop of Hippo himself.[210] In this connection, the Abbot of Stella through his influence on *The Spirit and the Soul* was to have an important effect on later Scholastic theology.[211] The reason for the affirmation of the identity of the soul and its powers is to be found in the desire to preserve that simplicity which it required in order to serve as the image of the substantial unity of the Godhead.

Concern for the classification and systematization of the powers of the soul appears explicitly in the fourth section of the work. In this area Isaac is in advance of William, who took greater pains in working out various systematizations of the body's organs and functions than those of the soul. Isaac (perhaps more the Scholastic here), cannot let such an interesting question pass. In this section he pursues the difference between the natural attributes which are identical with the soul and the accidental attributes (such as the four cardinal virtues) which are not. Isaac has two conceptions of virtue, an anthropocentric one originating in Stoic thought which defined virtue as "the habit of a well-instructed soul," and an anagogic view based on the Dionysian writings which, in the light of the central symbol of the golden chain of being, saw virtue as a form sent into man from above which enabled him to ascend to God.[212] This latter sense, which also appears in section twenty-one, is the more important one for the Abbot. The fourth section brings to a close the first major segment of the work which revolves around the implications of the threefold comparison of God, the soul, and the world.

We have spoken earlier about the importance of the drive towards systematic classification of the powers of the soul

---

210. E.g., That God is what he has and therefore cannot be subject the categories of quality and quantity, cf. *Tractatus in Iohannem* XLVIII,6 (ed.R.William, *CC* 36, 415-6).

211. The history of the identity of the soul with its powers has been exhaustively discussed by P.Künzle, *Das Verhältnis der Seele zu ihren Potenzem* (Freiburg/ Schweiz,1956).

212. Cf. *The Golden Chain*, 143-46; and R.Javelet, "La vertue dans l'oeuvre d'Isaac de l'Etoile," *Cîteaux*, 11 (1960), pp. 252-67.

for the particular form of theological anthropology displayed in these Cistercian writings. Introduced in the earlier sections, this becomes the main theme of the remainder of the treatise.

In the fifth section the implications of the Platonic division of rationality or reasonableness, positive appetite, and negative appetite are discussed; but in such a way that it is obvious that for Isaac they are based upon a prior division of the powers of the soul into the power of knowledge (*sensus*) and the power of desire (*affectus*).[213] Despite the importance of the doctrine of *affectus* in Cistercian and Victorine thought,[214] Isaac devotes only sections five and six of his treatise to it. He gives a fourfold division of desire based upon the interaction of time with the positive and negative aspects of appetite—joy (present positive appetite), hope (future positive appetite), pain (present negative appetite), and fear (future negative appetite).[215] These four powers serve as the basis for the virtues and vices; when well ordered, they are the sources of the four cardinal virtues, which, quoting from St Augustine, are asserted to be nothing more than different modifications of the power of love.[216] Isaac is aware that he has done no more than to touch upon the power of desire, as he informs us at the end of section six; it is obvious that in this treatise at least his major interest does not lie here. He is anxious to push on to the complex question of the classification of man's powers of knowledge.

Some investigators have seen in Isaac's varying classifications of the power of knowledge a pure eclecticism.[217] This

---

213. This division is so general that investigators of Isaac's theory of man have come up with very different theories concerning its origin. Among the abbot's contemporaries it is found in Hugh of St Victor (e. g., *De sac.* I, 10, 3); Bernard (e.g., *Asc.* 3, 1, 2); and especially Richard of St. Victor (e. g., *Benjamin minor* III; *Benjamin major* III, 13, etc.).

214. Cf. J. Chatillon, "Cordis affectus au moyen âge," *DS* I, 2288-2300.

215. These four divisions, also used in the eighth section of William's *Phys an*, were derived from Stoic moral theory and available to the medievals through a wide variety of sources, e. g., Chalcidius, *Commentarium*, chap. 194 (ed. Waszink, pp. 216-217); Augustine, *De civitate Dei* XIV, 6 (*ed. cit.* II, p. 421); Nemesius, *Premnon physicon* XVII, 1-6 (*ed. cit.*, pp. 95-96); and Boethius, *De consolatione philosophiae* I, met. 7 (ed. Rand, pp. 168-70).

216. *De mor. ecc. cath.* I, 15, 25 (*PL* 32, 1322).

217. P. Künzle, *op. cit.*, p. 66.

is not the case. The Abbot of Stella's attempt to synthesize
the wide variety of terms and classifications which he found
in patristic and contemporary sources may not have been a
completely stable one, but unlike the author of *The Spirit
and the Soul*, and even unlike William in his *The Nature of
the Body and the Soul*, Isaac brings a real systematic insight
to the problems of classification. Given the intellectualist
direction of the treatise, Isaac's main interest is to show how
man's ability to know demonstrates both his distance from
the divine nature and his ability to attain it. He does this by
means of an adoption, extension, and integration of two divergent systems of classification of the power of knowledge.

The first of these, which might be called the temporal
schema of the power of knowledge, is discussed in section
seven. Forethought (*ingenium*) as the power which looks into
the future, insight (*ratio*) as that which regards the present,
and memory (*memoria*) as that which contains the past, show
that man's intellectual ability, essentially involved in time, is
different from God's ability to grasp all things simultaneously
in one act of intuition.[218] Having made this point, however,
the Abbot of Stella is far more interested in showing how
man's power to know shows a similarity with the divine
nature that enables him to reach God. The rest of the treatise
is devoted to an explanation of the anagogic or ascensional
classification of the power of knowledge, the manifestation
of the golden chain that connects all the levels of the universe
with God.

The anagogic classification, introduced in section eight,
consists of five steps—sense knowledge (*sensus*), imagination
(*imaginatio*), reason (*ratio*), discernment (*intellectus*) and
understanding (*intelligentia*). It has long been noted that this
classification bears a striking resemblance to the four powers
of the soul mentioned in Boethius' *The Consolation of
Philosophy*.[219] Where then did Isaac's extra power of *intel-*

218. Künzle, *ibid.*, was the first to note that this unusual triad of powers
appears in the *Ysagoge in theologiam*, a work of the School of Abelard from the
early 1140's (cf. the edition of A. Landgraf, p. 70). Isaac develops it to a much
greater extent than the author of the *Ysagoge* does.

219. *Ipsum quoque hominum aliter sensus, aliter imaginatio, aliter ratio, aliter
intelligentia contuetur. De con. phil.* V, prosa 4 (ed. Rand, p. 388).

lectus come from? Boethius himself, in discussing the powers of the soul corresponding to the divisions of philosophy, makes use of both terms, *intellectus* and *intelligentia*.[220] This ambiguity enabled twelfth-century commentators, particularly Hugh of St Victor and Thierry of Chartres, to create the fivefold schema utilized by Isaac.[221] The Abbot of Stella, however, enriches the classification, making it capable of carrying a variety of meanings in a manner that suggests its symbolic power as a manifestation of the golden chain of being. Thus, the five steps are here compared to the five hierarchically ordered material components of the universe: earth, water, air, ether or the firmament, and the empyreum or fiery heaven. The anagogic significance of the whole is stressed by linking the five powers of knowledge to the four powers of desire mentioned in the last section to produce a ninefold schema of ascent that betrays its Dionysian significance by being compared with the nine choirs of the angels.[222] In section nine another favorite dimension of the schema is explored, its usefulness in classifying the various noetic objects in terms of their degree of immateriality. Sense knowledge perceives bodies, purely corporeal objects; imagination the likenesses of bodies, scarcely corporeal objects; reason the dimensions or forms of bodies (i.e., universal concepts), scarcely incorporeal objects; discernment, created spirits (i.e., men and angels), truly incorporeal objects; and

220. *In Isagogen Porphyrii Commentum* I, I, 3 (edd. C. Scheipss and S. Brandt, *CSEL* 48, pp. 8-9).
221. The earliest appearance of the schema is around 1130 in Hugh's *Miscellanea* I, 15 (*PL* 177, 485). Around 1140-45 (if we accept N. Haring's dating), we also find it in the second of Thierry of Chartres' commentaries on the *De Trinitate* of Boethius, the *Lectiones in Boethii De Trinitate* II, 30 (ed. N. Haring, *AHDL* 30 [1958], p.162). The development and use of the schema have been discussed by M.-T. d'Alverny, *Alain de Lille*, pp. 170-76; E. Bertola, "Di una inedita Trattazione Psicologica intitolata: *Quid sit Anima*," *Rivista di Filosofia Neo-Scolastica*, 58 (1966), pp. 571-75; and in *The Golden Chain*, chap. 4.
222. The Pseudo-Dionysius was responsible for organizing the angels into nine choirs in his *De caelesti hierarchia*. The Dionysianism of Isaac's classification resides primarily in its strong anagogic character. On the influence of the Pseudo-Dionysius in Isaac, cf. A. Fracheboud, "Le Pseudo-Denys parmi les sources du cistercian Isaac de l'Etoile," *Collectanea Ordinis Cisterciensium Reformatorum*, 9 (1947), pp. 328-41; 10 (1948), pp. 19-34.

understanding perceives God, the pure incorporeal. Isaac's description of the process of ascent is tied to his classification of the powers of the soul in a way that William's repetition of Augustine's schema of ascension is not.

Sense knowledge is discussed in section ten. Like William, Isaac's doctrine of sensation, based upon Augustine,[223] is one in which the soul takes an active part. Like him too it is founded upon the principle of like knowing like—each of the five senses operates by means of a congruency it has with one of the elements found in the objects it knows. Since the Abbot of Stella does not use sensation as the basic analogy for the mystical union, his treatment is less subtle and extensive than that of William.

Isaac is far more interested in the power of imagination, particularly in the crucial role that it plays on the border line between the material and the spiritual levels of reality.[224] As has been emphasized already, one of the most serious problems confronting both patristic and early medieval anthropology involved the union of the material and spiritual factors in man. Augustine had eventually confessed that the matter was a mystery; William followed him in this.[225] Isaac, on the other hand, uses the next three sections to discuss the problem in dependence upon Hugh of St Victor's work *The Union of the Body and the Spirit*.[226] The Abbot of Stella makes use of all three of the solutions current in the early twelfth century, union through number and harmony, union in the personality, and union through a physical medium;[227]

223. Isaac quotes from *De genesi ad litteram* XII, 16, 32 (*PL* 34, 319-20). For further background in Augustine, cf. *De gen. ad litt.* III, 4-5; IV, 34; and *De musica* VI, 10.

224. On *imaginatio*, cf. M.-D. Chenu, "*Imaginatio*: note de lexicographie philosophique," *Miscellanea Giovanni Mercati. II. Studi e Testi* 122 (Vatican City, 1946), pp. 593-602. G. Webb has seen the importance of *imaginatio* in Cistercian treatises, cf. *An Introduction to the Cistercian De Anima* (London, 1962, Aquinas Paper #36), pp. 15-18; but his analyses are untrustworthy at times.

225. *Phys an* 3 (712AB).

226. *PL* 177, 285-94.

227. First outlined by H.Ostler, *Die Psychologie des Hugos von St. Viktor*, *BGPM*, 15, 1 (Münster, 1906), pp. 62-89. Cf. C. H. Talbot, *Ailred of Rievaulx: De Anima*, pp. 41-44.

but these all appear within the context of the symbol of the chain of being—neighboring links on the chain must be sufficiently alike to be joined lest the unity of the cosmos be threatened. Section twelve, besides displaying some of Isaac's medical knowledge,[228] shows the cosmic implications of this doctrine of the joining together, or concatenation, of all things. The doctrine that "through two very apt median realities two diverse extremes can be easily and firmly joined,"[229] is as true in the great animal, or the world, as it is for man, the small animal.

Sections thirteen and fourteen of Isaac's treatise show a number of similarities with parts of William's *The Nature of the Body and the Soul.* First of all, the "bodily spirit" which played such an important part in the Abbot of St Thierry's *The Physics of the Body* is here clearly affirmed to be that which actually performs the work of vivification.[230] Isaac's use of the number and harmony theory of the relation of soul and body leads to a description of the body as the musical instrument which the soul uses in the manner of a skilled musician, another reminiscence of William. [231] Finally, the comparison between the manner of God's presence in the world and the soul's presence in the body in the fourteenth section, though Isaac's treatment is more extensive and detailed, is close to the tenth section of the second part of William's work.

In the fifteenth section the Abbot of Stella turns to the third level of the ascent of the soul, that of reason. What might be termed the more "Scholastic" side of Isaac comes out here in his Aristotelian doctrine of first and second sub-

228. The description of the six bones of the head and the seven vertebrae of the neck is probably based on Cassiodorus, *De anima* XI (ed. Halporn, p. 90); and Rabanus Maurus, *De anima* V, 9 (*PL* 110, 1114AD; 1119AB).

229. Very close to a passage in the Pseudo-Dionysius, *De divinis nominibus* VII, 3 (*Dionysiaca* I, pp. 407-08).

230. Isaac has a number of terms for the physical spirit: *spiritus corporeus, spiritus vitalis, spiritus pecoris,* and *sensualitas carnis.* As was remarked earlier, other passages on the function of the *spiritus* in Isaac's anthropology indicate a dependence on Constabulinus rather than Constantine the African.

231. *Phys an* 3 (712BC).

stance and his generalized notion of abstraction.[232] Systematically speaking, this heteronymous doctrine of reason ill accords with the rest of Isaac's epistemology, especially his Platonizing doctrine of sensation; but there were many precedents for the eclectic assumption of Aristotelian elements (known through Boethius) into a basically Platonic description of the activity of the knowing powers. Reason abstracts the universal concept, or second substance, from a body. The second substance is not a body; but because it cannot really exist apart from a body or first substance, it is described as the "first incorporeal," or the "scarcely incorporeal object." One use of this generalized doctrine of abstraction is explored in section sixteen. Like many other thinkers of the twelfth century, Isaac took an interest in the classification of the kinds of science. Here the Abbot of Stella introduces yet another dimension of his ascensional schema of the power of knowledge, that of the threefold division of sciences into natural science (physics), mathematics, and theology.[233] Sense knowledge and imagination can only investigate things on the level of natural science (the real state of the existence of corporeal things). Reason is active on the level of mathematical science (the rational state of existence); only understanding reaches the highest level of science, that of theology. One of the fundamental laws of Isaac's anagogy, the inability of a lower power to proceed above its appointed limit and the ability of superior powers to make use of the findings of the lower, is clearly displayed in this discussion.

The brief paragraph on the discernment is important in that it shows that Isaac, like Augustine,[234] but unlike the Pseudo-Dionysius, placed the human soul on a par with the angelic

232. This section should be compared with the similar treatment of first and second substance in *Sermon* 19 (1754A-1755D). An account of *ratio* in Isaac (not correct in all its particulars) can be found in W. Meuser, *Die Erkenntnislehre der Isaak von Stella,* Inaug.-Dissert. (Freiburg-im-Breisgau, 1934), pp. 25-31. Cf. also *The Golden Chain,* 170-4.

233. Found in Boethius's *De Trinitate* II (ed. Rand, p. 8), and much commented upon by the masters of Chartres. On Isaac's interest in the divisions of the sciences, cf. my article *"Theologia* in Isaac of Stella."

234. E.g., *De gen. ad litt. lib. imperf.* XVI, 60 (*PL* 34, 243).

nature and not in an inferior position on the chain of being. In the eighteenth section, the Abbot turns to the most important part of his treatise, the study of the understanding as the ground for man's union with God. This section is really a summary of the many aspects of the ascensional schema of the soul's powers that have appeared thus far. Especially stressed is the importance of the concatenation that binds these powers together. The lower levels on the chain of being are images and likenesses of the immediately higher levels, and are therefore joined together just as the four elements were linked in Platonic physics. "Therefore (in a manner of speaking) by this golden chain of the poet the lowest realities hang down from the highest, or by the upright ladder of the prophet there is an ascent from the lowest to the highest." The golden chain of Homer's *Iliad* (8, 18-27) had had a long history as an important symbol in the literature of antiquity.[235] Isaac undoubtedly knew of it through its appearance in *The Commentary on the Dream of Scipio* by Macrobius;[236] but the linking of the golden chain to the ladder of Jacob, a familiar symbol of ascension in Christian literature, suggests a direct connection with William of Conches who was the first to link the two symbols in his unpublished *Glosses on Macrobius* from the early 1120's.[237]

Unlike William and the compiler of *The Spirit and the Soul*, Isaac shows very little interest in giving definitions of the soul. The reason behind this hesitancy becomes evident in section nineteen. Philosophical definitions of the soul cannot capture its true essence; it is only when we see the soul as the image and likeness of the Wisdom who is the Second Person

235. Cf. P. L'Eveque, *Aurea catena Homeri: une étude sur l'allégorie grecque, Annales littéraires de l'Université de Besançon,* 27 (Paris, 1959); and L. Edelstein, "The Golden Chain of Homer," *Studies in Intellectual History Dedicated to Arthur O. Lovejoy* (Baltimore,, 1953), pp. 48-66. Lovejoy's own well-known work, *The Great Chain of Being* (Cambridge, 1936), misunderstands the medieval use of the symbol, as I have tried to demonstrate in *The Golden Chain,* chap. 2.

236. I, 14, 15 (ed. Willis, p. 58).

237. The text is published in *The Golden Chain,* Appendix, pp. 239-240. On the use of Macrobius at Chartres, cf. E. Jeauneau, "Macrobe, source du platonisme chartrain," *Studi Medievali,* 3rd series, 1 (1960), pp. 3-24.

of the Trinity that we can recognize the soul as the likeness of all things.[238] This microcosmic character of the soul is implicit in the many aspects of the five powers of knowledge; by them the soul has some similarity with all the levels of reality and therefore can in some way know all things. Whatever the original powers of the soul may have been, it no longer has the ability of itself to know God through the understanding. In typically Victorine fashion,[239] Isaac says that the three eyes of the soul have been hurt by man's sin, so that the eye of sense knowledge and imagination sees obscurely, the eye of reason scarcely sees, the eye of discernment and understanding sees almost nothing.[240] Having lost its ability to see God, the soul can no longer know itself or the nature of the angels. Original sin, then, and its effect, concupiscence, are viewed in terms of the master symbol as *cor-ruptio*, that which breaks the chain that should bind all things together.[241]

Isaac's final sections turn to the central theme of medieval Christian anthropology, man as the image and likeness of God. There is only one essential Justice which is God, shared in by just spirits by means of a participation of itself. How then is it possible for created things to participate in God? Isaac's doctrine of participation is Trinitarian in nature, being explained in terms of the triad originating with Hilary of

238. Isaac's assertion that the soul is defined by the philosopher as the *similitudo omnium* prompted W. Meuser, *op. cit.*, pp. 67-69, to claim that the Abbot had Aristotle's definition in mind (cf. *De anima* 431b). It seems more likely that he was thinking of a mysterious reference to Varro in Hugh of St.Victor's *Didascalicon* I, 1 (ed. C. H. Buttimer, Washington, 1939, pp. 5-6). In any case, the way in which Isaac explains his notion of the soul as *similitudo omnium* (based upon its likeness to the Word) is totally un-Aristotelian.

239. E. g., Hugh of St. Victor, *De sac.* I, 10, 2 (*PL* 176, 329-30); *De arca Noe morali* IV, 5 (*PL* 176, 670C-71A); and *In Hier. Cael.* III (*PL* 177, 976A).

240. For recent studies of Isaac's doctrine of original sin, cf. F. Mannarini, "La Grazia in Isaaco di Stella," *Collectanea Ordinis Cisterciensium Reformatorum*, 16 (1954), pp. 137-44; 207-14; L. Gaggero, "Isaac of Stella and the Theology of Redemption," *Coll. Ord. Cist. Ref.*, 22 (1960), pp. 21-36; and A. Hoste, *Isaac de l'Etoile. Sermons I*, pp. 338-39.

241. The suggestion comes from Gaggero, *op. cit.*, p. 26. While not explicit in the *Ep an*, it is clear in *Sermon* 54, the only other passage in Isaac referring directly to the golden chain (1874D-75A).

Poitiers,[242] used by Augustine in his work *The Trinity*,[243] and quite familiar to a number of twelfth-century authors.[244] Unlike William of St. Thierry, Isaac prefers Augustine's onto-logical and cosmological analogies. This one is useful to him in that since every creature must have existence or eternity, some form, and some gift, enjoyment, or use, all things in some way participate in the Trinity which is the highest Es-sence (Eternity), Form (or Image), and Gift.

The twenty-first section takes up the problem broached at the outset of the previous one, viz., given the fact that man has sinned and the highest eye of the soul is blinded, how shall he attain to God? The answer is given in terms of a further consideration of the participation of all creatures in God. The development of the argument begins from the in-vocation of the categories of creating and assisting grace: "The vessels then that creating grace forms so that they can exist, assisting grace fills so that they be not empty." Though some have seen in this popular division[245] a foreshadowing of the later Scholastic distinction between the natural and the supernatural orders,[246] this is surely incorrect.[247] Assisting grace is not a gift over and above the nature of man, but what sinful man in his historical condition needs in order for the faculties that he has from creating grace to operate correctly. The Augustinian cast to this doctrine is made more evident by an explicit appeal to the Bishop of Hippo's doctrine of illumination (understood in a very general sense) at the end of the section. The Abbot of Stella is here dependent on texts from the thirty-fourth and thirty-fifth of Augustine's

242. *De Trinitate* II, 1 (*PL* 10, 50).

243. *De Trinitate* VI, 10, 11 (*ed. cit.* I, pp. 496-98).

244. It is used by Peter Lombard, Aelred of Rielvaulx, Arnold of Bonneville, and Alan of Lille. Cf. R. Javelet, *Image et ressemblance*, Vol. 1, pp. 88, 200-01, 417-18.

245. Isaac also uses the distinction in *Sermon* 26 (1774D-75A). Among 12th century authors, it is also found in Bernard, Hugh of St. Victor, and Richard of St. Victor.

246. Meuser, *op. cit.*, pp. 43-45.

247. As seen by Mannarini, *op. cit.*, pp. 141, 144; R. Javelet, "La vertue . . . ," pp. 264-65; and A. Fracheboud, "L'Influence de St. Augustin sur le cistercien Isaac de l'Etoile," *Coll. Ord. Cist. Ref.*, 9 (1947), pp. 7-11.

Treatises on the Gospel of John.[248] Without entering into the difficulties connected with Augustine's own views on illumination, it seems that Isaac held to the necessity of illumination in order for the soul to reach the true wisdom (*sapientia*) which is the goal of its higher faculties of discernment and understanding, without necessarily claiming that direct illumination was always necessary for the limited knowledge (*scientia*) attained by the lower powers.

The final sections of the *Letter* summarize two of the most important facets of the anagogic process: its dynamic interconnection and its specifically Christian dimensions. The invocation of the movement of the theophanies down into the understanding and phantasms up to the imagination, very close to a text in John the Scot's *Periphyseon,*[249] is used to highlight the connections of the five levels. In section twenty-one the share of the whole of creation in the Trinity itself was discussed; now in twenty-three the role of the Holy Spirit, as closer in a sense to creatures, is to the fore. Augustine's analysis of the three functions of light—to be light, to shine, and to give light—are invoked as an analogy for understanding the mystery of the Trinity.[250] The light which illuminates the understanding to see the truth and the fire which enflames the power of desire to love virtue are Trinitarian in nature. The Spirit sent to us unites us to Christ who is historically the central link in the chain of being once broken by sin but now reunited through God's love.[251]

Though Isaac's treatise ends with the suggestion of a theory of mystical union, rather than a fully expounded theory, the power of his thought is evident even in these brief remarks. Union with God can take place only through the full actualization of both man's intellectual and affective powers. Although *The Letter on the Soul* concentrates on the intellectual ascent to God, it never forgets that only in the union of knowing (*cognoscere*) and loving (*diligere*) can God

248. *CC* 36, pp. 312-13; 318-19.

249. *Periphyseon (De div. nat.)* II, 23 (*PL* 122, 576D-77A).

250. *Soliloquiae* I, 8, 15 (*PL* 32, 877). Note again that it is a non-psychological analogy that is used.

251. Cf. R. Javelet, *Image et ressemblance*, Vol. 1, p. 153.

be reached.[252] Furthermore, this union re-creates the universe by forging anew the golden chain of being which is both identified with man (in his capacity as the microcosm) and is also the cosmic framework into which man fits. The union is nothing more than the building up of the body of Christ through the power of the Holy Spirit.[253] Isaac of Stella yields to none of his Cistercian peers in either profundity of thought or concentration of meaning.

THE SPIRIT AND THE SOUL

A slightly different procedure will be adopted in introducing the treatise *The Spirit and the Soul*. Thus far we have been able to give a fairly complete outline of the treatises along with a discussion of the sources utilized. Because of the length of *The Spirit and the Soul*, it will be impossible to go into as much detail. Unlike the works of William and Isaac, this text is largely devoid of originality, though not of importance. Instead of using past works, even through extensive citation, within a new framework and in the light of new organizing principles, it is dependent on almost pure quotation and paraphrase from earlier authors. Since a complete analysis of the sources of the work still awaits the attentions of scholars of medieval anthropology,[254] our main concern

252. For passages in his writings in which the Abbot discusses the union of *cognoscere* and *diligere*, cf. *PL* 194, 1708BC, 1723BC, 1730AB, 1744A, 1746D-1747A, 1774D, 1808A, 1822D, 1836D, 1843D, and this passage from section 23 of the *Ep an.*

253. Isaac is one of the most important witnesses to the doctrine of the Mystical Body of Christ in the 12th century, as is his fellow Cistercian William of St. Thierry. Cf. the discussions in E. Mersch, *Le corps mystique du Christ* (Paris, 1933), Vol. 2, pp. 142-48; H. de Lubac, *Corpus Mysticum* (Paris, 1944), pp. 121-22; A. Piolanti, "De nostra in Christo solidarietate praecipua Isaac de Stella testimonia," *Euntes Docete*, 2 (1949), pp. 349-68; and especially J. Beumer, "Mariologie und Ekklesiologie bei Isaak von Stella," *Münchener Theologische Zeitschrift*, 5 (1954), pp. 48-61.

254. The most complete appears to be the unpublished thesis in Polish of M. L. Lewicki, *Z badan nad zrodtami pogladow filozoficznynch Alchera z Clairvaux* (Lublin, 1955), summarized by the author in his article, "Une double thèse de philosophie sur Alcher de Clairvaux et Isaac de l'Étoile à l'Université de Lublin," *Coll. Ord. Cist. Ref.*, 18 (1956), pp. 161-64, "Les sources de philosophie d'Alcher de Clairvaux." See however, note 350 below.

64   *Three Treatises on Man*

here will relate to the questions of the origin and the influence of the work. Suggestions concerning the sources of the
individual chapters, based upon the work of D. Coustant, the
Maurist editor of the text, as well as upon more modern
studies,[255] will be provided in the footnotes to the translation.

With regard to the origin of the text, the identity of its
compiler (a better term than author here) is still in doubt. As
a matter of fact, we are not even sure that we are dealing
with what was meant to be one work. A. Wilmart, on the
basis of an investigation of the English manuscripts, thought
that the work was originally conceived in three volumes
(chapters 1-33; 34-50; 51-65).[256] Given the compilatory character of the whole and the variety of the sources used, the
possibility of different men working at different times cannot
be ruled out. The text translated here is the full version of
sixty-five chapters edited by Coustant and appearing in the
Patrologia Latina among the works of Augustine.[257] A shorter
version with different chapter divisions is frequently found
under the name of Hugh of St Victor[258] as the second book
of a four volume *De anima*, parts of which have been pseudo-
nymously ascribed to both Hugh and to St Bernard.[259] As can

255. Especially L. Reypens, "Âme," 445-46; P. Michaud-Quantain, "La classification de puissances . . . ," pp. 25-28; P. Künzle, *op. cit.,* pp. 66-72.
256. "Les méditations VII et VIII attribuéés à Saint Anselme. La série des 21
méditations," *RAM,* 8 (1927), p. 251, note 8.
257. *PL* 40, 779-832.
258. Noted in *PL* 177, 165-66, but without indication as to the differences.
259. These works are:
(1) *De cognitione humanae conditionis.* This is cited under Hugh's name in *PL*
177, 165-66; but is more frequently found under that of Bernard (sometimes as
the *Meditationes piissimae*) both in manuscripts and in *PL* 184, 485-507.
(2) *De spiritu et anima.*
(3) *De interiori domo seu de conscientia aedificanda (Domus haec).* The first
forty-nine chapters appear under Bernard in *PL* 184, 507-52, the fiftieth chapter
under Hugh in *PL* 177, 165-70.
None of the works are by either Bernard or Hugh, though they are deeply influenced
by both.
To be joined to these four are the opuscules:
(4) *De erectione animae mentis in Deum* appears under Hugh in *PL* 177, 171-90.
(5) *De diligendo Deo (PL* 40, 847-64), and the so-called
(6) *Manuale (PL* 40, 951-68).
These will appear in our notes below. For modern literature on this tangled mess, cf.

be seen from even this brief survey, we are dealing with literature whose genius does not lie in security of authorship nor
in clarity of the lines of the transmission of texts.

In most histories of medieval thought and spirituality, *The
Spirit and the Soul* appears as the work of Alcher of Clairvaux, the contemporary of Isaac to whom the *Letter on the
Soul* was addressed.[260] Since the work had long circulated
under the name of Augustine, it was Coustant, an editor of
the Bishop of Hippo, who first suggested that this and a
number of other treatises might belong to the little-known
Alcher.[261] This view was popularized by its appearance in the
Histoire littéraire de la France,[262] and has been uncritically
accepted by most modern authorities. A. Wilmart was one of
the first twentieth-century scholars to have some doubts
about Alcher's authorship,[263] doubts that were seconded by
C. H. Talbot.[264] G. Raciti in an important article has presented the most penetrating attack on the traditional position.[265] Raciti points out that everything we know about
Alcher from the works addressed to him by Isaac and Peter
of Celle indicates that he was a monk of a philosophical bent
with a special competence in physiology and medicine. The
poverty of both philosophical acumen and medical knowledge in *The Spirit and the Soul* makes it impossible to think
that this text is the work that Isaac requested from his friend
in chapter twelve of the *Letter on the Soul,* and weighs
heavily against the possibility of Alcher being considered as

---

P. Delhaye, "Dans le sillage de St. Bernard: trois petits traités *De Conscientia,*"
Cîteaux, 5 (1954), pp. 92-103; E. Bertola, "Di alcuni Trattati attribuiti ad Ugo di
San Vittore," *Rivista di Filosofia Neo-Scolastica,* 51 (1959), pp. 436-55; R.
Bultot, "Les 'Meditationes' Pseudo-Bernardines sur la connaissance de la condition humaine," *Sacris Erudiri,* 15 (1964), pp. 256-92; and G. Raciti, "L'Autore
del 'De spiritu et anima'," *Rivista di Filosofia Neo-Scolastica,* 53 (1961), pp.
392-94.

260. E. g., E. Gilson, *A History of Christian Philosophy in the Middle Ages*
(N.Y., 1955), p. 169; and J. Leclercq, F. Vandenbroucke, L. Bouyer, *La spiritualité du moyen âge* (Paris, 1961), p. 264.

261. "Admonitio in librum de spiritu et anima," reprinted in *PL* 40, 779-80.

262. Vol. XII, 683-86.

263. *Op. cit.,* pp. 251-52, note 11.

264. *Ailred of Rievaulx: De Anima,* p. 49.

265. "L'Autore del 'De spiritu et anima'," *op. cit.,* pp. 385-401.

the author at all.[266] There is a complete absence of any early tradition connecting the work with Alcher.

Raciti goes on to advance a new hypothesis concerning the compiler of the text. Since *The Spirit and the Soul* frequently appears with four other psychological texts,[267] and since these texts show the influence of Hugh of St Victor,[268] its ambience appears to be Victorine rather than Cistercian. On the basis of the ascription by Vincent of Beauvais in the thirteenth century of one of the related texts to Peter Comestor (d.1179), the general similarity with Peter's style as a noted compiler of books of source material, and Peter's retirement towards the end of his life to the abbey of St Victor, Raciti suggests him as the author and places the date of the work between 1169 and 1179.[269]

What may be said about this new hypothesis? First, it is evident that Raciti himself treats it as very provisional.[270] Decisions about twelfth-century texts for which there is no solid contemporary consensus on authorship can rarely be very secure. Nevertheless, while Raciti has rendered the authorship of Alcher scarcely tenable, the case that he makes for Peter Comestor is not very strong either. Against the hypothesis it might be argued: (1) the unity of style of the five treatises suggested by Coustant and Wilmart needs more investigation; and (2) there is a controversy over whether the text *The Difference of Soul, Spirit, and Mind* which Raciti uses to prove Victorine influence on *The Spirit and the Soul* is by Achard of St Victor or Gilbert of Poitiers.[271] Furthermore, there are both logical and historical gaps in Raciti's

266. *Op. cit.,* pp. 388-90.

267. Following Coustant and Wilmart, Raciti on p. 394 asserts that texts (1), (2), (3), (5), and (6) listed above in note 259 are from the same hand.

268. *Op. cit.,* pp. 394-96.

269. Pp. 396-400.

270. Pp. 400-01.

271. The most recent editor, N. Haring, made a strong case for Gilbert's authorship in "Gilbert of Poitiers, Author of the *De discretione animae, spiritus et mentis* commonly attributed to Achard of St. Victor," *Mediaeval Studies,* 22 (1960), pp. 148-91. J. Chatillon responded with a defense of Achard's authorship in "Achard de Saint Victor et le 'De discretione animae, spiritus et mentis'," *AHDL,* 31 (1964), pp. 7-35.

argument.[272] Two further points deserve to be mentioned: first, the eclectic mentality interested in compiling handy textbooks from authoritative sources was common to a number of theologians at work between 1170 and 1200 and not just a peculiarity of Peter Comestor; and second, the weight of evidence from the thirteenth-century use of the text indicates a Cistercian source.[273] It seems impossible at this juncture to make a definitive judgment about the authorship of the text, or even whether we are dealing with a text of Cistercian origin or only one heavily influenced by Cistercian speculation on man. The very shaky evidence we have seems to suggest production in Cistercian circles some time after 1170. In any case, given the influence that *The Spirit and the Soul* had upon later thinkers, it is an important witness to the role that the Cistercian *De anima* played in the wider world of medieval theological anthropology.

The extent of this influence makes the text more than worthy of inclusion here. In gathering together, even in a totally unsystematic way, so much traditional wisdom on the soul, it served as an admirable textbook or *vade mecum*.[274] Its popularity was at least partially due to the fact that anyone could find in it whatever pleased him in the matter of a definition of the soul or a classification of its powers, as long as he chose to neglect the different and sometimes opposed definitions and classifications also present in the work. But how did *The Spirit and the Soul* ever come to be associated with the name of St Augustine? As P. Michaud-Quantain points out, the concept of a neat classification of the powers of the soul, analogous to that given by Aristotle, is actually

272. E. g., logically, as when we are asked to make the leap from the demonstration of Victorine *influence* on the work to the necessity of a Victorine *ambience* (p. 395); historically, when we are told that Isaac's *Ep an* was popular among the Victorines from an early date without supporting evidence (p. 400).

273. Raciti, *op. cit.*, pp. 390-92, seems to want to reduce all this testimony to the original confusion by Philip the Chancellor between this text and Isaac's *Ep an*. The mistakes in ascription are so divergent as to make one original error the source of all the others somewhat improbable. The tradition of Cistercian authorship is the one constant.

274. This function was recognized almost a century ago by K. Werner, *Der Entwicklungsgang der Mittelalterlichen Psychologie* (Vienna, 1876), p. 1.

quite foreign to the mentality and sliding terminology employed by the Bishop of Hippo;[275] but although the work was also ascribed to Bernard, Hugh of St Victor, Isaac of Stella, and William of St Thierry at different times, its connection with the name of Augustine was the one that stuck. In an age that was so uncritical of the authenticity of texts, the error was made possible not only by the large amount of Augustinian material it contained, but also by an important factor in late twelfth-century theological speculation.

Western theology was being enriched in the last decades of the twelfth century by a variety of new influences. Not only the increasing familiarity with Aristotle, but the fact that the Aristotle being received was a Neoplatonized Aristotle was of great significance.[276] The reception of the philosophy of Avicenna (d.1037) and of other Arabic and Jewish philosophers, such as Ibn Gabirol (d.1070), all deeply influenced by Neoplatonism, was second only to that of Aristotle in importance. At this juncture, the medieval attitude towards the authority of tradition might have been expected to produce a negative reaction to the absorption of the heteronymous and indeed pagan ideas contained in the works of these thinkers. However, such rejection was to be a much more prominent feature of the thirteenth century than it was of the latter part of the twelfth. *The Spirit and the Soul* is evidence for a tendency which rather sought to open up tradition by attempting to bring it into line with new systems and ideas. This is at least part of the reason behind the concern of the text to incorporate Augustine into a changing intellectual world by using Augustinian material (or what was thought to be Augustinian material) to create an un-Augustinian classification of the powers of the soul. Furthermore, foisting off on the Bishop of Hippo such a diverse

275. P. Michaud-Quantain, "Une division 'augustinienne' des puissances de l'âme au moyen âge," *Revue des études augustiniennes,* 3 (1957), p. 248.

276. This period has been investigated by E. Gilson, R. de Vaux, M.-T. d'Alverny, and F. Van Steenberghen among others. For a survey that concentrates on some of the psychological issues, cf. E. Bertola, "Le Proibizioni di Aristotele del 1210 e del 1215 e il Problema dell'Anima," *Rivista di Filosofia Neo-Scolastica,* 57 (1965), pp. 725-51.

mélange of material surely encouraged the conviction that virtually anything could in some way be connected with aspects of the doctor's theory of the soul. *The Spirit and the Soul* is an important witness to the attitude of those who tried to be both open to the new currents of thought becoming available through translations from Greek and Arabic and still in harmony with the best aspects of tradition.[277]

It was due to this ascription to Augustine that the work came to play an important role in the evolution of one of the major themes of thirteenth-century Augustiniamism. The texts of Augustine himself on the question of the real identity of the soul with its powers are at best ambiguous;[278] but later Patristic and Carolingian sources, making explicit one side of the bishop's thought, clearly affirmed such an identity. Among twelfth century authors, although the beginnings of the contray opinion which asserted the real distinction are to be found with William of Champeaux, Peter Abelard, and others,[279] the Cistercians form a unanimous witness to the traditional doctrine. The identity thesis is one of the major motifs of *The Spirit and the Soul*, appearing in chapters 4, 7, 9, 13, 34, 35, and 37 among others. As P. Künzle has demonstrated, the sources for this doctrine are not to be found in the passages from Augustine himself which might be interpreted in this sense, but are rather from Isaac of Stella, Alcuin, and Isidore of Seville. Only the passage in chapter thirty-five goes back to an idea of St Augustine's by way of a text of Rabanus Maurus.[280] The assertion of the identity was to become one of the rallying

277. There is nothing of distinctly Avicennan character in the treatise itself, though Avicenna is present in the interesting *Quid sit anima*, a text of the end of the century edited by E. Bertola, "Di una inedita Trattazione Psicologica intitolata *Quid sit anima.*" Nevertheless, the context which accounts for the popularity of *De spiritu et anima* is that of the eclectic period in which Avicenna was becoming known at the end of the 12th and the beginning of the 13th centuries.

278. Cf. P. Künzle, *op. cit.*, pp. 24-29.

279. Künzle, *op. cit.*, pp. 43-62; and M. Ortuzer, "El ser y la acción en la dimensión humana (Pedro Abelardo, 1097-1142) y su gruppo, " *Estudios* (Madrid), 13 (1957), pp. 432-35.

280. *Op. cit.*, pp. 68-72.

points of the defense of traditional psychology against the encroachments of the Aristotelian teaching on the soul in the mid-thirteenth century. The reasons behind the spirited defense of this supposedly Augustinian view were, as has been mentioned before, of some theological weight—the traditional theologians did not see how the Aristotelianizing psychology with its distinction between the essence of the soul and its various faculties or powers could provide the kind of analogy between the soul and God which their own viewpoint encouraged. The influence and authority of *The Spirit and the Soul* played a not insignificant role in this dispute.

Of the popularity of the text there can be no doubt; Wilmart counted some sixty manuscripts in British libraries alone.[281] A brief sketch of the history of the text is important to flesh out an analysis of its significance. The work is first cited explicitly in *The Distinctions of Theological Terms*, a work of the late twelfth century from the pen of the widely-read Alan of Lille.[282] Towards the end of the same century it was also used as the basis for the first and second sections of the *Meditations* ascribed to Anselm of Canterbury.[283] There is a slight possiblity that it may have been known to Alfred of

281. "Les méditations VII et VIII . . . ," p. 251, note 8.
282. Intellectus, potentia animae qua comprehendit invisibilia, unde Augustinus in libro qui inscribitur *Perisichen,* id est *De anima*: Quinque sunt digressiones animae: sensus, imaginatio, ratio, intellectus et intelligentia. *Distinctiones dictionum theologicalium (PL* 210, 819D; cf. also 922Ab). On this work, cf. M.T. d'Alverny, *Alain de Lille,* pp. 71-73; and M.-D. Chenu, *La théologie au douzième siècle,* pp. 198-200. The reference to "de spiritu et anima secundum Bernardum et Augustinum" in the 1158 catalogue of the Prüfening library needs further investigation, since it goes counter to the other evidence and names of psychological treatises were extremely fluid. C. H. Talbot, *Ailred of Rievaulx: De Anima,* p. 50, claims that the work is cited in both the *Sententiae Berolinenses* (ed. F. Stegmüller, *RTAM,* 11 [1939], pp. 45-46), and the *De anima* of Dominicus Gundissalinus (ed. J. T. Muckle, *Mediaeval Studies,* 2,1940, pp. 99-101) — both from the latter part of the 12th century. The similarities, however, are general, and can be explained in terms of common patristic sources. There is, in short, no reason to question our probable dating of *De spiritu et anima* or Isaac's *Epistola* on the basis of Talbots' claims.
283. *Meditatio* VII, 1 = *De spiritu et anima* 49-50; *Meditatio* VII, 2 = *De spiritu et anima* 17. Cf. Wilmart, *op. cit.,* pp. 251-53. *Meditatio* VII is to be found in *PL* 158, 741-45.

Shareshal, the author of *The Movement of the Heart*.[284] Real popularity, however, came as the result of its appearance in the very influential *Summa on the Good* of Philip, the Chancellor of the University of Paris, written about 1230.[285] Philip attributes the text to Isaac of Stella.[286]

In the late 1230's and early 1240's the influence of *The Spirit and the Soul* is connected with the beginnings of Franciscan theology, the current which was to provide the center for Augustinianism in the thirteenth century. The *Summa* which is purported to come from Alexander of Hales (c.1185-1245), the Parisian teacher who by his entry into the order gave the Franciscans their first theological chair, seems to have thought the work came from the pen of Augustine.[287] John of La Rochelle, a disciple of Alexander and master at Paris from 1238 to 1245, made use of Isaac's fivefold schema as known through *The Spirit and the Soul* in both his *Summa on the Vices* and his *Summa on the Soul*.[288] In the mid-1240's, however, the polemical context in which the work was being utilized led to doubts about its authenticity and usefulness. Philip the Chancellor, while using it to corroborate his insistence on the identity of the soul and its powers, had recognized that it was only ". . .according to Augustine." Vincent of Beauvais (d.1264) thought it the work of Hugh of St Victor.[289] Albert the Great, while he used the work in

284. *De motu cordis* 15, 1 (ed. C. Baeumker, *BGPM* 23, 1-2, pp. 75-76) seems to be aware of the fivefold schema of Isaac, but whether he got this from the *De spiritu et anima* or not is not clear.

285. Raciti,*op. cit.*, p. 391.

286. IV. Item. Isaac in libro de anima et spiritu secundum Augustinum: De rationalitate oritur omnis sensus . . ., cited in O. Lottin, "La théorie des vertues cardinales de 1230 à 1250," *Mélanges Mandonnet* (Paris, 1930), Vol. 2, pp. 244-45.

287. *Summa theologiae* II, q. 59, m. 2. While the *Summa* contains material going back to Alexander, it is largely a compilation of his pupils not completed until c.1250.

288. Cf. P. Michaud-Quantain, "Une division 'augustinienne' . . ." pp. 235-37, 243; and E. Gilson, *A History of Christian Philosophy in the Middle Ages*, p. 330.

289. *Speculum naturale* XXIII, 25; *Speculum historiale* XVIII, 55; *Speculum doctrinale* XVII, 62.

dependence on Philip the Chancellor in some of his early writings,[290] expressed a negative attitude towards both its Augustinian authorship and its value in his *Commentary on the Sentences* (1245).[291] Nevertheless, Albert frequently cites it as belonging to Augustine, perhaps because of the Augustinian material it contained.[292] Thomas Aquinas followed his master both in an unqualified dismissal of the text when it disagreed with his positions,[293] and in moderate use of it (in his earliest works at least) insofar as it could be made compatible with his own strongly Aristotelian theory of the soul.[294] The doubts of Albert and Aquinas did not spell an end to the use of the text nor to its ascription to Augustine. The later history of *The Spirit and the Soul* remains to be written; but P. O. Kristeller has shown that it was influential on the thought of the fifteenth-century humanist, Pier Candido Decembrio, precisely because as a work of Augustine it escaped the humanist strictures against Scholasticism.[295]

Having investigated the influence of *The Spirit and the Soul*—its major claim to importance—a brief discussion of some of its themes may be of value in showing its affinity with the other texts in the present volume and its place in the

290. Raciti, *op. cit.*, p. 391.

291. Ad id quod de libro de spiritu et anima dicitur, negari potest quod non est Augustini, sed cuiusdam Guillelmi cisterciensis qui multa falsa dixit. *In I Sent.*, d. 8, a. 25, ad 2um. Cf. also *In I Sent.*, d. 10, a. 2. On the use of the text in Albert and Thomas Aquinas, cf. G. Théry, "L'authenticité du *De spiritu et anima* dans S. Thomas et Albert le Grand," *RSPT*, 10 (1921), pp. 373-77.

292. Théry, *op. cit.*, p. 376.

293. Théry, *op. cit.*, pp. 373-74, sees *In IV Sent.*, d. 44, q. 4, a. 3, sol. 2, ad 1 (c.1256), where Aquinas asserts the Cistercian origin of the text, as a turning point. After this he became increasingly hostile towards its utilization: e.g., ". . . liber ille auctoritatem non habet. Unde quod ibi scriptum est, eadem facilitate contemnitur, qua dicitur " (*Ia*, q. 77, a. 8, ad 1).

294. Raciti, *op. cit.*, p. 386, note 4, claims that when Aquinas and Albert agree with the text they cite it without comment, but when they disagree with it they highlight its inauthenticity. Raciti does not specify a series of texts within a chronological framework to support whether this is true throughout the careers of the two doctors.

295. "Pier Candido Decembrio and his Unpublished Treatise on the Immortality of the Soul," *The Classical Tradition: Literary and Historical Studies in Honor of Harry Caplan*, ed. L. Wallach (Ithaca, 1966), pp. 548-49.

Cistercian movement. Insofar as a very general analysis of the sources is concerned, it may be said that in the first half of the first section (chaps. 1-33), the dominant influence is to be found in Isaac of Stella's *Letter on the Soul*. The second section of the work (chaps. 34-50) depends more on Hugh of St Victor than any other single author. The third section (chaps. 51-65) is more eclectic and devotional in tone, with much more extensive quotations from the Scriptures. Throughout the work, especially since Isaac and Hugh themselves are both so deeply Augustinian, the aura, and even frequent verbatim citation, of the Bishop of Hippo are constantly recurring factors. One mark of the depth of Augustine's influence is in the strong emphasis on the mysticism of introversion to be found in a number of chapters (e. g., 14 and 27).

The title itself has something to tell us about the interests of the compiler. The distinction between the spirit (*spiritus*) and the soul (*anima*) was important to that wing of twelfth-century psychology which identified the term *spiritus* with the highest dimension of the soul.[296] This distinction is especially to the fore in chapter nine, which, in terms of the title at least, might be considered as the central chapter of the treatise. Of course given the author's dependence on Isaac of Stella, he also frequently refers to the soul's highest dimension as the understanding (*intelligentia*),[297] or even under the more Augustinian rubric of the mind (*mens*).[298] In his treatment of the physical theory of the vital spirit (*spiritus vitalis*),[299] and in the medical sections in chapters twenty to twenty-two,[300] the compiler shows that he belongs to the same school of interest as William and Isaac, though without sharing the expertise of the former.

A second major concern of the text is with the question of definition. William had contented himself with repeating the

296. M.-D. Chenu, "Spiritus . . .," pp. 211-13.
297. E. g., chapters 4-5 (781-82).
298. E. g., chapters 32, 34 (801-02, 803-05).
299. Chapters 14 and 33 (790,803).
300. Cols. 794-95.

definitions of Cassiodorus; Isaac was chary of any definition. Definitions, on the other hand, abound in *The Spirit and the Soul* This too is a sign of the period when the work was put together. The compiler undoubtedly saw his task as transmitting to a new theological generation a compendium of all that previous authorities had said by way of defining the various terms used in traditional psychology. The same holds true for the many classifications of the powers of the soul—classifications and descriptions from every possible source are juxtaposed with no thought of the possibility of contradiction.[301] It is obvious that the stress is on inclusiveness rather than consistency and system.

The range of reading indicated by the work is fairly impressive. As Lewicki suggests, in terms of the text's doctrine of God, Gennadius of Marseilles, Boethius, Bede, the Pseudo-Ambrosian text, *The Dignity of the Human Condition*, and Anselm are the dominant influences. Its doctrine of the soul looks to Cassiodorus, Isidore, Alcuin, Hugh, Bernard, and Isaac. Finally, Augustine and Macrobius (with a smattering of more recent material not noted by Lewicki), are the major sources for its knowledge of the body and physical reality.[302] Its theory of asceticism and mysticism is so eclectic that the only rule governing it might be enunciated as "make use of whatever is convincing and profitable." Almost all of the major themes of Cistercian mysticism appear at one time or another, not least of all the theme of self-knowledge that is emphasized in chapter fifty-one.

In a sense, despite its eclecticism and inconsistency, *The Spirit and the Soul* has much to tell us about the nature of the Cistercian *De anima*. In making use of such a wide variety of the anthropological tradition described in Part I of this introduction, and in transmitting this tradition to a new theological era, it points to both the theological limitations and the achievements of the monks who felt that the study of the soul was central to Cistercianism.

301. E. g., chaps. 11-12 (786-88) where a remotely Aristotelian theory of abstraction is found alongside an Augustinian theory of illumination.
302. M. L. Lewicki, *op. cit.,* pp. 161-62.

THE MEANING OF THE CISTERCIAN TREATISES ON THE SOUL

In their efforts to penetrate to the core of the astonishing success of the Cistercian movement in the twelfth century, historians have cast light upon the economic, the institutional, and the social factors that contributed to the rise of the order. Without denying the importance of any of these, the explanation that they afford of the early history of the Cistercians would remain seriously deficient unless attention were also given to the accompanying intellectual, theological, and religious factors. Did Cistercian theology have anything positive to contribute to the renewal of Christian thought, in the twelfth century? If so, was this contribution an important part of the attraction that the new order had for so many thousands of dedicated men? Or was Cistercian theology rather merely a negative alternative to the creative new trends of the time? Is Cistercian thought to be seen as a call only to the maintenance of traditional formulae and to the rejection of those developments which marked the beginning of a new era in the history of Christian reflection?

If one were to concentrate on a few of the more extreme statements of a Geoffrey of Auxerre, or even of St Bernard himself, it would be easy to say that Cistercian thought was largely a rejection of many of the new trends in twelfth-century theology. Part of the success of the order then might well have lain in its appeal to those who, temperamentally wary of innovation, were shocked by the excesses of the "new theology." The differences in the form and organization of the writings of the monks and those of the early masters of the schools only serve to heighten this impression.

There are, nevertheless, some very good reasons for thinking that upon close investigation this initial response proves a very shallow one. The attitude of the Cistercians to the theological variety of the twelfth century was both more nuanced and more positive than simple conclusions drawn from Bernard's attacks on Abelard and Gilbert of Poitiers indicate. Speculation on the nature, powers, and destiny of the soul shows how fully the Cistercian theologians entered into some of the crucial areas of contemporary discussion.

Cistercian psychological theory is a much wider topic than the term might suggest. What these twelfth-century monks were really concerned with when they penned *De anima* treatises is what today we would call theological anthropology—the meaning of the human situation in the light of revelation. While it cannot be denied that in many instances the Hellenic background to which the monks were heirs tended towards the neglect of the material and temporal dimensions of human existence, it is a gross oversimplification to think that this long tradition means nothing more than a shrinking of a full theological anthropology to a more narrow psychology. In the twelfth century a very full range of the problems implicit in the description of theological anthropology as reflection upon human existence in the light of revelation is evident in many of the *De anima* treatises.

Students of medicine at Salerno had already begun to seek insights from Arabic sources into the nature of the body and its relation to the soul before the small band of monks left Molesmes to found Cîteaux in 1098. School theologians at Laon were already turning their attention to the questions of the origin of the soul and the transmission of original sin while the early Cistercians were attempting to find the institutional and organizational modes to express the aims of their reformation of the monastic life. The great Anselm had already turned his attention to the problem of human freedom before Bernard entered Cîteaux in 1112. How then did the doctrine of man become a part of the Cistercian theological program?

Our evidence for the earliest decades of the Cistercian movement is sparse; the problems connected with the texts are intricate and await further investigation.[303] Recent research has begun to expose the complexity of the development in these years, but in terms of our present knowledge it does seem possible to say that there is no *explicit* concern for a new theological anthropology in the earliest stages of the

303. For a brief survey of the early documents, cf. J. Leclercq, "The Intentions of the Founders of the Cistercian Order," *The Cistercian Spirit* (Spencer, 1970), pp. 90-101.

Cistercian movement. Granted that the documents we possess are not properly theological, even in terms of unexpressed theological presuppositions there is no indication that the authors were conscious of the need for renewed speculation on the nature and destiny of the soul.

Though Bernard of Clairvaux is usually thought of as the magnetic leader of the second generation of Cistercianism, recent studies have shown that this picture too is over-simplified. In terms of his entry into the order in 1112, his close association with Stephen Harding, and his undoubted (though still unclear) role in the evolution of the fundamental documents, Bernard is both one of the founding fathers of Cistercianism and the man who propagated the ideal (or his version of it) to Christendom.[304] The ambiguous role that Bernard played has been investigated thus far mostly in terms of its institutional aspects, but a similar ambiguity may be found in the role that he had in placing theological anthropology at the center of Cistercian thought. While the Abbot of Clairvaux never wrote a *De anima* himself, it is obvious that a concern for theological anthropology focused upon the question of the soul is an important, even central, theme of his writings. The question of whether he is merely making explicit what was already implicit in the earliest stages of the Cistercian reform is thus a theological analogue to the question of the relation of his conception of the spirit and aims of the order as institution to the ideas of Alberic, Stephen Harding, and the other men of the first generation of Cistercians. It was Bernard who was responsible for the importance of anthropology in the Cistercian movement.

E. Gilson was among the first modern scholars to vindicate the theological significance of the Abbot of Clairvaux. In his book *The Mystical Theology of St. Bernard* he dealt specifically not with his theology as a whole, ". . .but with that part only of his theology on which his mysticism rests."[305] While

---

304. On the various generations of Cistercianism and the role of St Bernard, consult the studies of M. Basil Pennington, Louis J. Lekai, Augustine Roberts, and Jean Leclercq in *The Cistercian Spirit*.

305. *The Mystical Theology of St. Bernard* (N.Y., 1940), p. vii.

Gilson never says so explicitly, the most exact description of
the part of theology which grounds Bernardine mystical
theory would be that of theological anthropology. Scholars
such as J. Leclercq later made the same point more directly.[306] Indeed, the past thirty years have seen considerable
investigation of the dominant themes of the Abbot's theory
of man, especially those of self-knowledge and of man as the
divine image.[307] The most important recent contribution, W.
Hiss's *Die Anthropologie Bernhards von Clairvaux*, places
particular emphasis on Christian Socratism as the starting
point for Bernard's theory,[308] and on the connection between
his Christology and his anthropology.[309] In the light of this
research, it is evident that anthropology has become increasingly important in an evaluation of Bernard's theology.

Given the existence of such research, there is no necessity
to go into the complexities, details, and problems connected
with the thought of the Abbot of Clairvaux. Rather, in more
general fashion, the question of the meaning of the Bernardine emphasis on anthropology for the development of
the order will be pursued. This area, along with that of the
relation of Bernardine anthropology to other Cistercian
works, particularly the three treatises translated here, have
thus far received less attention than they deserve.

What must always be remembered about the anthropology
of Bernard is that no matter how systematic and profound it
may have been, it was never taken as an end in itself. Telling

306. J. Leclercq, *The Love of Learning and the Desire for God* (Mentor ed.,
N. Y., 1962), pp. 222-23.

307. Cf. E. Gilson, *The Spirit of Mediaeval Philosophy* (N.Y.,1940), Chap. XI,
"Self-Knowledge and Christian Socratism"; G. B. Burch, *The Steps of Humilty by
Bernard, Abbot of Clairvaux* (Notre Dame, 1963), "Introduction;" L. Bouyer,
The Cistercian Heritage (Westminster, 1958), Chap. III; E. von Ivánka, "L'Union à
Dieu: La Structure de l'âme selon S. Bernard," *Saint Bernard Théologien: Ana-
lecta Sacri Ordinis Cisterciensis,* 9 (1953), pp. 202-08; C. H. Talbot, *Ailred of
Rievaulx: De Anima. Mediaeval and Renaissance Studies, Supplement* I (London,
1952); "Introduction," especially pp. 23-27; M. Standaert, "La doctrine de
l'image chez S. Bernard," *Ephemerides Theologicae Lovanienses,* 23 (1947), pp.
70-129.

308. W. Hiss, *Die Anthropologie Bernhards von Clairvaux* (Berlin, 1964), pp.
31-41.

309. *Op. cit.,* pp. 20-21; 137-40.

man who he was had importance only insofar as it enabled man to do what he should. Theological anthropology was ordered to the life of the monk. It is perhaps too simple to say that the "New Monastery" demanded a new theory of man, because the subtle interaction of tradition and innovation found in Cistercian institutions is also manifest in Cistercian writings on the soul; but the statement does suggest something of the motivation behind Bernard's anthropological writings.

An investigation of the dominant psychological themes through which the Abbot expressed this very pragmatically oriented theory of man begins to indicate the effect that he had on other Cistercian authors. Dominant among these themes is that of self-knowledge, the "Know yourself" of the Delphic maxim, which both Gilson and Hiss assert is central to Bernard's thought.[310] The imperative of Christian Socratism, however, immediately raised several important questions to which quite divergent answers were given. First, from what sources was one to seek this self-knowledge? Certainly from the Scriptures and from the testimony of one's own conscience. Assuredly from the Fathers and the tradition of the Church as well. But could pagan philosophical and medical writings also be a source for self-knowledge? Even though the tradition of monastic expertise in medicine was a long one, Bernard's attitude towards medicine was on the whole ambiguous.[311] Many of his pronouncements were also heavily weighted against making use of pagan philosophy. Nevertheless, much of what Bernard received from Origen, Augustine, and others had its origin in pagan thought; and some Cistercian authors showed themselves far more positive towards philosophy and medicine than he had been.

The second major question concerned the basic theological truth at which one arrived as a result of the process of self-knowledge. Theologically speaking, for Bernard knowing one-

---

310. E. g., *SC* 23, 9; *JB* 9. For discussions, cf. Gilson, *The Spirit of Mediaeval Philosophy* pp. 209-28; and Hiss, *op. cit.,* pp. 31-41.

311. Bernard's attacks on medicine in *SC* 30, 10, and other places are discussed by Hiss, *op. cit.,* pp. 121-122, note 137; and Burch, *op. cit.,* pp. 58-60. It is a topic that demands further attention.

self meant knowing that man, made to the image and likeness
of God, had fallen from that high estate and become lost in
the *regio dissimilitudinis,* the land of unlikeness. Theological
anthropology explained the consequences of this truth and
provided the theoretical guidelines for the restoration of the
image and likeness. In the writings of Bernard this theoretical
basis took the form of a reflection on man as the image of
God which stressed human freedom as the *locus* of the
image[312] and considered the dynamism of the return to God
under the aegis of an intricate theory of love.[313] Bernard also
wrote extensively on the more practical and experiential
aspects of the return process, the life of asceticism ending in
the mystical experience which was to be the task of the good
monk.[314]

While the other Cistercian writers on anthropology never
disagreed that self-knowledge consisted in knowing that man
was the image of God, the manner in which they expounded
image theology showed considerable variation. In more traditional fashion than the Abbot of Clairvaux, many of them
tended to place the image in man's intellectual power rather
than in human freedom, and in their discussions of the restoration of the image they frequently used anagogical categories drawn from the mind's ascent to truth or even from
cosmic imagery as much as from an evolved theory of love.
Particularly in the latter area, however, many authors combined a variety of approaches. A general look at Cistercian
treatments of theological anthropology may suggest some
ways of characterizing this variety and relating it both to
Bernard and to the wider world of twelfth-century theology.

312. *De gra.* (c. 1128) is the treatise in which this is most fully expounded,
especially in Chap. 9. See the article by Standaert already referred to. As A. Le
Bail has remarked apropos of this treatise: "Ce titre serait aussi justemtne 'De
Anima.' Les Cisterciens du XIIe et XIIIe siècles ne comprenaient pas l'enseig-
nement de la spiritualité sans un traité 'De anima.' " cf. "S. Bernard," *DS* I, 1461;
1472.

313. Most clearly set forth in the *De diligendo Deo.* For a comparison of
Bernard and William of St Thierry on love, cf. J. Hourlier, "S. Bernard et Guil-
laume de Saint-Thierry dans le 'Liber de Amore'," *Saint Bernard Théologien*
(Anal. Sac. Ord. Cist. 9, 1953), pp. 223-33.

314. The *Sermones super Cantica* are the supreme expression of this.

Besides the works of the Abbot of Clairvaux, we possess a fairly extensive body of literature that may be described as representative of Cistercian anthropology.[315] Many of these *De anima* treatises are by noted Cistercian authors,[316] others, while anonymous, have such a distinctive Cistercian cast to them that we can consider them as representative of the Cistercian school.[317] A few texts, not written by Cistercians, have been influenced by Cistercian anthropology and bear witness to its major themes.[318] A study of this literature indicates that roughly speaking it may be divided into two main categories.

We find, on the one hand, moral-ascetical treatments based upon an analysis of *conscientia*.[319] In these treatises there is very little theory of the nature of the soul, of human freedom, or of the theoretical basis of the return to God. There is instead a concern for the practical aspects of the Bernardine program. Self-knowledge is still all-important, but it is self-knowledge that is gained through reflection on conscience as

315. If theological anthropology is as central to the Cistercian program as suggested, then a full investigation would call for an analysis of all the important Cistercian texts of the 12th century. Since this is clearly impossible, the concentration here will be on explicit treatments of the nature of the soul, usually in treatises specifically so named. Such a survey is adequate to expose the major lines of Cistercian anthropology.

316. The list would include: (a) William of St. Thierry's *De natura corporis et animae* (PL 180, 695-726); (b) Nicholas of Clairvaux's *Epistolae* 63 and 65 (PL 202); (c) Arnold of Bonneval's *De Paradiso animae* (PL 189, 1515-70); (d) Isaac of Stella's *Epistola de anima* (PL 194, 1875-90); (e) Aelred of Rievaulx, *De anima* (ed. Talbot); (f) Helinand of Froidmont, *De cognitione sui* (PL 212, 721-30).

317. These would include the anonymous compilation of four books *De anima* parts of which have been ascribed to Bernard, Hugh of St Victor, and even Augustine. (cf. Note 259 above). From the latter part of the 12th century we can also list :(a) *Tractatus de conscientia (Petis a me)* (PL 213, 903-12; PL 184, 551-60); (b) *Quid sit anima*, ed. E. Bertola, "Di una inedita Trattazione psicologica intitolata :*Quid sit anima,*" *Rivista di Filosofia Neo-scolastica*, 58 (1966), pp. 581-83; (c) *Quinque digressiones cogitationis*, ed. M.-T. d'Alverny, *Alain de Lille: Textes inédites* (Paris, 1965) pp. 313-17; (d) A few unedited treatises and fragments mentioned by M.-T. d'Alverny, *op. cit.*, pp. 182-83, note 87.

318. Especially the Cluniac Peter of Celle in his *Liber de conscientia* (PL 202, 1083-98); and less securely the canon regular, Hugh of Fouilloy, in his *De medicina animae* (PL 176, 1183-1202).

319. The primary texts here would be Helinand's *De cognitione sui*; numbers 1, 3, and 4 of the anonymous *De anima*; the anonymous treatise *Tractatus de conscientia*; and Peter of Celle's *Liber de conscientia*.

revealing to man the depth of his sinfulness and his need for God. Long discussion is given to all the aspects of the program of asceticism designed to lift man out of this slough of sin. It may seem questionable whether these highly allegorical and rather diffuse works are really to be considered theological anthropology or rather a form of pious reading. In themselves, their theological value is obviously small. As P. Delhaye has remarked in a study of three of these treatises, they must be viewed "in the wake of St Bernard."[320] It is only in respect to the importance of Bernard's thought that they take on some theological importance. Their authors have accepted the Bernardine theory of man as basic and thus view their task as merely drawing out and reemphasizing the practical moral conclusions of this anthropology. They see no reason to diverge from their master in the matter of theory. They also for the most part adhere to his suspicions concerning material drawn from philosophical and medical sources. The Scriptures, conscience, and a very generalized dependence on the Fathers are sufficient for them.

The moral-ascetical approach, however, did not exhaust Cistercian anthropology. We have also seen evidence of a more speculative and systematic attitude towards the problem of the soul, especially in the texts of William of St Thierry and Isaac of Stella. In the texts which display this approach there is greater evidence of the kinds of divergence from Bernardine positions mentioned above; these treatises are also among the best evidence for the intimate connection of Cistercian thought with other important theological schools of the twelfth century.

Needless to say, the two approaches, the moral-ascetical and the speculative-systematic, are by no means exclusive. Treatises may combine both approaches; the same author may write now largely in one vein, now in the other. Despite these divergencies, however, it is possible to point to a definite speculative tradition in the twelfth-century Cister-

320. P. Delhaye, "Dans le sillage de S. Bernard: trois petits traités *de conscientia,*" *Cîteaux* 5 (1954), pp. 92-103, studies the *Tractatus de conscientia,* the *Tractatus de interiori domo,* and the *De conscientia* of Peter of Celle.

cian authors, to enumerate the texts which best exemplify it,[321] and to summarize its major themes.

The central concerns of the speculative treatises can be summarized under three headings: the soul as mystery in itself, the soul as cosmic mystery, and the soul as divine mystery. The last of these areas is that most directly related to Bernardine anthropology; the former areas, while not absent from the Abbot's thought,[322] were less directly related to it. The soul as mystery in itself bespeaks the greater interest these writers took in systematic questions; their attention to the soul as cosmic mystery shows how the *De anima* treatises cannot be restricted to the study of the soul alone, but confront a much wider range of the problems of human existence in the material world.

The mystery of the soul in itself reflects one of the most typical aspects of twelfth-century theology, that passion for classifying and organizing the differing systems of thought and terminology which we have seen to be present in varying fashion in all three of our texts. In the area of psychology alone a bewildering variety of terms—*anima, animus, spiritus, mens, intellectus, etc.*—could be used for the soul. None of these words had a stable meaning. In the case of versions of Greek texts, the use shifts from translator to translator.[323] The same is true of the texts of the Latin Fathers; indeed, there is rarely a standard terminology found within a single author, as the case of Augustine so clearly demonstrates.[324] As M.-D. Chenu in his brilliant article on the various meanings of *spiritus* has pointed out, this semantic imprecision had a positive side insofar as it reinforced the analogical and symbolic mentality that was so important in the

321. Purer representatives of the speculative tradition besides William and Isaac would be Nicholas of Clairvaux's *Epistolae,* and the *Quid sit anima.* More mixed representatives would include Arnold's *De paradiso,* Aelred's *De anima,* and the *De spiritu et anima.*

322. Bernard does discuss the classification of the powers of the soul as mentioned below. On his handling of the union of the body and the soul, cf. Hiss, *op. cit.,* pp. 51-65; on his cosmology, pp. 118-20.

323. E. g., the differences in terminology between the translations of the texts of the Pseudo-Dionysius by John the Scot and John Sarrazin.

324. For a brief introduction to the vocabulary of Augustine, cf. L. Reypens, "Ame," cc. 436-41.

period,[325] but the positive aspect was clearly felt to have its limitations as is manifested by the attempt to give various coherent classifications of the powers or faculties of the soul during the century. The Cistercians took a leading role in this movement.

Bernard of Clairvaux was not indifferent to the question of the classification of the powers of the soul. He made use of the standard threefold description of powers reaching back to Plato: rationality, positive appetite, and negative appetite.[326] He customarily characterized the soul in terms of a triad taken from Augustine (reason, memory, and will), though the content he gave to this division was not Augustinian.[327] Nevertheless, the Abbot's main interests lay elsewhere.

This was not the case with William of St Thierry. William showed a strong interest in the classification of powers, and was unique among Cistercian authors (in this treatise at least) in being more systematic in the case of the classification of the organs and powers of the body than in the case of those of the soul. The unfinished treatise of Aelred, while it keeps closer to the heritage received from Augustine and Bernard and displays no interest in medical questions, still has as its major intention the desire to present a complete enumeration of the powers of the soul.[328]

This systematizing concern among Cistercian authors reached a peak in the work of Isaac of Stella. Not only was he interested in physiology and medicine; but, as we have seen, he also showed real creativity regarding the question of the classification of the powers of the soul. Though he made use of the threefold Platonic division, Isaac was more interested in developing two correlative schemas of man's rational powers: the temporal schema of forethought, insight, and memory, designed to indicate the difference between man

325. M.-D. Chenu, *"Spiritus,"* p. 223.

326. Bernard also occasionally uses the widespread division of the powers of the soul into *intellectus (sensus) et affectus*; e. g., *Asc* 3, 102 (cf. Hiss, *op. cit.,* p. 106).

327. Hiss, *op. cit.,* pp. 111-37; and von Ivánka, *op. cit.,* pp. 203-04.

328. Cf. the excellent edition and introduction already frequently referred to of C. H. Talbot; and P. Michaud-Quantain, "La classification . . .," pp. 182-83, note 87.

and God, and an anagogic schema of sense knowledge, imagination, reason, discernment, and understanding to show the way the soul can ascend to God. The anonymous work *The Spirit and the Soul* maintained this strong concern for classification, but lost the power of creative appropriation and systematization. In a combination of both moral-ascetical and speculative interests this diffuse treatise gathered together classifications of the soul's powers taken from a wide variety of Patristic and contemporary sources. Isaac's anagogic schema made an appearance in it, and, due to the authority that the work acquired when it was taken to be a product of the pen of Augustine himself, achieved a fairly wide diffusion in the later twelfth and thirteenth centuries. The same schema appears in five small anonymous texts from the end of the century which show Cistercian influence.[329]

Interest in classifying the powers of the soul is of importance in only some of the schools of twelfth-century theology.[330] In others the renewal of anthropology took the form of speculation on original sin, the origin of the human soul, and the mystery of human free will and grace, etc. Among those interested in classifying, the speculative Cistercian treatises have a surprising affinity with texts connected with the School of Chartres. This is particularly true of the interest of William of St Thierry and William of Conches in Arabic medicine.[331] Despite the differences between Cîteaux and Chartres and the personal quarrel of the two men, this resemblance is worthy of note.

The problem of how to define the soul was not the basic concern in this psychological approach. Only the treatise *The Spirit and the Soul* really busied itself with gathering together as many traditional definitions as possible. Since the

---

329. The *Quid sit anima* edited by E. Bertola; the *Quinque digressiones cogitationis* edited by M.-T. d'Alverny (Less probably Cistercian than the other treatises); and the three small fragments mentioned by d'Alverny, *op. cit.*, pp. 182-83, n. 87.

330. P. Michaud-Quantain's remarks on the completely negative attitude of the Victorines (*op. cit.*, pp. 32-33) are exaggerated.

331. On the anthropology of William of Conches, cf. Michaud Quaintain, pp. 28-32.

primary truth about the soul was that it is the image of God, the soul could not be adequately defined in itself, but always remained in some sense a mystery. A more serious concern in speaking of the soul in itself was the question of whether the soul was to be identified with its powers or whether there was a real distinction between its essence and its faculties. Despite the hesitations of some scholars about the position of Bernard,[332] the Cistercian theologians were unanimous in asserting the identity. As we have seen, one of the ways the assertion of the identity came to be a touchstone of orthodox Augustinianism in the thirteenth century was through its appearance in *The Spirit and the Soul*.[333]

The influence of medical literature played a major role in the second theme of the speculative tradition in Cistercian anthropology, that of the soul as cosmic mystery. Cistercian psychological treatises are truly anthropological precisely because in so many of these works the soul is also considered in relation to its own body and to the larger body of the world.

The relation of the soul to the body had always been one of the trouble spots in any Christian anthropology accepting the basic Hellenic distinction between the spiritual and material principles in man. As we saw in the first part of this introduction, in adopting a basically Platonic understanding of the soul as a spiritual substance in its own right, the patristic authors gained the advantage of cogent arguments for personal immortality, but were left with the difficulty of giving systematic theological expression to the unity of man. They had the choice, as A. Pegis notes, of either making the body accidental to the soul (the true man), or else of attempting to find an explanation for how two substances can come together to form a third without losing their indepen-

332. E. von Ivánka, *op. cit.*, p. 204; and P. Künzle, *Das Verhältnis der Seele zu ihren Potenzen*, p. 63, see Bernard as affirming the identity. For the less convincing opposing view, cf. W. Hiss, *op. cit.*, pp. 89-90.

333. The Cistercian views on the question are summarized in Künzle, *op. cit.*, pp. 63-74. On the whole question, cf. also M. Ortuzar, "El ser y la acción en la dimensión humana (Pedro Abelardo, 1097-1142), y su gruppo," *Estudios* (Madrid), 13 (1957), pp. 219-48; 431-63.

dence.[334] The patristic authors did not find the latter; but
since strict logic has rarely ruled in the history of theology,
the weight of the patristic tradition usually tried to avoid the
former alternative as well. Therefore, although the categories
used tended towards a devaluation of the temporal and
material dimensions of the human situation,[335] important
qualifications of this tendency were frequently introduced.
Logically impossible as it may be to bring temporality and
corporeality to systematic expression in terms of this tradition of theological anthropology, the unity of man was not
generally denied, especially in the case of the all-important
Augustine.

The speculative Cistercian authors, working within the
same mental perimeters, follow their patristic forebears in
this equivocation. This is especially evident in their concentration on medicine and physiology as a part of their program
of self-knowledge and their use of the theme of man as the
microcosm. If the soul is the true man, then there is no need
for being concerned about the structure and health of the
body; but if man is really a unity of body and soul, then the
knowledge of man demands a knowledge of his material side
as well. Just as the image of God lost through sin had to be
restored by a program of spiritual healing, so too the healing
of the body is both analogy and preparation for this operation. William of St Thierry, Isaac, and a number of other
Cistercians, all displayed such medical interest. Cistercians
were among the first theologians to make use of the new
Arabic medicine. No matter how crude and erroneous it may
seem today, we must remember that in the twelfth century
Arabic medicine was an important innovation. No matter
how puerile the analogies drawn between the operations of
the body and those of the soul as a way of mediating the
body-soul dichotomy, we must recognize that what was at
stake was an attempt by Cistercian authors to show that
"know yourself" meant knowing the material as well as the
spiritual aspects of man's nature.

334. A. Pegis, *At the Origins of the Thomistic Notion of Man,* p. 12.
335. Cf. M.-D. Chenu, "Situation humaine . . . ," pp. 25-26; 49.

How then did the Cistercians deal with the vexing problem
of the union of body and soul in explicit fashion? We have
already mentioned the three basic solutions available in the
twelfth century to the problem of the unity of man—union
through number and harmony, union in the person, and
union through a physical medium. Since none of these three
approaches is systematically coherent, elements of all three
are frequently found intermixed, as they are in Hugh of St
Victor's *The Union of the Body and the Spirit*, perhaps the
most important twelfth-century treatment. William seems to
have had no knowledge of Hugh's text; for him the joining of
body and soul is a mystery, as it had been for Augustine.
Isaac of Stella, on the other hand, showed many traces of
Hugh's influence, especially in his idea of the union as taking
place at the two extreme points of spiritual and material
nature, ". . .that is, in the imaginative faculty of the soul
which is almost a body and in the faculty of sensation of the
flesh which is almost a spirit."[336] What is operative here is the
hierarchical Platonic worldview, where the unification of
disparate elements and levels is effected by the multiplication
of mediating terms: "But it is not possible to combine two
things properly without a third to act as a bond to hold them
together" (*Timaeus* 31C). *The Spirit and the Soul* followed
Isaac in its discussion of the problem;[337] Aelred sought a
union in the physical medium of the sensual power (*vis
sensualis*) in a fashion that makes it difficult to judge whether
he actually knew Hugh's work or not.[338]

The theme of man as the microcosm, the world in
miniature, containing in himself something of every material
and spiritual level of reality, was another common way of
outflanking the implicit evisceration of materiality in the
body-soul dichotomy. This is a very rich theme with a long
and intricate history; it is present in a wide variety of

336. *Ep an* 11 (1881C).

337. *De spiritu et anima* 14 (789-90); and 38 (808).

338. *De anima* I (pp. 87-88). Cf. the comments in the Introduction by C. H.
Talbot, pp. 42-44.

Cistercian texts, including those of William, Isaac, and *The Spirit and the Soul.*[339] In terms of their treatment of the soul as cosmic mystery then, what can be claimed for the Cistercian treatises on the soul is not that they managed to escape from some of the ambiguities and tensions implicit in Platonic-Christian anthropological theory, but that they were aware of the issues involved in the precarious task of attempting to create a systematic Christian anthropology, and were bold and innovative in the use they made of traditional and contemporary resources in meeting these problems.

Whatever the importance of considering the soul in itself and the soul in relation to man's situation in material reality, the heart of the Cistercian view of man was the mystery of the soul's relation to God. The other elements had no meaning aside from this. There is no such thing as a purely philosophical theory of man in the Cistercian authors, no matter what differences of approach they may take. In the course of our consideration we have already had occasion to discuss how the treatment of the soul as image and likeness, fallen yet capable of returning to its former status, is the core of this theology. The speculative treatises tend to depart from the Bernardine theory of the image as being found in man's freedom to give greater emphasis to the intellectual nature of the image. William of St. Thierry was certainly more intellectualist than Bernard, though his most profound thought saw the full actualization of the image in the attaining of the resemblance through the union of the faculties of love and knowledge.[340] It is clear from the *Letter on the Soul* that Isaac of Stella considered the image to reside in man's intellectual faculties. As a matter of fact, in one of his sermons he repeated the twelfth-century commonplace that

339. Some microcosm texts: (1) *Nat corp.*; Prologus (695); *Phys an* 3 (710 CD); (2) *Ep an* 19 (1886A); and, of course, the whole five-fold schema itself; and (3) *De spiritu et anima* 6 (783).

340. Hourlier, *op. cit.*, pp. 225; 229-30; and O. Brooke, "The Trinitarian Aspect of the Ascent of the Soul to God. ....." pp. 123-24.

the image resides in truth, the likeness in love.[341] Even Aelred placed the image in the Augustinian triad of memory, reason, and will.[342] *The Spirit and the Soul* followed a similar intellectualist line.[343] The intellectualist tradition then played a much larger role in the speculative treatises than it did in either the writings of Bernard or of his followers of the moral-ascetical bent.

There are two further themes concerning the soul's relation to God which appear in the speculative treatises in distinctive ways: the description of the soul's ascent to God, and speculation about the nature of the mystical union itself. Images of ascension are by no means lacking in the writings of Bernard of Clairvaux—one need only think of the *The Degrees of Humility*. What might be called the anagogic mentality was common to all Cistercian anthropology, but there are special ways in which the speculative authors express this mentality. If we take two of the most compelling descriptions of the process of ascent to God, William of St Thierry's dynamic analysis of *anabathmon* and *catabathmon* at the end of *The Nature of Body and Soul,* and Isaac of Stella's fivefold ascent in *The Letter on the Soul,* we are stuck by the systematic and encompassing power of the symbols used. The system outlined in Bernard's treatise, the only ascensional pattern that rivals these two, is more directly practical and moral in its intent: more a description of the virtues by which the good monk mounts to God than a theory of the return of all things to their source through man the image and likeness of God.[344]

The process of the ascent of the soul to God leads us to the last of the major themes of the speculative treatises, that of

341. Sermon 16 (ed. Hoste, pp. 304-06, 1744A-B). This division first appeared in the *De dignitate humanae conditionis,* a Carolingian text circulating under the names of Augustine or Ambrose (*PL* 17, 1015-18). It is found in a wide variety of twelfth-century authors, including Hugh of St. Victor.

342. *De anima* II (ed. Talbot, p. 127). It is even found in some of the moral-ascetical treatises, e.g., *De cognitione humanae conditionis* (*PL* 184, 485C-87C).

343. *De spiritu et anima* 10; 34-35; 39; 63.

344. Cf. the analysis of G. B. Burch, "Introduction," *The Steps of Humility* (Notre Dame, 1963), pp. 3-112.

their theory of the union of the soul with God. One side of the tradition may be described as topographic, that is, it sought to locate the place in the soul (its highest or deepest dimension) where union with God actually occurred. This tradition reached as far back as the consideration of *Nous*, the highest, truly divine part of the soul, in Plato's *Timaeus*.[345] The history of the use of the Stoic term "the height of the soul" (*apex mentis*),[346] Augustine's speculation on "the mind" (*mens*) and "the more hidden depth of memory" (*abstrusior profunditas memoriae*), and Boethius's conception of the superiority of "understanding" (*intelligentia*), were among the important ways in which this theory of the higher dimension of the soul was transmitted to twelfth-century authors. M.–D. Chenu has described one aspect of the rebirth of such speculation in his study of the term *spiritus* in the twelfth century.[347] Other studies have contributed to the investigation of the theme among the spiritual authors.[348] The importance of thought about the higher dimension of the soul to Cistercian theological anthropology is obvious, and Isaac of Stella's analysis of *intelligentia* is among the most important Cistercian contributions to the topography of mystical union.

The other face of speculation about union with God is more dynamic, answering the question "What is the manner of this experience? " The goal of the Cistercian reform was to produce the kind of monastic milieu which would foster direct contact with God as its most important goal. Bernard had described this experience in terms of a theory of love in his *Sermons on the Song of Songs*. His theological doctrine of

345. E.g., the use of *Nous* in 51e, and of *daimon* in 90ad. On this question, cf. *The Golden Chain*, chap. 4.

346. Cf. E. von Ivánka, "*Apex Mentis*. Wanderung und Wandlung eines stoischen Terminus," *Zeitschrift für katholische Theologie*, 72 (1950) pp. 129-76. Reprinted in *Plato Christianus* (Einsiedeln, 1964), pp. 315-51.

347. Chenu, "Spiritus, le vocabulaire de l'âme . . . "

348. E.g., von Ivánka, *Plato Christianus*, pp. 352-63; J. A. Robilliard, "Les six genres de contemplation chez Richard de Saint-Victor et leur origine platonicienne," *RSPT*, 28 (1939), pp. 229-33; and R. Javelet, *Psychologie des auteurs spirituels du XIIe siècle* (Strasbourg, 1959).

the mystical union is also based on analyses of the nature
of love; both William and Isaac, as we have seen, are more
interested in analyzing the mystical union as resulting from
the union of love and knowledge, though Isaac never developed his thought to the extent that William did in his last
treatises. Furthermore, as J. Hourlier has pointed out,
Bernard's theology of the mystical union is largely expressed
in Christocentric terms while William's is also Pneumatic,
centered on the personal property of the Spirit as the union
of the Father and the Son.[349] Isaac's doctrine, tantalizing in
the brevity in which it appears at the end of the *Letter*,
appears closer to William, but with a specific and distinctive
invocation of the total body of Christ.

Our broad survey of Cistercian theological anthropology
with special emphasis on the speculative tradition puts us in a
position to assay some tentative conclusions concerning its
significance. That Bernard and the preponderance of the
Cistercian authors (not Isaac of Stella however) were suspi-
cious of the role of dialectic in theology and openly attacked
what they felt were perversions induced by its application is
well known. But this by no means should be taken to signify
that Cistercian thought was obscurantist or woodenly traditional in nature. Especially in the central area of theological
anthropology the Cistercian contribution was of real significance. Bernard's *Grace and Free Choice* is one of the most
original treatises of the age, particularly in its rethinking of
the theology of the image of God.

The *De anima* treatises of William of St Thierry and Isaac
of Stella are scarcely less original. Both works—though in
quite differing ways—display a systematic interest in anthropology as the theological ground for the life of prayer and
contemplation which will best help the monk to reach his
goal. They are more open than Bernard was towards utilizing
whatever traditional and contemporary thought they found
valuable for this project, as William explicitly announces at
the beginning of his work and as is clear from even a cursory

---

349. J. Houlier, *op. cit.,* pp. 228; 231-33.

perusal of Isaac's *Letter.* The use that William makes of
Arabic medical sources and the work of Gregory of Nyssa
proves how wide ranging his reading was. The Abbot of St
Thierry and William of Conches (whom he was later to
attack) are our first witnesses to the use of Arabic medicine
in Christian anthropological theory. Isaac of Stella also had
some acquaintance with Arabic material; but it is in the rich
variety of the patristic and contemporary sources he used, as
well as in the systematic way he went about his task, that he
shows his equality with William. Later anthropological
treatises in the Cistercian tradition, whether of the moral-
ascetical or speculative-systematic approaches, do not display
the same originality. Nevertheless, *The Spirit and the Soul,*
that compendium of old and new, was to be far more influential than earlier, more original, works in assuring Cistercian
anthropology a real influence in the history of medieval
theology.

   The final question to which we must address ourselves is far
less responsive to a direct and convincing reply. What role did
this theological anthropology have in the success of the
Cistercian movement? We shall never really know. It can
probably be safely said that few if any ever entered the order
because they were attracted by the kind of theology that was
being done by the Cistercians. One became a monk not to
write but to do and to live. Without denying the great
importance of the economic and social factors in the growth
of the order, the religious force involved in the presentation
of ideal monasticism was the central factor in its appeal to
the spiritual elite of Europe in the twelfth century. It was
insofar as theological anthropology contributed to the
understanding and actual living of this ideal, insofar as the
ideal monasticism evoked a theory of the ideal man, that the
Cistercian treatises on the soul had real significance in the
growth of the order.

Bernard McGinn

University of Chicago

A NOTE ON THE TRANSLATION

The vagaries of the terminology used in the three treatises translated here should be evident from the Introduction. In the interests of consistency and of providing some aid for the reader who may wish to get back to the original texts, standardized translations of the technical terms describing the soul and its powers have been attempted in the present versions. It should be noted that these have been the responsibility of the editor; any shortcomings, either in terms of the vocabulary chosen or of the application thereof are his responsibility and not that of the individual translators, despite the very considerable help he has had from the suggestions made by them in the original versions. The most important terms are set forth in the following outlines. The references are to the chapter divisions (e.g., #1, #2) in the translations and to the appropriate columns (e.g., 695-96) in the *Patrologia Latina (PL* 180 in the case of William; *PL* 194 for Isaac; and *PL* 40 for *The Spirit and the Soul).*

I. William of St Thierry—*The Nature of the Body and the Soul.*

Part I. The Physics of the Body.

A. The Four Elements and the Four Humors.

	fire (*ignis*)	— red bile (*cholera rubea*)	
	air (*aer*)	— blood (*sanguis*)	
#1 (695-96)			#2 (698B)
	water (*aqua*)	— phlegm (*flegma*)	
	earth (*terra*)	— black bile (*melancholia*)	

B. The Natural Powers (*virtutes*).

	appetitive (*appetitiva*)
	retentive (*contentiva*)
e.g., #2 (697C)	
	digestive (*digestiva*)
	expulsive (*expulsiva*)

C. The Spirits (*spiritus*). (N.B. These too are called "powers," i.e., *virtutes*.)

Spirit (*Spiritus*) #4 (700BC and in the later places indicated)	natural (*naturalis*)—in the liver; common to trees, animals, and men #5 (700C)		generation (*generativa*) nutrition (*pascitiva*) growth (*nutritiva*)
	spiritual (*spiritualis*)—in the heart; common to animals and men		(N.B. Also called the vital power, cf. 702D-703A) (N.B. spiritual power is also used in a wider sense, cf. 701BC.)
			sensation (*sensus*)
	animal (*animalis*)—in the brain (N.B. Most of its functions are proper to men) #5-7	forward lobe (*prora*)	imagination (*phantasia*)
		middle lobe (*media*)	reason (*ratio*) and discernment (*intellectus*)
		rear lobe (*puppis*)	movement (*motus*) memory (*memoria*)

Part II. The Physics of the Soul.

A. The Three Kinds of Organs.

#1 (709A)

in order to live—brain, heart, liver

in order to live well—e.g., organs of sense

in order to receive future goods—stomach, lungs, etc.

B. Soul and Intellectual Soul.

#3 (711BC)

soul (*anima*)

intellectual soul (*animus*)

C. Analogies Between the Soul and the Body.

        (1) the four elements = the four cardinal virtues
            (718A)

		hope (*spes*)
		joy (*gaudium*)
#8 (717D-719A)	(2) the four powers natural = the four passions	fear (*timor*)
		sadness (*tristitia*)
	(3) the three spirits and their effects (718B-719A)	natural → nutrition rationality → faith
		spiritual → vivification positive appetite → hope
		animal → sensation negative appetite → charity

D. Trinitarian Images.

             mind (*mens*)

(1) #11 (721B)   thought (*cogitatio*)

             will (*voluntas*)

             memory (*memoria*)

(2) #13 (722B)   deliberation (*consilium*)

             will (*voluntas*)

II. Isaac of Stella—*The Letter on the Soul.*

A. The Structure of the Soul (*anima*):

THE TWO BASIC POWERS   THE THREE PLATONIC POWERS (#4-5)

#3-Virtual or potential parts or powers (*vires sive potentiales partes*-1875A)

#4-Natural attributes which are really identical with the soul (*naturalia*-1877B)

I. #5-6: the power of desire (*affectus*-1878CD)

1. the positive appetite (*concupiscibilitas*)
   a) in something present-joy (*gaudium*)
   b) in something future-hope (*spes*)

2. the negative appetite (*irascibilitas*)
   a) in something present-sorrow (*dolor*)
   b) in something future-fear (*timor*)

II. #7-21: the power of knowledge (*sensus*-1879B) = 3. reasonableness (*rationabilitas*)

#3,7— the temporal pattern (1879BD)
   a) forethought (*ingenium*)
   b) insight (*ratio*)
   c) memory (*memoria*)

#8-23- the anagogic pattern (e.g., 1880AD)
   a) sense knowledge (*sensus*)
   b) imagination (*imaginatio*)
   c) reason (*ratio*)
   d) discernment (*intellectus*)
   e) understanding (*intelligentia*) (also called mind-*mens*, cf. 1881C)

B. The Union of Soul and Body:

#10-12
the union takes place in

1. the imaginative faculty or
   lowest point of the spirit   = fire (*ignis* 1882C)
   (*phantasticum animae*-1881C)

2. the faculty of sensation of
   the flesh or the highest   = the strength
   point of the body (*sensual-*   of fire
   itas carnis-1881C)   (*igneus vigor* 1882C)

‖

the animal spirit
(*spiritus pecorum*-
1881A)
the bodily spirit
(*spiritus corporeus*-
1881D)

C. The Anagogic Pattern and the Division of Sciences:

#16,20

understanding → c) theology (*theologia*-1884D)   concerns divine
    ↑   matters
discernment → (cf. #20—1886D-87A-on why it
    ↑   does not have its own science)
reason   → b) mathematical science (*mathesis,*   concerns the rational
    ↑   *mathematica disciplina*-1884C)   or theoretical state
imagination   a) natural science   concerns the real
    ↑   (*naturalis disciplina* 1884C)   or natural state of
sense knowledge   being

D. The Analogies of the Trinity:

(1) #20
(1887B)

Father   — the level of essence   — Eternity (*aeternitas*)
              (*essentia, esse*)
Son   — the level of form   — Form (*species*)
              (*species, imago, forma*)
Holy Spirit — the level of enjoyment   — Enjoyment (*usus*)
or Gift   (*usus*)
(*Munus*)

(2) #23
(1888CD)

Father   — light, i.e., existing and unbegotten (*lux*)
Son   — shines, i.e., light going forth and begotten (*lucet*)
Holy Spirit — illuminates, i.e., gives light (*illuminat*)

III. *The Spirit and the Soul.*

With regard to classifications of the powers of the soul, all of the terms already identified in William and Isaac will be translated in this treatise in the same way, *as long as they keep their technical sense*. Rather than to attempt to give outlines of the many classifications found in this text, the following summary of the translations of technical Latin terms may prove helpful.

1. *acies mentis*—penetrating power of mind - #2 (781)

2. *affectio*—affection - #20 (794)

3. *affectus*—(a) technically - power of desire (as one of the two fundamental powers of the soul)
    (b) non-technically - desire - e.g., #47 (814)

4. *anima*—soul

5. *animus*—intellectual soul

6. *appetitus*—appetite - #47 (808)

7. *cogitatio*—reflection - #38 (809)

8. *excessus*—ecstasy - #34 (804)

9. *ingenium*—(a) forethought - in Isaac's temporal schema
    (b) genius - in generic use, e.g., #38 (809)

10. *intellectus*—(a) discernment—when used as the fourth member of the Isaacan anagogic schema
    (b) intellect—when used as a member of the Trinitarian analogy of *intellectus, voluntas, memoria,* e.g., #35 (805)

11. *intelligentia*—(a) understanding—in the schema of Isaac
    (b) intelligence—when used as a member of the Trinitarian analogy of *memoria, intelligentia, amor,* e.g., #63 (827)

12. *phantasia*—phantasm - #32 (801). N.B. The same term appears in William as the name of a faculty and hence is translated as "imaginative power," cf. Book I, #7 (703A), while in Isaac, as in the present text, it signifies the product of a faculty and is thus translated as "phantasm," e.g., #22 (1888B).

13. *sensualitas*—sensation - #34 (804)

14.   *sensus*—this is the most difficult term of all to attempt to do justice
      to. It can take the following meanings:
      (a) an individual sense faculty, e.g., sight (as in William and
          Isaac)
      (b) the five faculties of sensation in general (also in William)
      (c) the actual experience of sensation (in William and *The
          Spirit and the Soul*)
      (d) the content of sense knowledge (in Isaac)
      (e) the power of knowledge in general (in Isaac and *The
          Spirit and the Soul*)[350]

350. As the present study was going to press, the work of L. Norpoth, *Der pseudo-
augustinische Traktat: De spiritu et anima* (Institu für Geschichte der Medizin der
Universität zu Köln in Verbindung mit der Ruhr-Universität Bochum, 1971) came
to my attention. According to the report given by D. Aschoff, "Der pseudo-
augustinische Traktat *De spiritu et anima*," *Revue des études augustiniennes*, 18
(1972), 293-94, this work is the fullest account of the treatise presently available,
and confirms some of the positions taken above, e.g. on the Cistercian origin of
the compilation.

WILLIAM OF ST THIERRY

THE NATURE OF THE BODY AND THE SOUL

TWO BOOKS WRITTEN UNDER THE NAME OF
THEOPHILUS
THAT IS, A LOVER OF GOD

THE NATURE OF THE BODY AND THE SOUL

PROLOGUE

AMONG THE GREEKS the answer of the Delphic Apollo is well known: "Man, know yourself." So also Solomon, or rather Christ, says in the Canticle, "If you do not know yourself, go forth."[1] For he who does not dwell in his own domain through the contemplation of wisdom, necessarily enters into that of others through the vanity of curiosity. The power of knowledge of the thinking man is hardly enough, without the help of grace, to know himself, and even this is of no value unless from the knowledge of what he is he rises to him from whom he is, to him who is above him. It is an unfortunate and stupid mistake to expend the forces of one's mind on other things when nature, indeed the God of nature, has enjoined such an important work within oneself. And so we shall make a thorough investigation of our microcosm, our little world, man, both within and without, that is in soul and body, so that through our understanding of what we can see and perceive in ourselves we may rise to the Author of all things, visible and invisible. We shall first say something about the nature of the body, then about what is proper to the soul. But realize that what you read is not my own; rather I have gathered together here what I have found in the books of philosophers and physicians, and also in ecclesiastical writers, and not merely their ideas, but their very words, spoken or written, which have been published.

1. Song 1:7. On the Delphic oracle see below, p , n. 123.

BOOK ONE

THE PHYSICS OF THE HUMAN BODY

THE FOUR ELEMENTS AND THE FOUR HUMORS

E VERY ANIMAL BODY is formed of earth, that is, is a composite of the four elements. It is one thing that is formed from the earth, but several things go into its make-up. What makes it up are the four elements. Each element has a quality that is proper to itself: fire, heat; air, wetness; water, coldness; earth, dryness. But fire, because it is mobile, takes on the quality of dryness. It is hot and dry. Air, because it is beneath fire, takes on the heat that is proper and natural to fire. It is hot from fire, wet of itself. Water is beneath air, and so takes on wetness from it, while it is cold of itself. Earth is below water so it is cold from it, dry of itself. According to Hippocrates, if the animal body were made up of only one element, it would never feel pain, because it would have no way to feel pain, being one existing thing.[2] But muddy earth becomes water; rarefied and heated, evaporated water becomes air; condensed and collected air becomes water; and so on. Thus corruption comes about.

From these four elements four humors are created in the animal body and so are called its children. They serve the physical body just as the elements serve the world. They provide the substance and order for the life and health of the

---

2. The source of this doctrine may be Constantine the African's *De locis communibus (Pantegni)* 1, 25, where Hippocrates is cited as teaching the mixing of the four elements in the human body, though the idea of the presence of all the elements being the source of the possibility of pain is absent. See the treatment of sources in J. M. Déchanet, *Oeuvres choisies de Guillaume de Saint-Thierry* (Paris:- Aubier, 1944), pp. 59-61.

body, if they are present in the proper manner and order and are not corrupted by vice or neglect. Otherwise just as water by condensation is changed into earth, and muddy earth into water, so too the humors when they corrupt one another or are corrupted by one another corrupt and destroy the body which they ought to vivify and order. And so the body finds its proper, primary and natural make-up in the coming together of the elements. If these are balanced and well put together so that opposites are not attacked or destroyed by opposites, but rather hot is tempered by cold, cold by hot and so on, a good mixture is produced, and a harmony in nature produces *eucrasia*,[3] a good balance of the four qualities. When nature is in balance, it is impossible for the human body to be infected with any disease, that is if it is, as has been said, eucratic, of a proper mixture. But when these are out of balance, it is necessary for the body to change. But this is discussed elsewhere. Now we must see how the four humors come to be and are nourished.

THE FOUR HUMORS AND THE PROCESS OF DIGESTION

2. Any food, from whatever source it is taken, is made up of the four elements, as we have indicated is the case with the body. But in how many ways and what dissimilar ways, in regards to hotness and coldness, dryness and wetness, the elements can be in the things that can be eaten, the *Book of Degrees* shows.[4] When food is taken, the mouth first breaks it down into fine particles with the teeth and tongue. The tongue moves the food into position, the teeth tear it and crush it. So prepared, the food is passed on to the stomach through the throat and the esophagus, being tasted for hardly the space of a psalm.[5] The esophagus is a long, round, hollow

3. A possible source for the term *eucrasia* is the discussion of the theory of the soul as *crasis* or harmony in the *Premnon physicon* of Nemesius, bk 2, 39-51.

4. A work of Constantine the African (c. 1020-1087) on the different degrees of heat in medicines.

5. The PL text has here *palmi,* but "for the measure of a palm" as a time measure does not make much sense. On the other hand, it is natural for a monk to

organ, rough on the inside. It has long hairs within, some directed crosswide, some directed upwards toward the mouth. The hairs directed upward naturally attract food; those directed crosswise squeeze the food, and by squeezing convert it into juice and slowly pass it into the opening of the stomach.

The stomach has two openings, one at the top and one at the bottom. They are also called gates because they are closed and opened at times. The upper opening of the stomach is closed when food has been received until it is digested. The stomach, taking from the digested material the nutriments that it finds suitable, passes the rest out into the intestines through the lower gate. The stomach accomplishes this through four powers natural to it: the appetitive, the retentive, the digestive and the expulsive. Some other parts of the body also have these powers; especially those four parts which are considered fundamental: the brain because of its animal and sensitive powers, the heart because of spiritual power, the liver because of natural power and the genitalia because of reproductive power. The appetitive and digestive powers cause desire; the retentive power serves digestion by restraining the food lest it return the way it came, squeezing it and gradually passing it further down bit by bit, in good order for digestion. The desire, retention and expulsion of the stomach, just as the work of the esophagus, is accomplished with the help of some hairs. These extend lengthwise and crosswise through the stomach. The intestines below the stomach also have these hairs. This digestion which is accomplished in the stomach is the first digestion, a boiling brought about by natural heat.

What leaves the lower opening is received into the duode-

---

speak of a short space of time as being "for a space of a psalm." See *Regulations of the Order of Cistercians of the Strict Observance* (Dublin, 1927), p. 64: "He remains standing in his stall for the space of two verses (of a psalm);" p. 65: " . . . remaining at the presbytery step for the space of a *Pater*;" p. 173: "For the space of a *Miserere* (Ps 51)." We would therefore emend the text to read *ad mensuram psalmi*.

num intestine, so called because its length is twelve fingers. As soon as digestion is completed and the matter changed, the waste is eliminated. The other intestines receive what is passed on, three smaller interstines above nearer the opening of the stomach and three larger ones below. There is here one small intestine in which what has been passed on is held for a short while until, by a second digestion, the juices are further purified and refined, and what is pure and refined is sent to the liver through the mesentric veins. It should be noted that in the course of digestion there are foods which change and are not changed, such as scammony extract, and other foods which change and are changed, like onions and garlic, which are both food and medicine. The liver receives the juice through the veins just mentioned and through the portal vein, and changes it into its own nature for redistribution.

Whatever in it is fiery, the reddish bile takes to itself as nourishment; whatever airy, the bood; whatever watery or wet, the phlegm; whatever gross and earthly, the black bile. Thus the four humors are produced in the liver, and from the liver distributed through the whole body. If they act according to the rules of nature, cooperating with one another and aiding one another, they will produce a single state of healthiness, even though their qualities are diverse. The reddish bile, since it is hot and dry, refines the blood by its warmth. It flows along with the blood, without any acidity, itself quite refined, so that the blood may provide suitable nourishment to those members which are delicate and require refined food. But blood, because it is hot and wet, modifies the dryness of the red bile with its own wetness. Phlegm, since it is cold and wet, complements by its coldness the warmth of the blood, and by its wetness it aids the dryness of black bile, which is cold like itself.

THE FOUR HUMORS, BLOOD AND PHLEGM

3. Note how these offspring of the elements work as their parents do. In the same way that the elements work in the larger world outside, so do the four humors work in the

smaller world which is man, the microcosm, as has been said. They harmonize one with the other in their diversity, and by their harmony they produce a most beautiful unity in their order. There also arises from digestion that subtle and sweet vapor, which gently touches the brain and closes its lobes so that it puts to rest all its actions: this is sleep. In sleep, with all the powers of the soul suspended, only its natural power is active; and at that time it works the more energetically because all nature is leaving it free. The soul, resting within, with all the troubles of the senses being shut out, turns over within itself the past, present and future, and these are dreams.

Since these four humors are created and formed in the liver, each one does not have its own proper appearance, but like the liver itself (which appears to be of blood) they all have somewhat the appearance of blood; and each of them is distributed to nourish and control the whole body through its pathways, the veins and arteries.

The different humors are produced in this manner. First in the middle of the stomach food is whitened, that is, it is made like phlegm. Then in the lower part of the stomach, close to the liver, it becomes a watery blood. Boiled in the liver, it becomes blood. When it is further boiled it turns into reddish bile; and when excessively boiled, into black bile.

Reddish bile, leaving the liver, passes into the body in many ways. Through a vein it passes to the lower intestines with a certain amount of pain and causes the feces that remain to be eliminated. In this case one who compels nature before the urge comes undermines his health. One also injures his health if he puts off the needs of nature when the urge comes. Through another vein the reddish bile enters the stomach and there causes digestion and appetite. It is also distributed to other parts of the body. Finally the gall bladder receives the refuse. For it is the function of the gall bladder to purify the blood of reddish bile, lest staying in the blood it inflames it. When the bile is allowed to dominate excessively, it produces the worst infirmities, causing everything to become inflamed.

The blood leaves the liver through two veins, the concave

and the portal, and through the veins and venules it spreads itself through numberless parts. One vein enters the stomach and brings food, if there is any, from it to the liver. Another enters the side of the stomach, bringing food from the liver to nourish the stomach itself while it digests food. Another going to the spleen draws off from the liver the waste matter from the blood. But before the vein arrives there, it is divided into many parts and is sent to nourish the flesh. This vein is called by physicians the pancreas for it is proper to the blood to nourish the body.[6] It is also proper to blood to imitate a quality of air (whose nature, as has been said, it shows), insofar as like air it allows itself to undergo many changes. If the blood is thick and turbid, this indicates excessive heat and humidity; if it is thin and watery, it indicates coldness of the liver; if it is reddish and fetid, it indicates an infection of reddish bile and its own putrefaction; if foamy, flatulence; if congealed and watery, it indicates too much phlegm and a defect in the eliminative function, for what ought to be eliminated through urine, perspiration and other means is remaining in the blood.

Phlegm is half digested food, and so is cold and wet. It sometimes serves to nourish the body when blood is deficient. Boiled down, it is changed into blood. If phlegm is discharged as liquid and with no taste, it is natural; if sweet, it is infected with blood; if salty, with red bile; if bitter, with black bile. If it is glassy and congealed, this is caused by cold. From its effects its type can be recognized. If natural phlegm is excessive, it quells the appetite for food and drink because of the abundance of moisture in the stomach; it reduces the taste of food and drink, just as water mixed with any food usually diminishes its taste. If sweet phlegm is predominant, all food tastes sweet and is quickly digested; if salty dominates, one eats less, his mouth tastes bitter and he desires to drink. The bitter phlegm rather weakens the appetite and disagrees with food; the food is not digested and collects in

6. "Pancreas" comes from the Greek *pan*: all, and *kreas*: flesh, as the blood nourishes all flesh, the whole body. However, the etymology of William's *panagras* is not so clear.

the lower part of the stomach, while the upper part is left empty and hungry. Glassy phlegm destroys food and drink, causing stiffness through excessive cold.

These four humors, passing to the upper parts of the body, are there purged by natural purification: red bile through the ears, black bile through the eyes, phlegm through the nose and mouth. But it is urine which strains and purifies the blood. Because of their wetness and abundance, blood and phlegm more easily move through the body and dispose of their own waste, discharging it through the kidneys and bladder; and so they have no proper organs as do red bile (the gall bladder) and black bile (the spleen). Black bile has its seat in the spleen, where it is blackened by the blood of the liver. From there it is sent to the mouth of the stomach to strengthen the appetite.

THE THREE SPIRITS OR POWERS

4. This is the way the humors that come from digestion in the liver are distributed. From the heat of this digestion a certain vapor comes forth and generates a spirit which is called "natural." This spirit vivifies the liver itself and enables it to serve the demands of natural powers. Three powers share in directing the body. A power is an operative habit residing in an organ which enables it to carry out its proper function. There is the natural power in the liver, the spiritual power in the heart and the animal power in the brain. All the functions of the body flow either from the soul and nature, or from nature alone. What is ruled by the soul and nature is animated; what is from nature alone, inanimate. The inanimate does not concern us now. But in the animated organs, it is necessary that some power of the soul and nature be present by which they are able to carry out their functions. The nature of this power is known from its activity. In our desiring, retaining, digesting and eliminating a natural power is exercised; in our feeling and free motion, an animal power; in our inhaling and exhaling, a spiritual power. Natural power is common to trees, beasts and men; spiritual power to beasts and men; animal power in some animals and not in others.

For imagination and memory are perfect only in rational animals.

THE PRODUCTION OF THE THREE SPIRITS

5. The natural power is threefold; that is, it has three powers: generation, nutrition and growth. The generative power is found in sperm, the nutritive power in the process of vegetation, and growth in the development from small to large. These are principally the work of blood which has the power of nutrition and growth. The gall bladder, spleen and kidneys aid the blood by cleansing it of its superfluities. The gall bladder draws off red bile lest it inflame the blood; the spleen absorbs the waste material in the blood; and the kidneys pass the liquid waste into the bladder to be eliminated, in the same way as the intestines receive the remnants of food from the stomach for elimination. All these are operations of the natural spirit which arises out of the liver, augments and directs the power, and watches over its activity, just as the spiritual spirit in the heart and the animal spirit in the brain.

There are three spirits, three powers ruling and giving life. As the natural spirit has its origin and seat in the liver, so the spiritual spirit has its in the heart. For the heart is the source of spiritual heat. The lungs, the tissues and the muscles of the chest nourish it. Muscles are nerves and flesh combined. By their movement cooling air is drawn in, and by a sort of digestive process warm befouled air is expelled.

Spirit is the power of the powers for performing their actions. For the spirit is a kind of force of the soul through which its powers perform their acts: the natural power in the liver, the spiritual power in the heart, and the animal in the brain. These three powers or three spirits are founded in these three principal members, the liver, heart, brain, and from them spread through the whole body.

The spiritual spirit or its power centered in the heart causes expansion and contraction. Expansion occurs when the heart expands itself and the arteries to draw in air (sometimes just enough, sometimes too much) and very thin blood from the veins, For unless the heat of the heart is so tempered, it would burn the heart itself and everything around it. Hence the heart is said to rest in the bosom of the lung as in the lap of its nurse, continually drawing air into itself to sustain its life. If this inhalation is in any way obstructed, it always returns as long as it finds any air on which to feed. If this is entirely wanting, the heart dies. Hence physicians say that man cannot live more than seven days without food, nor more than seven hours without air. Therefore the spiritual power is that which gives life to everything, that from which everything living in the body lives. This is the spiritual spirit. This spirit, as has already often been said, is born in the heart and goes through the arteries to all the members of the body, augmenting and directing the spiritual power, and watching over its activity. The arteries leaving the heart serve the heart by carrying the vital spirit everywhere. They are hairy, having hairs inside and out. Those outside stretch lengthwise to draw heat or breath from the bottom of the heart and to cause the arteries themselves to expand. But other hairs inside placed crosswise compress the breath and expel the befouled waste. This is the first digestion of the spiritual spirit. Then the spirit, ascending through arteries on the right and left of the neck called "juveniles,"[7] enters the brain. The juveniles enter the cranium. The cranium is the seat of the brain, the covering of the head in which the brain is contained. It is made up of many bones, both because of the vapors, so that through openings between the joints of the bones they may have a way of leaving, and also to allow the veins and arteries to enter. The "juvenile" arteries, bearing the vital spirit, penetrate the cranium going right to the seat of the brain. Under the brain they spread in all directions like a net, so that beneath the warmth of this net the spirit may again be digested. There the spiritual spirit remains and is purified by digestion. From this digestion the animal spirit is created. Then through the two arteries curving back above the net it leaves and is borne to the forward lobe of the brain, where, again refined and purified, it eliminates its contaminants through the passage in the palate and the nostrils. And this is

7. These would seem to be the carotids.

its third digestion. It passes then to the rear lobes[8] through the passage between the forward and rear lobes, and there creates memory and movement, just as in the forward lobes it creates imagination and sensation. The forward lobes are the anterior part of the brain located in the front of the head, and the rear lobes are the posterior part of the brain placed in the back of the head. Each of the functions has its own dwelling, a certain lobe in which its power is contained. Between them is the middle lobe which contains reason and discernment.

THE THREE FACULTIES OF THE BRAIN

6. It is to be noted that the brain does some things by itself and some things by its functions. Reason stands in the middle as queen and lady, differentiating us from beasts. Imagination is in the front and memory in the rear. They act through their own power. Animal power, that is sensation, which is also in the forward part, works through the five senses. And motion, in the rear, works through the nerves that lead from the posterior lobes. We maintain that the reason, imagination and memory act of themselves. Although there seems to be imagination and memory also in brute animals, just as there are sensation and motion (otherwise a dog would not recognize its master and a bird would not return to its nest), it must be stated that they have neither memory nor imagination. Rather they have a greater power of sense. Where their soul is without reason they rely on a sensitivity that is an integral part of their body. All their soul has is sensitivity and motion. Hence it has a more intense movability and members more adept for motion.

Some philosophers called this spiritual spirit the spiritual soul, for they wanted the soul to be corporeal. But this is wrong. For the spiritual soul is a substance made to the image of God. It is like God, and so exists in its body in some way as God exists in his world; it exists everywhere in the body

8. William uses the words *prora* and *puppis*, bow and stern, quite consistently to signify the forward and the rear lobes of the brain.

and is entire in each point. It is entirely present in natural operations, entirely in the spiritual operations, entirely in the animal operations. In natural matters it works subtly, in animal matters more subtly, in spiritual, with the greatest subtleness. It does some things naturally, some things actively and passively, like an animal, and some things through its own power and according to its own nature, that is spiritually. Whether a power is natural, animal, or spiritual, it is not the soul, but an instrument of the soul. But let us return to our topic.

All these activities of the spirits have their origin in the heart, come from the heart. Because the heart burns naturally with such heat, as has been noted, by its very heat it draws to itself whatever can moderate it. Its form is such that it has two auricles. The right auricle receives the vein from the liver through which it draws blood to itself. The left opens out on to a large artery, supplying the vital spirit everywhere through all its parts. It must also be noted that throughout the body arteries and veins do come together and through the abundance of pores which a provident nature created in them, they communicate with each other. The arteries give the veins the vital spirit; the veins give the arteries natural nutrients. Thus the blood in the arteries does not lack nourishment, nor does that in the veins lack animal spirit. But let us return to the spirit.

THE SPIRITUAL POWER AND THE MOTION OF THE BODY

7. We have said that when the spiritual spirit passes into the rear lobe of the brain it brings memory and motion into operation there: memory of itself, motion through its functionaries the nerves. In the same way in the forward lobe it produces imagination of itself, and sensation through its functionaries the five senses. To discuss the spiritual actions of the spirit is difficult; it is somewhat easier to talk about what it does through its functionaries in the body or outside the body through sensation and motion.

To begin with motion, the moving power created in the brain passes through what is right at hand. For provident nature placed seven pairs of nerves in the brain itself. These, passing through suitable openings, by themselves or through other nerves coming from them and subdividing, move what is to be moved, and control what is to be controlled in the area of the head and neck and down to the diaphragm, that is, to the middle of the body cavity. For the five senses give to each its motion and its power of sensation. It gives these also to the brain, tongue, throat, and the other organs, as has been said, right down to the diaphragm. But because this moving power is based in the brain, the animal would be very slow and sluggish in its movements if the power for all its free movement were dispensed from there through all the parts of the body, even to the soles of the feet. So nature has provided a suitable auxiliary for the brain which extends to the lower parts of the body, and bears its power of operation and sensation to all areas of the lower part. The nerves are the natural causes of motion, and muscles with nerves cause sensation. They are delicate members easily set in motion by foreign humors. Nothing in the body suffers a sense of pain that is not controlled by these. For the pain that we feel when a bone, or a nail or anything of this kind is injured is not felt in the bone or nail but at their point of contact with flesh and nerves. If the nerves were to extend from the top of the body to the bottom, they would not only be easily broken because of their length but also sensation and motion would be weakened. For this reason there is a nerve, called in Arabic the *nucha*,[9] descending from the brain, from the end of the posterior lobe, through the vertebrae of the back, the bones of the spine, to the lower part of the body. This nerve is also called the brain of the back or the spine.

Like the brain, this nerve is clothed and covered over with certain warming and nourishing membranes. For the brain when enclosed in the cranium has between it and the hard-

9. This term is a common one in Arabic medicine and is found in both the texts of Constantine and in the *De differentia animae et spiritus* of Constabulinus (d. 935).

ness of the bone two membranes: one very soft and light by which it is warmed (hence called by physicians the *pia mater*) and another stronger one (called the *dura mater*), by which it is protected from the hardness of the skull. So also the brain of the back, the *nucha*, has a *pia mater* and a *dura mater*. In addition it has two other membranes, made up of ligaments, which protect and cover it. If all the coverings are damaged down to the *pia mater*, and the *nucha* remains intact, there is no danger. But if the *nucha* is injured or cut, everything below loses sensation and movement, while what is above remains uneffected. For example, if it is cut at the first vertabrae below the skull, everything around and below this point is deprived of sense and motion. From this *nucha* sensation and motion are supplied to all members placed around or below it, through nerves leaving from both sides. In this way voluntary motion reaches from the brain to the rest of the body.

Motion comes from the rear lobe of the brain. This is smaller than the front lobe, because the operation of the front lobe is of greater dignity and extension and this lobe contains more instruments of operation than the rear. The front lobe is also softer than the rear. The rear must be harder so that it can withstand motion more easily; the front softer, so that the seven pairs of sensitive nerves that arise from it may quickly perceive sensations. The rear lobe has only a few nerves leaving from it causing motion and sensation. By these and by all the nerves leaving the brain nature brings about sensation and motion, and more agile motion and more acute and more noble sensation. But, because the general movement and sensation of the body proceeds from the nerves of the rear lobe and of its mediator, the *nucha*, both motion and sensation are especially assigned to the rear lobe.

THE ANIMAL POWER AND SIGHT

8. Now we must pass to the animal power of the animal spirit. Since it manifests itself mainly in the five well-known senses of the body and in their actions, it seems that we

should examine these senses more closely. First we will consider sight whose small but marvelous organ, the eye, was scarcely ever examined or investigated by some of the best minds among the philosophers and physicians.

How much more noble the eyes are than the other senses nature itself shows, since it placed them in front of the seat of reason, and closest to it, as the sense most like it in power and most necessary for studying those things which are around and beneath it. The organs or instruments of the eyes that bring sight from the brain are the optic nerve, humors, and sheaths. The optic nerve proceeds from the brain itself, from under the *pia mater* where it is born and warmed. Lest its weakness be injured by the bones of the skull as it passes through, it is wrapped in a small sheath of *pia mater*. It goes to the eyes, giving them the power of sight, and is anchored in the middle humor, the crystaline. There are three humors and seven sheaths producing or helping sight.

The humor in the middle is called the crystalline. It is, as has been said, the basis for sight. Its shape is round so as not to be injured easily, but flattened on one side, so that sight may be steadily directed. Below or behind the crystalline humor is located the vitreous humor in this fashion. The first sheath is placed below or around the crystalline humor. It is called the retina, because it is composed of veins and arteries in the form of a net.[10] Its function is to refine the blood coming to it lest the coarser substance of blood damage the crystalline humor. The crystalline humor is the proper instrument of sight, receiving its name from crystal because of its clarity. From this retina, not through veins and arteries with which there is no connection here, but naturally, the vitreous humor draws[11] the blood. Converting food into its own nature, it supplies nourishment to the crystalline humor. But between the retina and the vitreous humor there are yet two sheaths, the *secundia,* so called because it holds the second place, and the *scliros,* or hard sheath, to protect the eyes from the inside from excess humors and other super-fluities.

10. Retina comes from the Latin *retis* or *rete*: net.
11. Reading *sugit* instead of *fugit* in the PL text.

Over these three sheaths is the vitreous, or glass-like, humor. The optic nerve, not single but twofold that it might have the power to give each eye its spirit of sight, is joined to this.

Outside the vitreous humor is the fourth sheath (called because of its tenuousness, the *arenea*, the "spider web") so placed that it might easily attract the humor and by its lightness may soften both humors. For over this is placed the crystalline and then the *evagaidos* or albuminous humor (like the white of an egg) which nourishes the crystalline humor from the outside by its humidity and protects it from the air, lest it dry out. After this is the *uvea*, a sheath shaped like a grape. It is the receptacle for tears. After this is the *cornea*, hard as horn, which protects the *evagaidos* from exterior damage. It also holds the crystalline humor, lest the use of the eyes be overly extended and sight dry up or weaken, as in the case of fish which never close their eyes and so run into nets. The seventh sheath is the *conjunctiva*, which contains and connects everything. This is the whiteness that appears in the eyes. It does not cover but surrounds the *uvea*.

Now the optic nerve coming from the brain is hollow, so as to supply enough spirit for sight. When it reaches the eyes it so spreads as to surround the vitreous sheath. The spirit of sight, leaving the brain, strikes the sheath and illumines the eye. This brings it about that the crystalline, which is the most transparent and clearest, quickly adapts itself to colors. For the spirit for seeing, clarified in the hollow of the nerves, leaves and passes to the clarity of the crystalline humor, and from there, going outside, mixes with the air of day. When it mixes with the air they are both easily and very rapidly changed. For the air and the spirit mix easily with the colors of the things seen. The spirit that goes out from the crystalline humor and is changed, quickly changes the crystalline. When the mind which is in the lobe of the brain senses this change, it discerns exterior things by their colors; through colors it understands the shape, quantity, and motion of bodies. The very clear air of day gives as much help to this spirit as the brain gives to the nerves. For the nerve carries sensation and motion from the brain and brings it to its members. Likewise the exterior air carries the changes in visible colors and the spirit brings the same change into the mind.[12]

Every sense experience changes the one experiencing it in some way into that which is sensed or there is no sensation.[13] This then takes place in the eye when the exterior splendor unites with the interior spirit. And this happens without any delay. In this way sight occurs in the eye. Sight, if it is refined and strong, sees both far and near perfectly; because it is strong, it sees remote objects; because it is refined, it discerns well what is to be seen. If sight is strong and coarse, it sees distant objects because it is strong, but imperfectly because of its coarseness. If it is weak and refined, it sees what is near perfectly because of its refinement, but not what is far off because of its weakness. Weak and coarse sight does not see far because of its weakness nor perfectly because of its coarseness. And that is that concerning the eye.

THE ANIMAL POWER AND THE OTHER SENSES

9. The nose: the two passages of the nostrils are necessary for two reasons. The more important is to draw in breath and odors; the other, to eliminate coarse waste coming from the brain. These passages admit odors to the forward lobe of the brain; they do not create them. Two small organs similar to breasts are the instruments of smell. They are placed near the *dura mater* and through an opening in it reach up to the brain; below they reach down close to the nose. In this way they bring about the sense of smell. The fumes from odorous bodies, dissolved and mixed with the air, are drawn in through the openings of the nostrils by these breasts and are transmitted to the brain. They change the fumes which they

12. This theory of sight is a common heritage from the ancient Greeks. It is found substantially in Empedocles (fifth century BC) and his commentator Theophrastus (c 371-287 BC). For a clear expression of it see Plato, *Timeus* 45b-d. A source closer to William's time is Constantine's *De oculis*.

13. This is an application of the famous Platonic axiom: "Only like knows like." William applies this extensively in his mystical writings.

have drawn in to the lobes of the brain into their own nature. The mind senses this change and thus the sense of smell is produced. The inhalation of air into the brain is necessary, because it does the same for it as breathing does for the heart. When the brain expands, air is drawn in to refresh it; when it is compressed, superfluous vapors are expelled. When air is drawn in by expansion of the lungs, the nose and the throat, the sense of smell operates. In this way then things to be smelled are smelled: through the breast-like organs, which we have described, vapors dissolved from odorous bodies and mixed with air are conveyed to the brain.

A pair of nerves proceeding from the brain and spreading out in the ears produces hearing. The openings of the ears themselves are covered with cartilage for two reasons: lest anything get into the ear that might impede hearing, and to help gather the voice that comes that it might enter the ear with strength. These two nerves spread over the opening of the ear, and completely cover it; this covering is for hearing what the crystalline humor is for sight. The voice strikes the air. This movement or disturbance of the air comes to the ears, and entering is gradually changed. For the motion of the nearby air strikes nearer air, and so on in succession. Thus vibrating, it penetrates the ear until it reaches the covering of nerves mentioned above and these themselves naturally take on the same vibrations. Both vibrations are similar, because they both involve the air. This motion is conveyed to the mind by the nerves, and the mind discerns the nature of the voice received, and thus hearing takes place.

The tongue is the instrument of taste and speech, having near itself veins continually supplying it with saliva. These veins begin at the base of the tongue in the manner of arteries. From them the phlegmatic moisture called saliva flows out. Another nerve comes from the brain and spreads through the tongue to give it the sense of taste. This comes about as follows. When the thing to be tasted contacts the tongue, nature causes the tongue to be changed into the nature of the thing tasted. The change affects the nerve, and through it transmits the taste to the mind to be distinguished and judged, and thus we have the sense of taste.

Touch is like the other senses, because it is changed into the substance of the thing which is touched. This change is sent to the mind through the nerves, and in this way the mind senses the change. All the senses have proper organs except touch. Touch belongs to the whole body except for those parts which lack nerves, like hair, nails and so forth; these sense only where they are connected to the body, because at that point there are nerves. To conclude our treatment of the senses, we can say, nothing is experienced in the body which does not sense, and there is no sensation that is not ruled by the nerves.

MAN'S TRUE DIGNITY IS IN THE SOUL

10. It must also be noted that the senses correspond to the four humors about which much has been said above. For sight is fiery in nature, hearing airy, smell vaporous, taste watery, touch earthy. What wonder, since also the ages of each man correspond to the various humors? For adolesence up to the twenty-fifth or thirtieth year is likened to blood, which nourishes through wetness and warmth. For whatever grows, grows through humidity and heat. Up to this point man grows in strength and height and length and width. Then follows young manhood, like reddish bile on account of its dryness and heat: its heat consumes the wetness of youth and so is dry (for less humidity leads to dryness). Young manhood, which maintains the body perfect without loss of strength, ends around thirty-five or forty. Old age, cold and dry, is likened to black bile. It is cold because the wetness which in young manhood is dried out. This comes to an end at about fifty-five or sixty. Then comes the period of debility, naturally the driest and coldest, but accidentally humid because of indigestion and the abundance of phlegm.

We have now written about the exterior man. But not exclusively exterior. We have written about some things that are inside the body of man and are not entirely subject to the senses of man. But by reason and experience physicians and philosophers have discerned these, they have been able to reach this far in their search for the dignity of human nature. Yet they have failed most absurdly in this, that among these things they have thought to include that part of man by which man is the incorruptible image of God and is preeminent above other living things, namely, his rational soul. They simply commend and salute the beauty of man, how he naturally stands erect above other living things, showing that he has something in common with heaven; how throughout the length of his body there exists a balanced unity in the distinction of members, with a beautiful equality of members on right and left; how the whole body is ordered by weight and measure and number.

Let us pass on to the soul. For the balance in the human body is evident from the equality of members, and careful experiments in measuring can show the measure. For physicians tell us that if a man lies flat on his back with arms and legs extended and a compass is centered on his navel, it can be revolved in all directions without an interruption, equally touching each of his extremities. Concerning number the matter is clear enough. To pass by exterior members, which are evident to all, there is no doubt that everything inside has its number as well. For even the bones have been counted by those who specialize in such matters; two hundred and forty-one have been found to be in every human body. And so also with the nerves. Seven pairs of nerves have been found to leave the brain; from the *nucha* thirty-two pairs and one unpaired. What else? It is certain that veins, muscles, and everything that is in the body have each a definite number. But, as we said, let us pass on to the soul, and let us not limit ourselves to what philosophers or scientists of the world think or guess about it, but consider briefly what the Catholic Fathers have learned from God and taught to men.

BOOK TWO

PHYSICS OF THE SOUL

T HE SOUL, AS THE PHILOSOPHERS OF THIS
world say, is a simple substance, a natural species, an
organ distinct from the matter of the body and its
members, and having the power of life. Now according to our
teachers, the teachers of the Church that is,[1] the soul is
spiritual and its own substance. It is created by God. It is
life-giving, rational and immortal, but changeable in regard to
good and evil. It is said to be its own substance because no
other spirit receives the flesh or body to share its sorrows and
joys.

The way it vivifies the body is wonderful and ineffable. We
know that there are three basic functions in the body for the
sake of which everything else in us is there. Some things exist
simply for the sake of life,[2] some that we may live well, and
some to provide for the propagation of new life. There are
three organs, which we have discussed at length in the first
book, the brain, the heart and the liver, without which
human life could not exist. Everything else is an added good,
which nature gives to man that he may live well, such as the
organs of sense, etc. They go to make up our life, but in such
a way that even if many of them are lacking for any reason,

1. In this first chapter or section William depends on Cassiodorus, *De anima* (PL
70:1283) and Gregory of Nyssa, *De hominis opificio* (hereafter cited as *De hom*),
30. For the latter work, William uses John Scotus Eruigena's translation. At the
beginning of each section we will indicate our author's sources when these have
been identified.

2. Omitting *bene* here which is found in the PL text. It seems to be in this
phrase by the slip of some copyist.

nonetheless man can still live. But some of these, added by nature to the constitutive elements of life serve the organs of life, in such a way that without them the latter would not be able to function. These would be the stomach, the lungs and some others. For the lungs indeed cool the fire which is in the heart by the air inhaled in breathing, if they did not do this, the fire of the heart would burn itself and everything around it. The stomach provides food for the organs, without which nature would soon fail. There are many things serving and aiding these, each in its own way. For the power of life is not drawn uniformly from some one thing in us, but, with the God-given soul as its source, nature breathes into many parts its life-giving influences and causes, making the whole necessary and almost inscrutable collection into one living being.

THE THREE BASIC ORGANS[3]

2. However, passing over the many and varied organs which nature employs to strengthen and beautify life, let us first consider the fundamental principles of life: the brain, heart, and liver. First, the brain, whose important function in the control of life is shown in a negative way by the fact that it cannot receive even the slightest injury without death occurring at once. The covering or membrane of nerves which encloses the brain (called by the Greeks, the *hymen*) is the source and cause of all voluntary motion. A spirit freely set in motion descends from it through the nerves and flows through them to every part of the body. It gives for the body's motions[4] a direction which is varied and manifold, exceedingly swift and versatile and adapted to every activity. From this comes the turning of the neck, the raising and lowering of the head, the mobility of the jaws, the rapid movement of the eyes and eyelids, the various functions of the hands. From this is the rhythmic motion of the legs and

3. Dependent on *De hom* 30 and Claudius Mamertus, *De statu animae* (hereafter cited as *De statu*), 1, 21, 1-2.

4. Reading here with Déchanet *motuum* in place of the *mortuum* found in the PL text.

feet in walking and all the other movements of the joints with the nerves relaxing or tightening, working as though by a kind of natural mechanism. This spirit of life for voluntary action receives its command to move in the brain, its seat, and readily brings about each act in each member according to a certain plan of nature.

In regard to the heart: if its natural warmth is extinguished, death follows as the body immediately becomes cold. From this it is evident that there is a source and cause of life also in the heart. From it tubular channels and many kinds of arteries proceed, some springing from others, which furnish fire and vital spirit to the entire body. But because it is absolutely necessary for some food to be provided by nature for the heat of the heart (for fire does not have continued existence of itself unless it is nourished by suitable food or matter), streams of blood rise out of the liver as from a kind of spring. With the help of the veins they flow everywhere through the body bearing a warm spirit, lest one defect arising from another destroy nature. For every superfluity has such a corrupting effect.

Thus through this efficient and orderly arangement the rational soul united directly to the body shows its power to sustain life and promote natural growth, more obscurely indeed in its first appearance, but more clearly through the processes of nature and careful study. For just as the sculptor who is creating a man in stone first cuts out a rough form and then the distinct lines and beauty of his figure, so God, the author of nature and creator of body and soul, formed man in his image and likeness,[5] more obscurely indeed in the beginning, but more clearly and more perfectly in the consummation of his work. In the fashioning of the organs the beauty of the soul is foreshadowed by analogy, imperfect in the imperfect, but perfect in the perfect to come. It would have been perfect in the beginning, if nature had not been corrupted in its beginnings through malice. For this reason we are born like animals, and the image of our Maker cannot

5. Gen 1:26.

shine in us immediately, nor without long and hard labors. Man is led to his perfection by a long way through the material and animal properties of his soul.

Let every man give thanks to his Creator, not as much as he ought but as much as he can, for in his beginnings he granted him the perfection of every creature. By his almighty power he granted him existence with the stones, seminal life with herbs and trees, sensual or animal life with the beasts, and even added rational life with the angels.[5 bis] But in whatever way herbs and trees seem to live, however brute beasts and animals seem to have a soul, it is yet certain that all these things, alive though they be, do not have a soul, nor do they rise to the dignity of the human condition. In seeds some animal activity indeed appears, but it does not go as far as the motion that comes through sensation. Life is there even though there be no soul. For the existence of this life, all the elements, each in its own particular way have come together. Earth is there in their substance, water in their sap, air in their growth, fire in their germination. And although it is rare that things lower in order are always affected by superior things, it happens thus. After the cold of winter heat returns with the return of the stars through the rotation of the heavens. The heat first affects what is closest to itself by nature and place, the air. For air is just below fire, just as it is above water. Through the roots of trees or plants it then draws water from the depths of the earth. But fire, which naturally seizes upon all the elements, draws the warmed air to itself. And so, through the pith of trees, just as fire draws the air, so does the air draw water, and water earth. It is just like the way we can draw water from a lower elevation when we wish, through a straw. These four elements together produce the harmonious melody of life in the trees; if any of them is present either in excess or defect, the tree will first grow sick, and then die as though overcome by languor. Brute animals, through their free movement and sensation seem to live in a somewhat higher way than herbs or trees. But they have not yet the perfection that comes from the gift of reason and understanding.

5bis. A common them. See Claudius Mamertus, *De statu* 1,21; Gregory the Great, *Hom. in Evang.* 29 (PL 76, 1214B). See *Ep an* 19, and *The Spirit and the Soul* 6.

THE HUMAN SOUL AS INCORPOREAL AND UBIQUITOUS[6]

3. Therefore we say that the human soul alone is true and perfect, capable of every action. If we say that something else that shares life is animated, we speak incorrectly, for a perfect soul is not in these things. They have only some of the animal operations which are in man in his beginnings. Brute animals are completely governed by their senses, and in this regard they are powerful. In these they are more powerful than men who nevertheless surpass these senses by reason. These senses are like a gently-flowing stream where it meets an obstacle that impedes its progress. It bursts forth with greater force. But the spirit of man is far different. For it rules and judges the senses. As a queen, reason sits in the central castle of its city, with the gates of the senses open in all directions. It recognizes by their face and dress each of the domestics bringing in familiar things and the strangers bringing in foreign wares, and receives and puts each in its place of knowledge. It distinguishes each by its kind, its cognates and its class and gives each its room in the memory. Of its nature the intellectual soul is something wonderful. And through its powers it shares itself with each of the senses and receives the proper sense knowledge. No wise man can doubt that the intellectual soul is something other than sensation. For if it were located in one sense, it would have only one sort of operation according to that sense. But it is simple and non-composite, even though it does reach out in many directions in the operation of the various senses. In its simplicity it has variety yet it is one in its variety. Even more, because in a simple thing nothing can be considered to be other, it is not one thing when touched, another when smelled, another when tasted, and so forth.[7] See then how much the functioning of the senses of the rational man differs from that of the brute animal.

Let all the conjection and vain reasoning of those who

---

6. Dependent on *De hom* 10-12 and 15.
7. William might be refuting the Platonic theory of multiple souls; (e.g., *Timaeus* 69d-71b), known through a number of patristic witnesses.

would place intellectual power in certain parts of the body be stilled. Some of them would say its seat is in the heart, others contend the soul is in the brain, and each brings forth his own physiological arguments. Conjectures concerning corporeal things can be reduced to some kind of arrangement of bodies, but the intellectual soul must be seen to govern all the individual parts by a mysterious power and union with each. If those who argue for the heart point to Scripture where it speaks of God "searching hearts,"[8] we would point out that it also says: "God searches the kidneys."[9] Therefore he who remembers the heart also remembers the kidneys, and the intellectual substance is found either in both kidneys and heart, or in neither. The author of nature wishes the association and bond between the intellectual substance and the corporeal to be ineffable and beyond our comprehension, so that by the law of nature the incorporeal might neither exist within nor be held within the body, nor be encompassed by the body, nor be found outside it. For in some way beyond the understanding of reason the intellectual soul approaches nature and, fitted into it and about it, is considered in so far as possible to be placed neither within nor enclosed by nature, nor outside and enclosing nature. Rather in a manner which cannot be expressed or understood, it is able to be completely permeated by nature and still effect its own operations. For the whole of the intellectual nature is not in any one part but in the whole. It is not located within, in the cavities of the body, nor is it forced out when one gets fat, or anything like that. For its purposes it uses the whole body as if it were a musical instrument. One who knows how to play a musical instrument, when he finds a suitable instrument, plays well. But if the instrument is worn by rot or age or damaged by some accident, the player loses nothing of his art, but the instrument remains silent or produces poor sound. So it is with the intellectual soul. It takes possession of the whole instrument of nature, and touches each part with its intellectual operations as is its wont. In those which

8. Jer 17:10.
9. Ps 7:10 (Vulgate).

are properly disposed, it accomplishes what it desires: but in those which are not up to par, its operation is sluggish and inactive.

THE BODY AS THE INSTRUMENT OF THE SOUL[10]

4. Hence nature prepares and adapts the instrument of the body to the use of reason in everything. For example, look at the hands as they are joined to the body. You will find nothing like them in any irrational animal. See how much this adds to the harmony in the instrument of the human body. All the beasts have feet here where men have hands. Although nature has given man hands for many life functions in war and in peace, yet before all it is for this: if man had no hands his mouth would have to be fashioned like those of quadrupeds so he could take food from the ground. The length of his neck would have to be increased, his nose shaped like that of a brute animal. He would have to have heavy lips, thick, coarse and projecting, suited to cutting fodder. The fleshy part around the teeth would have to be solid and rough, as in dogs and other animals that eat meat. Thus if hands had not been provided for the body, an articulated and modulated voice could not exist. Man would have to bleat or low or bark or make some other kind of animal noise. But now, with the hand serving the mouth, the mouth serves reason and through it the intellectual soul which is spiritual and incorporeal. This is something not shared with irrational animals. When the intellectual soul touches the speech organs, like a plectrum, it expresses in speech its own interior motion. It is like a musician who by accident is without voice and yet wishes to make music. He displays his art through other voices, through pipes or string instruments. So it is with the intellectual soul discovering various insights. Since it itself is incorporeal and has no speech of its own, it satisfies itself by expressing its thoughts through the bodily senses.

The hands may also furnish another great service to reason.

10. Dependent on *De hom* 8-10.

For it is a great gift to reason that we can speak through our hands by writing, that the sounds of letters can in some way be compressed into characters made by our hands. Thus hands and mouth serve reason together. Hands write for future times or absent ones; the mouth most easily and promptly speaks whatever reason interiorly suggests. For the breath pushed through the trachea from the lungs, by its impetus, produces in the trachea the sound of the voice. Then, as in a flute, through certain circular movements of some membranes, which serve as so many carriages, the voice moves upward to where the jaws, teeth, and tongue, like plectrums, swiftly form a whole variety of sounds adapted to use. The lips, opening and closing, serve the same function as the fingers of the flute player do on the holes of the flute. From a great variety they form one melody. In this way man naturally produces words, but the ordering of them belongs to reason.

If therefore, as has been said, the lips had a rough and laborious task to perform in feeding man, the mute and interior soul would not be able to exercise its reason through this distinctive organ of speech; and unable to communicate with one another, we could not be rational. But now the hands undertake this service and leave the mouth apt and free to serve reason. The intellectual soul, which expresses its own activity by speaking, perceives the activity of others through the ears, eyes and other senses. It has such an inner capacity that all these perceptions come together, no matter from what source they have come. The soul also has its pens by which it records them in the memory, some more carefully and hence more permanently, others more negligently, and so sooner erased.

MAN AS THE IMAGE OF GOD[11]

5. And so, in the image of him who created it, who is unmoved in himself while giving movement to all else, there

---

11. In this chapter William has drawn sections from many different places in *De hom*: 11, 8, 14, 18, 2 and 4.

is one power, the innate intellectual soul itself, which runs through all the instruments of the senses and registers every occurence. Through the ears it hears, through the eyes it sees, and so on. In this it is quite unlike him in whose image it is, because God does not come into contact with beings by means of different powers. It is absurd to think of anything being received and a multiple activity of receiving in the simplicity of the Godhead. But it is not required that an image in no way differ from its prototype. For that would be identity, not an image. Therefore it is not necessary that the image imitate the example of its examplar in regards to his divine nature and the incomprehensibility of his essence. For if the nature of the image totally embraced its exemplar, it would no doubt be greater than what it comprehended. Indeed from the fact that the rational soul does not even attain perfect knowledge of itself it is seen to image the nature of the divine incomprehensibility.

The fact that man stands erect indicates something else. The erect man, reaching toward heaven and looking up, signifies the imperial and regal dignity of the rational soul. This shows that man has received from the Creator dominion over all the beings that look down, and that he has much in common with what is above if he maintains the dignity of his inborn likeness, namely, that the intellectual soul command reason, and choose only what is useful. They are lacking this dignity who slavishly serve the lusts arising from the senses, making reason, which is naturally the mistress serve the desires of nature. For when the intellectual soul does this and follows the natural desires of the flesh or the senses, it becomes the minister of those whose lord and judge it ought to be. And thus the corporeal nature freely imposes on the intellectual soul both its feelings of grief and its desire for happiness. Such men have put off the image of the Creator and have put on another image, one that looks at the ground like an animal, one that is beastly. For the likeness of man to God is not a thing of passion. Voluptuousness does not liken him to God's transcendent nature. Fear and ferocity, desire for some things, hatred for others, are far from the character of divine beauty.

These movements, and the like, human nature takes from the irrational. Nature has armed the beasts with them for self-preservation, but in man they are the passions of the soul, and indeed passions by which man made to the image of God suffers himself to be lowered to the image of beasts. Truly passions, because they are against nature. Hence David says, "When man was in honor he did not understand; he has been compared to senseless animals and made like unto them."[12] For, as has been said, what is natural in beasts is vice in man. For carnivores are driven by ferocity; the love of pleasure serves the fertility of animals, fear protects the weak, fright *a fortiori* the weaker, gluttony the corpulent. From none of these do animals or beasts suffer passion, because none of these things which flow from libido are matters for sorrow in irrational beings. But human misery, admitting these passions with an open heart and augmenting their beginnings both in number and strength by its deliberate cooperation, produces a most turbulent and undescribable generation of vices. Love of pleasure springs from man's likeness to irrational beings, but increased by man's faults it begets through lust such a great variety of sins that no one can find the like among irrational animals. Certainly reason with its reasonable desires rejects these things with all their kindred, yet with the help of man's thoughts, they increase. So from anger is born madness, envy, lies and treachery. All these are evil effects of a degenerate soul. For if passion were deprived of the help of thought, like a bubble it would soon disappear.

All these things, as has been said, have entered into the constitution of man from his animal nature. The author of nature gave them to him to serve him. In giving man a soul with the body, mixing the divine with the earthy, God gave reason a twofold opportunity. He wished that through relationship and association with both, man might enjoy the one and use the other, enjoy God through his more godlike nature and use the goods of earth through the related senses.

12. Ps 48:13, 21 (Vulgate).

The Supreme Artisan indeed made our nature suitable and apt for its regal role. In the formation of the soul, and also in the very shape of the body, as has already been sufficiently indicated, he prepared such an animal as would be equipped to rule, one not prone on the earth but standing erect toward the heavens.

THE MISERY OF THE EXTERIOR MAN[13]

6. The rational soul, when it understands and preserves its honor, is something noble and lofty. It is far removed by nature from rustic lowliness and degeneracy, since it is free and able of its own power to command all things and make them serve its wishes, governing them by its authority. This is proper to one with royal dignity. For this reason man is born defenseless, devoid of natural protection, to such an extent that whereas nature appears a happy mother at the birth of other living things, for man she seems a sorrowful step-mother. She gives to other living things coverings of various kinds, shells, bark, thorns, hides, shaggy coats, bristles, hair, down, feathers, scales, fleece. She also protects the trunks of trees against cold and heat with a double layer of bark. Man alone does she cast naked on the naked earth on the day of his birth, to weep and cry right from the start. No other animal does she bring to the light of day for so many tears so soon. In all ancient and recent history, Zoroaster alone, that inventor of the magic arts, is said to have been born laughing,[14] so that he who was to attack the established nature of things by his evil arts would stand out by his own unnatural and ill-omened beginning. Then poor man, so that he may know that he is imprisoned, is immediately put in swaddling bands with all his members tied together. His eyes and mouth alone are left free to give vent only to tears and cries. And this is equally true of him who is born in happy

13. The last part of the chapter comes from *De hom* 7.
14. The source for this remark concerning Zoroaster is Augustine, *De civitate Dei* 21, 14, who takes it from Pliny, *Historia naturalis* 7, 15, the earliest Classical appearance. It is also found in the Persian tradition.

circumstances, be he the son of an emperor or king. Bound hand and foot, he lies there as he begins his life, an animal weeping because of his punishment; but he has only one fault, he has been born. The folly of those who think from these beginnings man is born for pride! The first hope of strength, the first gift of time, makes him like a quadruped. How long is it before man's first successful steps? How long before mouth and tongue first form words? How long before he takes food? How long before solidity comes to the palpitating skull? Add to this that of all the animals poor man alone is born knowing nothing except how to cry. By great labor on the part of his mother or nurse or of himself everything must be learned that man ought or could know naturally. And then finally when at some point human dignity seems to have reached its fulness and to be stabilized or confirmed, immediately come sickness, medicines, and finally the cares of burial. Nothing has a life or health that is more fragile, nothing is more burdened with the care of life and health. By some sudden accident, it is cut off or crushed to ruins; it is terminated by poison from some worm or herb, or snuffed out by some beast. And it can hardly be guarded even by the most watchful care and constant flight from everything that in any way has the power to harm it. Man is vulnerable through the weakness of his body to everything that nature places under his feet by virtue of his reason. Poor man is brought into this life lacking everything that is useful. To judge by external appearance he seems miserable rather than blessed. He is not armed with a set of horns, nor a pointed hoof, nor with claws or teeth, nor with a deadly tooth or fang as are so many animals, nor is his body covered with a coat of hair. Man alone is slower than those that run swiftly, smaller than those of great size and more open to attack than those protected by natural armor.

MAN'S PREEMINENCE RESIDES IN REASON[15]

7. And how, someone will say, can one who is such be said to possess power over everything? Truly in every way. First

15. Dependent on *De Hom* 7, 4, 16.

of all, because human reason masters the power of harming in all the things beneath it. It either carefully avoids it, or forcefully destroys it and puts the thing to his own use. For what seems to be a lack in our nature gives man an opportunity to exercise power over the things subject to him. Man would perhaps despise this power if he had no need of the service of these things. But now for this reason the things useful to us for this life are scattered among all the things that are subject to us, so that the authority by which God has raised human nature above them is necessary for us. For the slowness of our body and the difficulty it has in getting around has subjugated the horse and forced it to serve. And again man has forced other animals to carry his burdens. The nakedness of his flesh has made it necessary that man put sheep to his service. Lest he eat grass like an ox, he has subjected the ox to himself for the cultivation of the land. He also has the dog, a kind of living sword against ferocious and hostile beasts and a guard while he sleeps at night. He has iron, sharper and stronger than horn and hoof, which provides him with arms, not like the savage beast's, burdening him by nature at all times, but arms that can be taken up and put down according to reason. This same iron gives him armor, helmet and breastplate stronger than the crocodile. What more? All creatures serve man and fight for him as their king.

So see and embrace, O man, the dignity of your nature. Do not think yourself so much as being vile because of your body which the animals excel, as of great worth because of your interior endowments which excel everything that lives and that does not live. For according to your inner dignity you are born to a royal estate. For to be made in the image of the Almighty, what else is this than to be immediately granted a royal nature? To draw an example from human custom. Those who make images of kings or lords make the image like the original, and show the royal dignity with purple robes. And men are then accustomed to speak of the image as the king. And so with human nature. Because it was created to rule others, it was chosen through likeness to the King of all as a certain animated image sharing with God, the chief exemplar, both dignity and name. This dignity is not proclaimed by a purple robe nor by a sceptre or a crown, for God's exemplarity is not in these. Rather for the purple robe man is clothed with virtue which surpasses all royal emblems; for the sceptre, his insignia is unending beatitude; and for the royal diadem, he is crowned with the crown of justice. Thus he is seen in all these things carefully taking on the form of the Supreme Exemplar in his royal dignity. For in this, that man is said to be made to the image of God, it is as if it were said that God made human nature sharer in every good. For God is the fullness of all goods, and man is the image of God. Therefore in that he is capable of the fullness of every good, the image is like unto his Exemplar. For the form of every good is in us, virtue, wisdom, and everything that can be thought to be better. Likewise he expresses his dignity in this, that his intellectual soul is free from every necessity and subject to no natural power. It has within itself a will able to do what it desires, it has the power of free judgment. For it is a voluntary power and without compulsion, but what is forced and suffers violence is not a power. This intellectual soul or soul in general is given by God, and from the soul is our natural life.

THE NATURE OF THE SOUL AND ITS FUNDAMENTAL POWERS AND FACULTIES[16]

8. Given the soul, it must be asked what it is, why it is, how it is. When we seek what it is, the question concerns natural science; why it is concerns reason; and how it is concerns morality. What it is no one comprehends. For its matter is nothing, it is a spiritual thing, an intellectual thing, the thing most like God. Why is it? The man who does not wish to understand this does not deserve to live. Its end is to live according to reason. How it is follows from its living according to reason. Just as the body consists of four life-giving elements, so too, the rational soul possesses four elemental

16. Cf. Jerome, *Commentarium in Evangelium s. Matthaei* 2, 13.

virtues: prudence, temperance, fortitude, justice. Of these four quasi-elements, the rationality of the soul is formed: that rationality which is the way of living according to reason. For these four elemental virtues, divided into many parts, give birth in the soul to the beginnings of many other different virtues.

Just as the soul uses four powers, the appetitive, retentive, digestive, and expulsive, in administering material life in all of the principal parts of the body, so also it administers rational life through four passions, hope, joy, fear and sadness. And just as the whole of bodily life operates through three powers, the natural power in the liver, the spiritual in the heart and the animal in the brain, so spiritual or rational life acts through three powers: rationality, the positive appetite and the negative appetite. And as the three former powers producing vivification and the animal power in the brain pro-life could not continue, namely, the natural power in the liver producing nutrition, the spiritual power in the heart producing vivifaction and the animal power in the brain producing sensation, so for ordering or perfecting rational or spiritual life in rationality there is founded faith, in the positive appetite, hope, and in the negative appetite, charity. For although faith which human reason establishes has no merit, nonetheless because it is founded in rationality, it is as if by nature always accustomed to be avid for reason. Hardly anything is credible to it unless either proper authority or reason itself shows it in some way reasonable. How much affinity there is between the positive appetite and hope is easily shown; indeed it is useless to make the effort to show it.

But the negative appetite and charity seem so opposed that one would seem to exclude the other. But it is a certain fervor of spirit that gathers this diversity into one; there is fervor in anger and fervor in charity. But I do not speak of beastly anger, but rather of human or rational anger. For there is a beastly anger, and there is a rational anger. Rational anger is divided into two kinds, zeal and discipline. Hence this habit of mind is nothing other than love of God and neighbor and hatred of vice. And it is hatred of vice because it is love of God and men. Beastly anger is divided into three kinds: fury, where there is no quantitative measure, madness, where there is no end, and what is called "coitus," the anger which only revenge satisfies just as coitus satisfies the desire of the flesh. Rational anger is fostered by charity; nevertheless charity is fostered by the anger in which it is founded, for unless anger had gone before charity would not follow. For justice cannot be loved unless iniquity is hated.

Therefore just as the life of the body is controlled and preserved by the powers in the liver, the heart, the brain, and the effects of these powers, as has been said, so virtues control and preserve the life of the spirit. But also, as the former are impeded in their various operations, either from weakness due to defects or strain due to excesses, and the body suffers or becomes infirm, so also can the virtues be affected. An affected rationality often produces of itself presumption, heresies, and the like; the positive appetite, concupiscence of the flesh, concupiscence of the eyes and the pride of life; and the negative appetite, beastly anger, cruelty and hatred.

THE SENSES[17]

9. The soul has animal senses. It has nonetheless spiritual ones. But it works so wonderfully, so powerfully, in both that human discernment can hardly comprehend it. For the soul is something invisible and incorporeal, and yet through the senses it does something invisible and corporeal about a visible body. For a sense is one of the five invisible bridges between the invisible incorporeal and the visible corporeal, all in the same body. The soul is invisible and incorporeal, yet wondrously it does something invisible and corporeal about the visible body; it is sight, hearing, taste, smell and touch. For sight is one thing, the eye another: hearing one thing, the ear another, and so for the rest.

The interior sight of the soul is brightened by prudence, darkened by folly; its hearing is offended by fallacy, soothed

17. Dependent on *De statu* 1, 6,2; 21,5.

by truth. Equity smells sweet to the rational soul, iniquity and uncleanness stink. It grows thin on vanity, fattens on virtue. Miserable is the companionship of folly, happy the association of wisdom. The soul is all eye, because it sees all, and sees the whole that it looks at. But the exterior man neither sees entirely, because only the eye sees, nor does he see all that he sees, because he does not see everything of any body that he sees. Moreover it is the same for hearing as for sight, for smell as for taste or touch, for this unity or power cannot exist in body.

THE MANNER OF THE SOUL'S PRESENCE INSIDE AND OUTSIDE THE BODY[18]

10. Since the soul is something invisible or incorporeal, as we have said, and for this reason not localized (for nothing incoporeal is), it must be asked, so that we may study the soul itself more clearly, whether it is truly proven that it is not localized. Like the divinity is it absolutely outside those categories which are proper to bodies and bodily things? None of these relate to the divine essence although it is the first and supreme substance. It cannot be said what kind it is, for it is incomparable; nor how great, for its greatness is not quantitative; what it has, for there is nothing that it does not have; how it is, for it is its own mode of being. Nor may one seek the characteristic of one who has all, nor the place of him who is not localized and is entire everywhere, nor the time of the eternal, nor the act of one who rests and who possesses all in his rest, nor the passion of the impassible. Because the human soul has no mass, it has no quantity. However, because it is subject to changing desires, it has quality. But because it is not localized in place, it is not qualified by location. The soul is in its body somewhat as God in the world. Everywhere, and everywhere entire. It is entire in each sense, so that the entire soul senses in each; it is entire in each part, so that the entire soul gives vegetative and animal life to the whole body. For this reason it is said in a sense to

18. Dependent on *De statu* 1, 2, 19-24.

be localized. The same is true of the other categories. Therefore the divinity is subject to no category, the soul to a few,
the body to all. For the soul acts not through place, but
according to its various desires, pleasant or painful. Although
without the body it can be spiritually soothed or afflicted
through desire, nonetheless the whole of the body without
the soul feels neither pleasant nor painful things. For the soul
has a fuller and more active power in its actions than the
body. Hence it is that even while it administers the body and
gives it sensation, if at any time it raises itself through the
internal gaze of the mind to high and eternal truths, it in a
certain way leaves the bodily senses and ceases to be localized
by them, so that it does not see things placed before them,
does not hear sounds in the vicinity, does not understand the
page the eyes are reading. By a marvelous and in a way Godlike power, it is at the same time completely present in contemplating heavenly things by discernment, completely
present in the sensation or act by which it is acting (although
it does not sense what it does), and completely present in the
body which it is vivifying. It is the same soul which senses:
the same which does not understand what it senses: the same
which, neither sensing nor understanding, quickens and
vivifies the body through which it senses what through itself
it does not understand. The soul is also its own power. For
what it thinks is an accident, but it is by its very own substance that it thinks. And so also with the will. To will something is an accident, but the willing itself is its substance.
Therefore, it thinks as a whole, because it is all thought; it
wills as a whole, because it is all will.

THE SOUL'S WAY OF SEEING AND THE SOUL AS AN IMAGE OF THE TRINITY[19]

11. See, I beg, how we progress into the image of him who
created us. For if the thinking soul is all thought, if it is all
will, obviously the all-loving soul is all love. But God is said

19. Here William draws on a number of texts in *De statu*: I, 24, 2; II, 2, 1-2; 4,
2; III, 9, 3; 11; II, 2, 3; I, 26.

to be and is love.[20] But that love is such that by it only the good can be loved, and only well loved. But the love which is the human soul can, by the change of its desires, both blaze with heavenly charity for higher things which for the soul is God alone, and descend to lower things with a damnable love. The soul, created in such majesty and dignity, in the image of its Creator, contemplating itself and him, pauses a little in itself. It looks at its power, not without fear, and pondering whether there be anything above itself to which it must pass, it discovers that everything changeable or movable can be moved only by one who is unmoved. It understands about itself that even if it does not move locally it does move through desire, and that there is some more stable support above it that moves neither in place nor in time. Because, as has been said, nothing is moved except by something unmoved, the soul sees that it necessarily stands still so that it can move the body in space and time, just as God, stable in himself, moves the soul in time. The soul finds itself the mean between God and the body because it is unlike any body since it is the image of God, and nevertheless it cannot be equated with God because, although it had its beginning from him, it is not made out of him nor descended from him.

The soul realizes that it sees incorporeal things of itself, corporeal things through the body; but also that it sees corporeal things of itself without the body. It indeed sees, not to mention other things, the interior components of the body, the brain with its three lobes, intimately united to each other and the mass of the liver lying in its place, clinging to the threads of the spleen.[21] the diaphragm hanging from the stomach, the heart bearing without intermission, the pathways of the veins and the network and roots of the nerves, the bone joints and the hollows of the lungs and countless other things. Whatever the soul thinks of, any place or any region, it is there, even though it cannot contemplate them in themselves. It contemplates whole scenes, the courses of the rivers,

---

20. 1 Jn 4:8.

21. The *regulis alienis* of the PL text should read *regulis lienis* as is indicated by the close dependence of the passage on *De statu* III, 11..

the faces of men, and so on. Although it does not see them, for they are bodily and can be seen only with bodily eyes, yet the soul is present wherever its thoughts go, without seeing the places with the physical eye. So too it is present where it gives life, where it does not see, where it vivifies the internal organs of its body.

And in this too it recognizes in some way in itself the image of its Creator. It sees him as the illuminating light,[22] and itself as the light able to be illumined. More, it sees that the things present in itself, the mind, thought and will, in some way respond to the image of the supreme Trinity. For when the soul thinks of anything, what it is thinking of is wholly in the mind, and the whole of what it remembers at any moment it thinks of wholly at the same moment; and it wills to think and remember, that is, it loves to have a mind and thought. When it remembers that it thinks, it certainly comprehends the whole thought with the whole mind. When it thinks of its love or its mind, it thinks of all its love and of all its mind by a total comprehension. With the whole of its love the whole loves the same total mind and its same thought, since it loves to remember and think and to love itself. And if the whole of each, all at the same time, loves, thinks or remembers itself, the three all together will be no greater than either the whole mind recalling, or the whole thought thinking, or the whole love loving. When the soul sees this within itself, indeed sees that this is itself and hears God in some way speaking to it, it sees the resplendent truth, it listens to Christ preaching and saying, "I and the Father" and my charity are not three, "but one,"[23] we are one God. You, rational mind, with your thought and your love are one man, made to the image of your Author, though not created his equal. You have not been begotten, you have been formed. You are not the one who forms. Withdraw from things which are beneath you. They are less formed, less beautiful than you are. Come up to the Form that gives form so that you may be more beautiful. Constantly unite yourself to this

22. Jn 1:19.
23. Jn 10:30.

Form, for you will receive more from its beauty the more the weight of charity presses you against it. From this you will be stabilized as the image of him from whom you took your origin."

THE DIGNITY OF MAN IN CHRIST[24]

12. Truth says this and other things to the ear of the heart,[25] instructing us within. When any soul hears this, although human misery is always prompt to envy, it will no longer have any reason to envy the angels. For such a man and the angels and God are all one spirit, as the Apostle has said.[26] They are one in God, according to the Gospel.[27] This is especially so since the Head of man, the man Christ, truly and perfectly assumed by Truth itself, by the Son of God, into oneness of person, merited once to hear what no angel could ever have heard. For he heard from God the Father, "This is my beloved Son in whom I am well pleased."[28] And so let holy humanity rejoice, glorified in its Head, Christ. Let it, exalted above the angels, exult in itself, since it heard an angel worshiped by a man, refuse the honor and say with devout humility and sweetest charity: "Do not do that, for I am your fellow servant and one of your brothers."[29] Let even the least wayfarer of the kingdom of God who is still in this world presume to exult, because, as the same Truth testifies, his "angel always sees the face of the Father."[30]

MORE ON THE IMAGE OF THE TRINITY[31]

13. But let us return to the image of the Trinity. Just as nothing exists without God the Creator, that is, the Holy

24. Dependent on *De statu* I, 26.

25. S. Ceglar sees an influence of Augustine here in the use of the expression "ear of the heart;" cf. *William of St Thierry: The Chronology of his Life with a Study of his Treatise* On the Nature of Love, *his Authorship of the* Brevis Commentatio, *the* In locis, *and the* Reply to Cardinal Matthew (Ann Arbor: University Microfilms, 1971), p. 278.

26. 1 Cor 6:17
27. Jn 17:21
28. Mt 3:17

29. Rev 22:9
30. Mt 18:10
31. Dependent on *De statu* II, 6.

Trinity, so absolutely nothing can be which is not both one and threefold. Every soul, as has been said, subsists in three undivided parts: memory, deliberation, will. And every body is one and yet has measure, number, and weight.[32] The soul by its three is made capable of the latter three: that is, it can judge the measure, number, and weight of all bodies. For the image of the Trinity proceeds from the supreme being who is God, through the middle being which is the soul, to the lowest, bodies, impressing its mark on bodies while giving knowledge to souls. As the soul contemplates all these things by discernment, it is no longer delighted in its own beauty alone but also in the Form that gives it form. By contemplation of that form it becomes ever more beautiful; for to study that Form is to be formed. Whatever is drawn toward God is not its own, but his by whom it is drawn.[33] Blessed is that soul, truly blessed. If it prays, as the Apostle says, it does not itself pray, but "the Holy Spirit" prays for it "even to sighs beyond description."[34] If it speaks, through it the Spirit speaks mysteries. Whatever it does, not itself but the Spirit works in it, in all things, distributing everything to each as he wills.[35] For just as the body lives from the soul, so does the soul live from God, sighing for him alone, continually breathing only him as the living body breathes air, remaining completely in God through faithful affection, and having him whom it loves remaining in it through his almighty operation. It lives as one spirit with him. For the will of the Father and Son, the Holy Spirit, by an inconceivable grace, with unutterable joy, by most secret inspiration, in a most manifest operation, conforms the will of the soul to himself, uniting its love to himself with spiritual omnipotence. He becomes

32. Wis 11:20

33. In this sentence William twice uses the word *afficitur. Affici* is a special word for William found frequently in his writings. As he employs it it is not easy to translate adequately. It expresses the twofold idea of a very intimate union and a blow or wounding. God by his illuminating grace "affects" the soul. At the same time, the soul is stricken, wounded, "affected"—and united, "glued" to God. See *On Contemplating God* 3 (CF 3:39), 7 (CF 3:47), 11 (CF 3:53); *Golden Epistle* 170 (CF 12:67).

34. Rom 8:26

35. 1 Cor 12:11

so united with the soul that, as has been said, when the soul prays with sighs beyond description, it is rather the Spirit who is said to pray. And this is the prayer of the Son to the Father: "*I will* (that is, I bring it about by the power of my will which is the Holy Spirit) that as I and You are one in substance, so they also may be one in us through grace."[36] One in love, one in beatitude, one in immortality and incorruption, one even in some way in divinity itself. For "to as many as received him he gave the power to become sons of God."[37]

THE SEVEN GRADES OF THE ASCENT TO GOD[38]

14. But let us consider the steps from the bottom to the top by which the soul striving for perfection ascends in its progress to its Author. The soul's first step is to give life to this earthly and mortal body by its presence. It gathers it into one and holds it together, not letting it dissolve and waste away. It causes its nourishment to be distributed among its members equitably, giving to each its due. It preserves harmony and measure in its beauty, growth and reproduction. But all this man has in common with trees. For we also say that these live, we see and confess that each of them is preserved, nourished, grows and reproduces according to its own kind.

And so, rise to the second step and see what the soul can do in the senses, where life is more clearly and manifestly perceived. Here there is nothing in common between us and trees rooted to the earth. The soul reaches out by touch, and senses and discerns hot, rough, smooth, hard, soft, light, heavy. It also distinguishes innumerable kinds of tastes, odors and shapes by tasting, smelling, hearing, and seeing. And in all these things the soul approves and desires those which are according to the nature of its body, and rejects and flees those contrary to it. In sleep and dreams it withdraws

36. Jn 17:21
37. Jn 1:12
38. Dependent on Augustine, *DQA* 33:70-76.

from these senses for a certain interval of time, letting their activity be restored by a kind of vacation. During this time the soul turns over within itself the crowds of images which it has drawn in through them. Often gesturing and moving the soul is delighted by the ease with which it can move the body. Without labor it coordinates the motions of the members. It does what it can to foster sexual intercourse; and in this companionship and love two natures become one body. But again the soul can do all this in animals. No one will deny it.

And so, rise to the third step which is now proper to man. Think of memory, not as recalling things brought into the soul through the senses, for this pertains to animals, but in the recollection and signs of the numberless things that have been committed to memory and retained there: so many skills of craftsmen and agriculture, the construction of various cities and buildings, the many wonders of architecture, the invention of so many signs: letters, words, gestures, sounds, pictures and paintings; the many languages of the nations, rivers of eloquence, all sorts of songs, many ways of playing and relaxing, musical skills, precision in measurement, mathematical abilities, present conjectures of the past and future. All these are great and completely human, but still these are a common heritage, in part of learned and unlearned alike, and in part of good and bad alike. In these three degrees you see what the soul can do in the body.

Therefore, look up and mount to the fourth step where goodness begins, and all true praise. For here the soul dares to put itself above not only its own body, by which it acts its part in the world, but even above the body of the world itself. It dares to think of the world's goods as alien to itself, and to judge and condemn them in comparison with its own power and beauty. In order to delight more in God, it withdraws itself more from all sordidness. It wishes nothing for another that is does not wish to happen to itself. It follows the authority and precepts of the wise, and through them tells itself to believe in God. In this daring of the soul, wonderful as it is, there is still labor and great and bitter conflicts against varied troubles and allurements. For in the business of purgation it undergoes the experience of death.

When this is accomplished, that is, when the soul is free of all corruption and washed from its stains, then finally it most joyfully possesses itself in itself and fears absolutely nothing for itself nor is anxious about anything for any reason of its own. This then is the fifth step. It is one thing to achieve purity, another to hold on to it; the purity that does not suffer itself to be again defiled is something entirely other than the act by which the soul restores itself from its defilement. In this step the soul conceives in every way how great it is. When it realizes this, then with a certain mighty and incredible confidence it goes to God, that is, to the very contemplation of truth, and that highest and most secret reward for which it has worked so hard.

But this action, the desire of understanding those things that truly and ultimately are, is the supreme gaze of the soul. There is none more perfect, better, or more direct. This is the sixth step in its activity. For it is one thing to cleanse the eye of the soul, lest it look in vain or boldly look and see unworthily, another to guard and strengthen its well-being and another to fasten a calm and direct gaze on that which is to be seen. In these last two steps you see what the soul can do in itself. But note that those who want to have that peaceful and direct gaze, first, before they have been cleansed and healed, are so repelled by the light of truth that they think that there is not only no good but even much evil in it. They decide that the name of truth does not belong to it, and while cursing the medicine, they take refuge in some licentious and miserable pleasure in the darkness that their malady can bear. Hence by divine inspiration and very much to the point was it said by the Prophet: "Create a clean heart in me, O God, a direct spirit renew within me."[39] For a direct spirit is, I believe, one by which it comes about that the soul cannot deviate or err in speaking the truth. And this is not given unless the heart is first cleaned, that is, unless thought itself

39. Ps 50:12 (Vulgate)

has first restrained and cleared itself of all cupidity and all the filth of mortal things.

The very vision and contemplation of truth is the seventh and last step of the soul, now no longer a step but the permanent state to which the previous steps lead. He who enjoys it alone understands what are its joys, what is fruition of the true and supreme good, what is the breath of peace.

THE DYNAMISM OF ASCENT AND DESCENT

15. Therefore the faithful soul, burning with desire and not sluggish in zeal, makes its *anabathmon,* that is, its ascension and, disposing the steps in its heart,[40] it arrives at the place which God has prepared for it or put at its disposal. It lives, as the Apostle says, the life of God,[41] a spiritual life in the joy of the Holy Spirit, in the hope of the sons of God, in contemplation and imitation of supreme justice. It lives also as long as it lives here, as long as it sees here in part and obscurely as through a mirror,[42] so using its natural passion that, though in the flesh, it does not live according to the flesh. It becomes almost impassible,[43] since its very passions are not passions for it but virtues. It does not fear except with a chaste fear. It is not sad except because it is kept from the kingdom. Rejoicing in the breadth of charity, it joyfully runs the way of the commandments of God,[44] believing all things, hoping all things, bearing all things,[45] and peacefully loving because of the contemplation of its goal. And it can sweetly rest in hope in what it enjoys and suffers and awaits as long as there remain faith, hope and charity, these three.[46]

40. Ps 83:6 (Vulgate)
41. Cf 2 Cor 4:11; Eph 4:18
42. 1 Cor 13:12
43. This is the traditional Greek concept of *apatheia.* For a thorough discussion of the Greek tradition concerning this, see T. Ruther, *Die sittliche Forderung der Apatheia* (Freiburg, 1949), 3-19. A succinct but quite adequate consideration of it can be found in John Eudes Bamberger, "Introduction" in Evagrius Ponticus, *Praktikos, Chapters on Prayer,* CS 4 (Spencer, Massachusetts: Cistercian Publications, 1972), pp. lxxxii-lxxxvii.
44. St Benedict's *Rule for Monasteries,* Prol. 49.
45. 1 Cor 13:7
46. 1 Cor 13:13

For when death is taken up in victory[47] and that which is in part is done away with,[48] there will no longer be faith or hope, but only the reality. Then the greatest of all, charity,[49] will reign and exult in that victory, with fear and sorrow destroyed, faith and hope transformed. And then it will enter into the joy of the Lord,[50] in which the blessed soul will enter happily to live eternally and to rise again in its own proper body in a wonderful manner, so that what shared in the work may also share in the glory in eternal life.

In contrast, the unhappy and wretched soul, if it may indeed be called a soul, which kills itself and is in itself dead, makes a *catabathmon*, that is, a descent to a lower place. Indeed, not a descent but a ruin, so that "what is filthy may become filthier still."[51] It does and suffers all that is contrary, separated from the life of God.[52] For, created in the image and for the vision of God, it ought to have begun here to savor God, but instead it began to lose its taste, and going away from the face of God as did Cain,[53] it dwells in a region of unlikeness, in the land of Naid, that is land of "commotion."[54] Banished from virtue, it is subject to vices; estranged from the peace of the sons of God, it is in turmoil in itself. Distorting natural skills into wickedness and cunning, it becomes malicious. It plunges itself shamefully into animal pleasures and those of the senses and abandons itself to lust. It becomes like the horse and mule which have no discernment.[55] Prudent only to do evil, it no longer knows how to do well. It has no care for itself, no memory of God. Hence it is imprisoned by its pact with its passions which it abuses miserably. It fears only what is troublesome to its senses; rejoices only when pleasures are at hand; is saddened only when this is taken away. In all things it is like an animal

47. 1 Cor 15:54
48. 1 Cor 13:10
49. 1 Cor 13:13
50. Mt 25:21
51. Rev 22:11
52. Eph 4:18
53. Gen 4:16
54. This is the interpretation of Origen: *Homilia in Jeremiam* 21:10; PG 13:540b. Naïd comes from the Greek Septuagint. The Hebrew text has Nod.
55. Ps 31:9 (Vulgate)

or beast, except, as was said above, what in them is natural is
a vice in the human soul.

Yet by the continual practice of wickedness this soul is
sometimes so numbed by its excessive boredom that it too in
some way becomes impassible or insensible. Yet it does not
escape any of the very harsh and rugged ways of the flesh by
zealous striving for wickedness, but rather it is enslaved to its
own corruptions: avarice and concupiscence of the flesh or of
the eyes, and worldly ambition.[56] Thus it lives as long as it is
enclosed in the tomb of the body. But when it has been torn
away from it, almost like the brute animals to which it feels
itself likened, it dies with the whole body. But, although it
has completely lost its true essential virtue about which
Wisdom says, "Fear God, and observe his commandments,
for this is the whole of man"[57] yet by the most just judgment
of God it is not permitted entirely to die. It remains passible
but only for grief, excluded from all joy, separated from
every hope, having no fear of sorrow but rather entirely enslaved to sorrow itself. Something living remains life-giving in
it, but it lives only to suffer. It is passible to be punished and
tortured, life-giving so as to give life again to the body to be
tortured with it, with which it always wishes, if it could, to
sin always. How much better it would have been for it if like
the soul of an animal it had completely died with the body,
so that it be not punished forever! Only the difference in
their loves makes this difference between the blessed soul and
the damned. In the one love is the guardian of its natural
dignity, but in the other it degenerates into carnal bestiality.

56. 1 Jn 2:16
57. Eccles 12:13

THE LETTER OF ISAAC OF STELLA
ON THE SOUL

THE LETTER OF ISAAC OF STELLA
ON THE SOUL

TO HIS BELOVED ALCHER
Brother Isaac commends himself
and all that is his.

YOU COMPEL ME, MY DEAR BROTHER, to
know what I do not know and to teach what I have not
yet learned. For you do not wish us to teach you what
we learn in Scripture about the soul, that is, what the soul
may have been like before sin, or what it may be like under
sin, or what future sort of soul may exist after sin; but rather
you wish us to teach you about its nature and powers—how it
may be present in the body, or how it may depart, and other
things which we do not know. And yet we are not permitted
by you not to know. We do confess as true what you heard
from us in our community gatherings. And by this you are
spurred on to hope for something more. Yet when we agree
to obey your entreaties and turn our mind toward the
matter, it escapes us, flies away, and in some way vanishes.
From this very fact we learn that our soul bears a great
likeness to the divine nature which restrains an unworthy
investigator of it with the words: "Turn away your eyes from
me, since they have made me fly away."[1]

2. There are then three realities—the body, the soul, and
God; but I profess that I do not know their essence, and that
I understand less what the body is than what the soul is, and
less what the soul is than what God is.

Perhaps you are astonished at this and you should be. Nevertheless, in this body which corrupts the soul and weighs
upon it, where the earthly dwelling also presses the power of

---

N.B. This translation, made from a corrected text prepared from three manuscripts, differs in some particulars from the edition of Tissier found in PL 194.

1. Song 6:4

knowledge down into the depths[2] and earthly limbs and
dying members weaken what has been pressed down, the
body, which is necessarily darksome, is the first of these
three that the soul encounters in its activity. Darkened by it,
the soul can see but obscurely. But insofar as it escapes from
this darkened smoke, it will indeed see more clearly. And so,
insofar as its discernment is higher and purer than sense
knowledge, the soul is able to see itself more clearly and
more surely than the body, and insofar as the understanding
surpasses discernment, it can see God himself better than the
soul. The truth of every essence is in God; in the soul, the
image of something appears, but in the body there is scarcely a vestige of anything. God alone is truly simple; every
body is truly composite; but the soul can be said to be each of
these in respect to each. If some body is simple, the soul
which is superior to every body is even more simple, but God
alone is the most simple because he is the most high.

3. It is on this account then that God is all those things
which he possesses because he is all that is his. The body can
be none of the things it possesses because it is nothing at all
of the things that belong to it. The soul, however, standing
midway between these natures is a mixture so that it is some
of the things that it possesses and is thereby simple, and is
not at all some other things and is thereby not truly simple.
To add another argument to something already certain: God
has neither quality nor quantity. For when it is said what he
is like or how great he is, nothing else is predicated of him
than what he is. The body, having both quality and quantity
is neither. The soul does not have quantity because it is not a
body, and does not lack quality because it is not God.

If it is nevertheless ever said to have quantity or parts, this
must be understood by virtue of analogy rather than as expressing the truth of its composition. For it has powers or
natural potencies, according to which it is said to have virtual
or potential parts, such as forethought, insight, and memory.
If these are truly quantitive parts of the soul, they are neces-

2. Wis 9:15

sarily souls, and it would follow that the soul will consist of as many souls as it has parts. For every part is of the same nature as its whole. Every part of a body is body, and every part of the soul, if it has quantitative parts, is a different soul. Therefore, as there are innate parts of the soul (forethought, insight, memory, and the like) it is necessary that they be not quantitative parts since they are identical with it, namely, the same nature, the same essence, altogether the same soul. For the soul and the insight of the soul are not two essences but one; different properties indeed, but one essence. Certainly, as properties, as St Augustine says, the soul is one thing and insight is another; notwithstanding, insight is in the soul and the soul is one. But the soul does one thing, insight another. The soul lives, insight has judgment; and though they be one, only the soul supports life, only insight supports wisdom.[3] Therefore it is obvious how the image of divinity in the soul shines out here, in that although there is a plurality of natural properties in it, there is only one nature, and although none of these properties is the other, none of them is anything else, but is different from the others.

4. The soul then is rational, positively appetitive (concupiscible), and negatively appetitive (irascible)—a kind of trinity of its own, as it were. It is this entirely, nothing more or less, and this whole trinity forms a certain unity of soul and is the soul itself. Therefore, the soul has natural attributes and is itself all of them; for this reason it is simple. It also has accidental attributes and is not identical with them, and therefore it is not completely simple.

The soul is not its prudence, its temperance, its fortitude, or its justice. It is therefore one with its powers but not with its virtues. For we must remain in the city until we are clothed, that is, our powers are clothed, with strength from on high.[4] For the powers are able to receive the gifts which by habit become virtues. Furthermore, just as there is an inborn heat in fire which warms those who approach, making an

3. I have not been able to locate this quotation *verbatim* in Augustine, but the sense is close to *De Trinitate* 15, 17(28).

4. Lk 21:49

accidental heat in them from that nature by means of which they have the ability to heat, and an inborn light illuminating those drawing near from that nature by which they have the ability to be enlightened, so too in the divine nature there is an inborn gift and primal goodness, giving light and heat in the form of wisdom and justice in those who draw near, clearly creating in that part the virtue by which they can be enkindled and illuminated. Thus the text: "Approach and you will be illuminated;"[5] and the other: "Draw near to me and I will draw near to you;"[6] and again: "The love of God is poured out in our hearts through the Holy Spirit who has been given to us."[7] Note that the powers are sometimes spoken of indifferently as virtues, as in the gospel where talents are given to each according to his own virtue.[8] And the term "virtuous men" is derived from "powers," just as "learned men" is indirectly derived from "virtue." For he who gives to each as he wishes does not fill all the powers of all men with his grace, but gives some to one group and some to another. The more fortunate are those who are rich in many graces, if they are the better ones about which the Apostle Paul says: "Earnestly desire the better gifts."[9] The Lord Jesus, all of whose powers of soul were endowed by strength from on high, is said to be full of the Holy Spirit,[10] full also of grace and truth,[11] and perhaps this is true of him alone of whose fullness we have all received![12]

There are therefore both natural and accidental attributes of the body, but none of them is the body itself. There are neither natural nor accidental attributes of God, but whatever is of God is totally, solely, and eternally the one God. There are natural attributes of the soul which can be nothing else but the soul itself, and there are accidental attributes

5. Cf. Ps 33:6 (Psalm references are according to the Latin Vulgate)
6. Jas 4:8
7. Rom 5:5
8. Mt 25:29
9. 1 Cor 12:13
10. Lk 4:1
11. Jn 1:14
12. Jn 1:16

which cannot be anything but different from the soul itself. But if it should be thought that there are also some natural attributes of God, since the Father has a natural Son and he a natural Father, and both have something natural, the one fatherhood, the other sonship. God nevertheless generally differs from the body and the soul in that he has no accidental attributes. He differs from the body because he is his natural attributes, from the soul because he is all his attributes, except for what is predicated relatively of one person in respect to another. The soul is in no way all its attributes, nor does it differ from its accidental attributes by relation or property alone, but rather by a difference in essence.

5. Since it has been placed in the middle, the soul ought to be in harmony with both extremes, with the highest being in its superior part and with the lowest being in its inferior part. As has been said, according to its properties the soul has a depth, a mid-point, and an apex, although according to essence all are one. The total essence of the soul is fully and perfectly contained in these three: reasonableness, positive appetite, and negative appetite. The prophet, wishing to show that a complete and perfect human soul would be present in Christ, said: "That he may know how to reject evil and choose good";[13] having immediately before said of the reality of his body, "He will eat butter and honey."[14] By this he meant to say he would truly experience in his flesh both labor (butter is made from milk by constant churning with great labor and weariness) and repose (honey is sweet of itself), insofar as experience knows through reason to choose the good, that is, the honey, through the positive appetite, and to reject evil, that is, the butter, through the negative appetite. For this reason, we whom he taught about himself by his own example may learn from the bitter things which we suffer to flee those that are more bitter, and from the sweet things of which we have a foretaste to desire those sweeter still. Thus following him we may finally attain to him

13. Is 7:15
14. Ibid.

who by frequent trials nourishes us and by consolations from time to time soothes us.

Through reasonableness the soul is of a nature to be given knowledge of things below itself or above itself or even in itself or on a par with itself. Through the positive and negative appetites the soul is moved to seek or to reject a thing, to love it or to hate it. Therefore, every power of knowledge in the soul arises from reasonableness, while every power of desire comes from the other two. The power of desire is fourfold, insofar as what we love, we either rejoice in as present or hope for as future; while in the case of hate, we are either already plunged in sorrow or else are in fear of being made sorrowful. Thus joy and hope arise from the positive appetite, while sorrow and fear come from the negative. These four powers of desire of the soul are like the elements and common matter of all the virtues and vices. For the power of desire gives a name to every action. Since virtue is the habit of a well-trained soul, the powers of desire of the soul must be trained, organized, and ordered to their proper goal and operation by reason so that they may give birth to virtues. Otherwise, they will easily fall into vices.

6. When love and hate are ordered prudently, modestly, strongly, and justly they issue in the virtues of prudence, temperance, fortitude, and justice which are universally said to be like the roots or hinges of all virtues. "For," as St Augustine says, "that which is spoken of as the fourfold virtue is love's variable power of desire, so that temperance is love keeping itself whole and pure for God, fortitude is love overcoming all things with ease for the sake of God, justice is love serving God alone and for this good commanding everything else to be subject, prudence is love which discerns those goods which help us to God from those which hold us back from him"[15] In like manner, as it is said, every motion of the soul by which it is moved to choose or reject, to love or hate something above itself or below itself, in itself or on a par with itself arises from the positive appetite and the negative

15. *De moribus Ecclesiae catholicae et de moribus Manichaeorum* I, 15, 25; PL 32:1322.

appetite. From the positive appetite comes the initial emotion, titillation, delight, and love; from the negative appetite comes emulation, anger, indignation, and hatred. If all these are satisfactorily, properly and fully ordered in the soul through hatred of the world and self, the soul will advance in the love of neighbor and God, in contempt for temporal and inferior things, and the desire of eternal and higher things. But these remarks, touching upon rather than explaining the power of desire, are enough.

7. The power of knowledge, on the other hand, arising from reasonableness, varies and is variously named insight, memory, and forethought, due to the division of time into present, past, and future. Forethought is that power or thrust of the soul by which it reaches out and concerns itself with the discovery of things unknown. Forethought searches out unknown matters, insight judges the things found, memory preserves matters already judged and presents things to be further determined. Forethought therefore brings what it has uncovered to insight, memory brings back what it has hidden, but insight is placed so to speak over present matters, and, as if it were the mouth of the mind, always either chews what the teeth of forethought gather or ruminates on what the stomach of memory presents. For everything that we know does not always occur to us, nor is everything that is known present in the view of the thinker. Rather the hidden word which is expressed exteriorly by the mouth is only gradually and piece by piece drawn out of the memory, and formed in the mouth of the mind. This is also the reason why to God nothing is future or past, but all things exist at one and the same time and are always present to his gaze. All things are said to be present to him eternally and immovably in the Word, that is, in the *Logos*, in the act of the mind which at one and the same time and always ponders with him and speaks to him. For which reason the whole of his every act of knowledge about everything is called neither memory nor forethought, but Word. Certainly, insight, memory, forethought, three in activity, are one according to the essence of the soul and are identical with the soul itself. And just as there are various

activities of the power of knowledge because of time, even though it is one in the soul and is the soul itself, so also because of what it seeks and does to know, the power of knowledge is said to be multiple and is given many names.

8. Thus sense knowledge, imagination, reason, discernment, and understanding are enumerated. All these in the soul nonetheless are nothing else than the soul. Properties are distinguished by various activities, but there is one rational essence and one soul. For just as the life by which the soul lives (not how it lives) is nothing else than the living soul, so also any power of knowledge by which the soul learns (not by which it is taught) is not other than the soul knowing. Nor is the soul's will as a faculty able to be other than the soul willing.

Just as in the visible world there are as it were mounting steps: earth, water, air, ether or the firmament, and the highest heaven itself which is called the "empyrean," so too there are five stages to wisdom for the soul as it makes its pilgrimage in the world of its body: sense knowledge, imagination, reason, discernment and understanding. For reasonableness is led to wisdom by five steps, just as the power of desire is led to charity by four.[16] Through these nine stages the soul which lives in the spirit, journeys into itself by the powers of knowledge and of desire as if on internal feet. It advances in the spirit even unto the seraphim and cherubim, that is, to the fullness of wisdom and the consuming fire of charity. May the soul through practice have in itself the virtues for which it has faculties through nature, so that as it is called a heaven because it is the seat of wisdom it may be decorated in itself with its own heavenly orders and may be regulated by the virtues. It will be easy for someone with leisure to compare these stages to the names and orders of the angels.[17]

9. By sense knowledge therefore the soul perceives bodies; by imagination, the likenesses of bodies. By reason it perceives the dimensions of bodies and the like. This is the first incorporeal object which nevertheless needs a body to subsist

16. See above, n. 5, p.
17. This is done in the *Treatise on the Spirit and the Soul,* see below, Section 5, pp.

and through it is in place and time. By discernment the soul goes beyond everything that is a body or of a body or is in any way corporeal to perceive the created spirit, which has no location but cannot possibly exist without duration since it has a changeable nature. Finally the understanding, in one way or another, and insofar as it is permitted a created nature above whom is the Creator alone, immediately beholds him or who alone is the highest and purely incorporeal being— he who needs neither a body to exist, nor location to be somewhere, nor duration to be at some time or other.

10. Sense knowledge is therefore compared to earth since it does not transcend the body. (Every body is to be considered as earth.) Sense knowledge is that power of the soul by which it perceives the corporeal forms of bodily things as present. Though it is not a body, it is described as "bodily," because it does not transcend the body, as already said, or because it makes use of bodily instruments. Because of the number of these instruments it is said to be fivefold, although within it is one. As water poured into a basin sends out varying streams through many openings that differ due to their type and position, though within the basin it is one and the same water, so sense knowledge, one and the same on the inside, varies because of the kind and position of its instruments and exercises its power towards different objects. For within, not only in the imaginative faculty of the soul which is the lowest point of the spirit, but also in the animal spirit which is the highest point of the body, sight, hearing, smell, taste, and touch are all together, though, as had been said, in different instruments they perform different tasks. Fire, for instance, shines in the eyes which by their setting, fiery nature and composition are adapted to light. Air, thin, pure, and neighbor to fire sounds in ears fitted to its setting, composition, and resonance. The remaining comparisons are obvious. For dense air, filled as it were with fumes, by odors or evil smells affects the nostrils and water flavors the palate. Earth, however, is joined to the sense of touch, especially to that of the hands and feet by which we are more frequently in contact with the earth. For the rest, since the animal body is primari-

ly of earthy stuff, wherever the sense of touch is found in it,
there too is the spirit.

11. Imagination arises from sense knowledge, and due to its
differences there is variety in imagination too. Imagination is
that power of the soul which perceives the corporeal forms of
bodily things which are not present. Sense knowledge perceives real bodies through their actual present qualities, different ones in different ways as has been said. Imagination
however perceives the likenesses and images of these real
bodies. For this reason it is called "imagination." Since these
are not true bodies, nor truly qualities of bodies, imagination
has a certain distance from bodily things, is somewhat vaporous though not yet incorporeal. It is the ultimate effort of
the bodily spirit, but not the achieving of the incorporeal.
For it is impossible for that which is a body to be so attenuated that it becomes a spirit, or for that which is a spirit
to be thickened into a body.

Everything which is born of flesh is always by nature and
essence flesh, and what is born from spirit is in like manner
spirit.[18] There are some things, however, that are similar in
each, namely the high point of the body and the low point of
the soul, through which body and soul can be easily joined
in a personal union without confusion of nature. For things
that are alike take delight in each other and are easily bound
together; such things do not shrink from each other because
of unlikeness. Therefore, the soul which is truly spirit and
not body, and the flesh which is truly body and not spirit,
are easily and aptly united in their extremities, that is, in the
imaginative faculty of the soul which is almost a body and
in the flesh's faculty of sensation which is almost a spirit. The
high point of the soul, that is the understanding or mind
(concerning which there will be a discussion later), bears the
image and likeness of its superior, God, so that it could be
ready to receive him and was taken up even into personal
oneness when he wished it without any change in its nature.
So too why should not the high point of the flesh, the facul-

18. Jn 3:6

ty of sensation, bearing the image of the soul, take hold of
the essence of the soul in personal union? In the animal's
power of knowledge and memory is not there some image of
reasonableness, and in its power of desire some image of
man's will, and in its rejections, of man's power of disapproval?

12. The bodily spirit (which indeed is truly a body) by the
natural power of knowing distinguishes among many things,
by the power of positive appetite chooses, and by the nature
of negative appetite rejects. Although brute animals which
are thought to have nothing at all beyond a corporeal nature
do not lack these things, nevertheless the human body is
better fitted to the rational makeup of the soul as a dwelling
place. It is as if the body were brought to obedience and
harmony by the plectrum of the best of harpists with his
well-ordered and harmonious cadences or measures. As it is
written: "Wisdom built herself a house and carved out seven
pillars."[19] This verse is anagogically referred to the natural
creation of the rational mind which is called the dwelling and
home of divinity. Allegorically, however, it signifies the spiritual building up of the Church. Nonetheless, historically and,
as it were, fundamentally, it speaks of the structure of the
human head which is the seat of the soul and in a sense the
house of reason. For the head, composed of six bones, is
supported by the seven columns of the neck, something you
who are distinguished in medicine know better than I.

If, perhaps under divine prompting, you were not loathe to
write us an accurate letter about the structure of the human
body, you would receive something written in return from
us. You could write about how the soul gladly assumes the
body as the instrument of its activity and enjoyment. How it
guards it with great care, unwillingly leaves it go, and having
let it go awaits it with desire, and upon receiving it exults
with the gratitude, as John said, "of harpers playing upon
their harps."[20]

In the meanwhile we will pursue what has been begun. This

19. Prov 9:1
20. Rev 14:2

discussion suffices for the manner in which the body and
soul, of contrary natures as you have stated, agree and are
able to exist together. For through two very apt intermediaries two diverse extremes can be easily and firmly joined;
something that is easily seen in the structure of the great
animal, as some call it, that is, of this world. The most apt
intermediaries for the soul and the flesh according to what
has been said are the faculty of sensation in the flesh which is
mostly fire and the imaginative faculty of the spirit which is
said to be a fiery force. They may be described in many
ways. As someone says speaking of souls: "Fiery is the
strength in them and heavenly its origin."[21]

13. Here perhaps someone might say: "If the soul resides in
the body through that faculty of sensation which is the
bodily spirit, why after the departure of the soul does not the
body live on by that spirit which is certainly life? " To which
we respond that while the condition of the faculty of sensation remains unimpaired and the tempering necessary for
vivification is present, the soul will never leave. But when
the body is distempered and broken, the unwilling soul departs,
taking all its possessions along with it, namely, sense knowledge and imagination, reason, discernment, understanding,
the positive appetite and the negative appetite. In life the
soul is moved by these last two to delight or to pain.

The body is like an instrument which at first, whole, tempered, and arranged that it might contain a musical strain and
resound when touched, now, on the contrary, lies in pieces,
broken and useless. The instrument has indeed perished, but
the strain or song has not, unless you were to think that a
song is for all that a sound alone. For the soul which is not a
body is not able to be in a place, nor come to a place, live
there or leave there. So too the song or musical strain is
present in the musical instrument or in the page of an an-
tiphonary while the cords or notes are aptly arranged. When
they are arranged it approaches, when they are confused it
departs; so also is the relation of the soul with its body. And

21. Virgil, *Aeneid* 6, 730

if you ask where is the soul after the body, I ask where is the song after the page or after the sound, where is the meaning after the spoken word, where is the judgment after the spoken line, where is the number after the thing numbered?

Put down four stones and three and there are seven. Take them away, and are not four and three still seven? Therefore things that can be numbered or have been numbered, if you will, are like a kind of body of number itself, as the spoken line is of the judgment, the spoken word of the meaning, and the modulation of the voice of the song. By all of these incorporeal things are as it were held fast by bodies, now and then drawing near, now and then departing. But you might say that the comparison agrees more with God, who is purely and completely incorporeal, who is in all things in himself, than it would with the soul. And so it is. As I said at the beginning, I can make a philosophical statement more securely and easily about God than about the soul, and about the soul than the body. The soul still possesses the image and likeness of divinity, and so it is altogether necessary that it should be similar to him in nature.

14. God then is everywhere in himself; the soul, wherever it is, is in itself to a certain degree. For this reason the soul, after it departs from the body, is where it had previously acted in the body. God is still where he was before he made the world, where he would be if the world were to cease to exist. God is infinite and unlimited, and therefore though he exists in himself he is said to be everywhere. The soul is neither, and therefore though it exists in itself, it is acknowledged to be both finite and limited. Nevertheless neither finitude nor limitation have location except by natural potencies and powers. Its natural potencies and powers are the same as itself. Therefore the essence itself is finite and limited so that when it is said to be in a certain place, it is denied to be elsewhere.

The soul is present in so far as it can act; beyond this it has no power. God on the other hand is omnipotent. Therefore the soul remains invisible and without location and is visible in the body through the body, just as the meaning remains in

the letter and is visible through the letter. God is altogether
invisible in every creature, and through the creature itself is
seen by those who have eyes to see.[22] He will be seen more
fully and more perfectly by new spiritual eyes in the new
heaven and new earth.[23] For the whole of creation is as it
were the body of the divinity and the individual parts like
individual limbs.

Just as God is in the whole and whole in each of the parts,
but remains in himself, so also the soul is in its whole body
and is in itself whole in each of its members. God is truly of
this manner of being, the soul to the likeness of that truth.

Therefore since the soul, as has been said, is incorporeal and
for this reason without location, by means of that part by
which it is said to be almost bodily, it is also found to be
nearly fixed in place. On this account therefore just as by
sense knowledge the soul is engaged with bodies, by imagination it is concerned with the likenesses of bodies and of
places. In those likenesses the soul appears to itself to do or
undergo something, whether waking or sleeping, whether
deprived of the senses for an hour or completely irrational
(whether this happens through itself or some other spirit
good or evil). It is never able, whether in the body or out of
the body, to pass beyond the body in what belongs to sense
knowledge, nor beyond bodily likenesses through imagination, inasmuch as it has received these powers only for these
activities. By means of these powers it neither sees nor will it
see God beyond it, the angel on a par with it, it in itself, nor
even the incorporeal forms of bodies beneath it.

15. There remains, therefore, reason, the third step of the
soul to wisdom (as has been said). Reason then is that power
of the soul which perceives the incorporeal forms of corporeal things. For it abstracts from a body, not by an action but
by reflection, those things which are founded in a body; and
although it sees that they do not subsist in reality except in a
body, it still perceives that they are not a body. Obviously,
the "nature of body" itself according to which every body is

22. Cf. Mk 8:18; Rom 1:20
23. Cf. Is 65:17

a body is undoubtedly no body at all. Nevertheless, it never subsists outside the body, nor is the "nature of body" to be found except in a body, though this nature is found not to be a body nor the likeness of a body. Hence it is perceived by neither sense knowledge nor by imagination. Therefore reason perceives what neither sense knowledge nor imagination can, namely the natures, forms, differences, and proper accidents of corporeal things. These are all incorporeal, but not outside bodies; subsistent beings only by reason. For second substances are only found to subsist in first substances. How much less subsistence belongs to those beings whose being it is to be in some subject. These are the beings which above we have rightly called the "first incorporeal." Although they are not body, they are not yet able to be called spirit, because though they are abstracted to be sure from the things in which they exist, they in no way subsist in themselves. For they need a body in order to exist, and for this reason location in order to be somewhere, and duration in order to be at some time or other. As already said, beings of this sort subsist only in other beings, even though other beings are in a sense from them. Indeed second substances are in the first, but the first are from the second.

16. There are then diverse states of existence of the things with whose perception sense knowledge, imagination, and reason are concerned and active, viz., the real and the rational (or the natural and the theoretical, as some prefer). From this source those two branches of study are explicitly distinguished, that is the natural and the mathematical. Mathematics is called "science" in that the rational state of existence of things which sense knowledge does not know and which imagination does not conjecture subsists as a whole in reason and in scientific knowledge rather than in actuality.

Sense knowledge and imagination thrive on the level of the natural states of the existence of corporeal things, but without reason they are insufficient. They do not rise to the rational level, but remaining below, from a distance as it were point out the incorporeal form to reason as it rises. Certainly they are able to bring reason itself to this point, but they

cannot accompany it up to the incorporeal forms of corporeal things.

Yet that branch of study which they call "theology" rises
even higher in that it deliberates about divine matters. In
some similar proportion reason is able to assist it, but in no
way able to attain it. For it has its boundaries and is limited
by proper borders. The sun, freeing itself from the depths
and obscured by some misty haze from waters and swamps,
at first gleams redly rather than shines, and then coming
forth more clearly blazes out into the freeness of the purer
air when it has trodden the mists underfoot. So too the soul,
rising up from the animation of the flesh alone into sense
knowledge, and through it and after it into imagination
(where stained by the phantasms of bodies it is still feeble),
at last, after it has evolved above all this, towers up and
gleams forth in the purity of reason. But discernment surpasses reason both in rank and in power, just as the firmament,
as completely free from all the dullness of earth as it is from
the fluidity of water and the moisture of air, surpasses the
lower atmosphere. Dull and heavy, sense knowledge lies
underneath like the earth which imagination like water surrounds. Reason is compared to the thinness of air, encompassing and penetrating and discerning everything below it in,
as it is said, the pendulum of abstraction. Discernment is
compared to the solidity of the firmament, and itself discerns
the real state of existence of spiritual natures. Then understanding seems to be compared to the very fine and thin,
totally fiery, highest heaven.

17. Therefore discernment is that power of the soul by
which it perceives the incorporeal forms of truly incorporeal
things. We call that truly incorporeal which does not need a
body in order to exist, and for this reason neither does it
need location in order to be somewhere, even though it is not
a completely pure incorporeal being, since it is not able to
exist without duration. For a pure incorporeal being is simple
because it is completely self-sufficient.

18. By means of sense knowledge then, as has been said,
the soul perceives bodies; by imagination, that which is

scarcely a body; by reason, the scarcely incorporeal; by discernment, the truly incorporeal. By understanding, it perceives the pure incorporeal which does not require a body in order to exist, nor location in order to be somewhere, nor duration in order to be at some time or other, nor a cause in order to be from somewhere, nor a form in order to be something, nor some class of subject in which to subsist, or which it may stand by or follow after. But, as has been said, it is completely self-sufficient; it exists by means of itself and is identified with itself.

The true but not pure incorporeal being is some kind of image and likeness of the pure and true incorporeal being; and that which we have called the "scarcely incorporeal" being is an image of the former. That which we said is "scarcely bodily" is an image of the "scarcely incorporeal." The highest body, fire that is, is joined to the "scarcely bodily" by a kind of likeness, and air to fire, water to air, earth to water. Therefore (in a manner of speaking) by this golden chain of the poet[24] the lowest realities hang down from the highest, or by the upright ladder of the prophet[25] there is an ascent from the lowest to highest. Just as Wisdom affects the order of things from one end to the other, that is, from the highest to the lowest, it also, drawing them in strength from the Archetype into their proper states so that they are what they should be, sweetly sets all things in order,[26] directing and ruling through being what he has drawn from nothing into existence. So also the soul, the image of that Wisdom, had it not fallen away, by freely gazing upon him everywhere would follow him, admiring and loving, searching out and praising in everything the power drawing all things from nothing into existence and the Wisdom ordering all things through being and the Goodness supporting all things lest they fall back into nothingness. It rejoices exceedingly like the Psalmist: "How you have

24. The reference is to Homer. See my study, *The Golden Chain: A Study in the Theological Anthropology of Isaac of Stella*, CS 15 (Washington, DC: Cistercian Publications, 1972), especially pp. 61ff.
25. Jacob, Gen 28:12
26. Cf. Wis 8:1

delighted me in your creation, Lord, and I will rejoice in the works of your hands. How great are your works, Lord; your thoughts are altogether too deep."[27] And in another place: "I will meditate upon all your works, and will be occupied with your marvels."[28] (The works pertain to creation, and the marvels to conservation.) And in another place: "Wonderful are your works, O Lord, and my soul knows full well."[29] Wonder gives rise to inquiry; inquiry merits knowledge.

19. Therefore the soul has that by which it may inquire and know, for made to the likeness of total Wisdom, it bears the likeness of all things in itself. Hence it had been defined by a philosopher as the likeness of all things.[30] By means of sense knowledge therefore, as has been frequently said, it inquires after and knows bodies; by imagination, the likenesses of bodies; by reason, the dimensions of bodies, both the similarities of the dissimilar and the dissimilarities of the similar; by discernment, the changeable spirit; by understanding, the unchangeable God. The soul then, possessing in itself powers by which it may inquire about everything, through them also has a manner of existence similar to everything (though it is one)—similar to the earth through sense knowledge, water through imagination, air through reason, the firmament through discernment, and the heaven of heavens through understanding. Or similar to metals and stones through essence, grasses and trees through life, animals through sense knowledge and imagination, men through reason, angels through discernment, God through understanding it sings psalms to its Creator with thanks and praise saying: "Your wisdom is marvellously beyond me, it is strengthened, and I cannot reach it."[31] This knowledge is described by the soul as strengthened in that it is not able to attain it, because the soul itself has been weakened in respect to what it ought to have beheld and possessed. And so in another place there is the

27. Ps 91:5-6
28. Ps 76:13
29. Ps 138:14
30. The philosopher referred to is probably the Roman author Varro. See *The Golden Chain*, 118-9.
31. Ps 138:6

lament and complaint: "My iniquities have encompassed me, and I am not able to see"[32] And again: "The light of my eyes is not with me."[33] And: "My eye has been clouded by anguish."[34]

20. Only the eyes of concupiscence (namely of man, that is, of the spirit) have been enlightened and opened to curiosity and those of the flesh (that is, of woman) have been opened to pleasure. The eye of sense knowledge and imagination has been clouded so that it sees rather obscurely, the eye of reason so that it scarcely sees, the eye of discernment and understanding so that it sees almost nothing. For who sees himself? Who knows himself? I refer to the terms "image and likeness of God," and "according to the image and likeness of God." He who knows one or the other of similar terms, knows both; and he who does not know one or the other, knows neither. Therefore, the soul which through itself ought to know God above itself, has lost the capacity to know itself in itself, and the angel on a par with it.

By the power of discernment then by which the angels act, they see themselves and our soul; nevertheless, they are not able to be seen in their nature by souls in return, because the soul has been weakened and is not able to open its eye to see them. For this reason when they wish to show themselves to men, they either depend upon sense knowledge on the outside through an assumed body, or upon imagination within through corporeal likenesses.

Since sense knowledge and imagination have their sphere in natural things, reason in mathematical things, and understanding in theological things, discernment scarcely constitutes its own branch of study. For the incorporeal nature whose incorporeal forms it perceives is located midway between bodily nature and God as we have said. It has natural attributes which it is, and they cannot be perceived by it otherwise than through abstraction. It also has its accidental attributes which, when abstracted and looked at in their own

32. Ps 39:13
33. Ps 37:11
34. Ps 6:7

nature, belong to a higher order and require the understanding itself by which God is seen. For the natural virtues,
considered in their height and source and natural essence, are
all one and supreme—the principle of all, the nature of natures, and the essence of essences. Whence discernment gives
place partly to natural studies and partly to theological. For
what else is the essence of justice than the God whose participation is termed virtue? And are not there as many varieties
of participation as there are individual shares of justice? Essential justice, however, is one. It is not a quality, nor an
accident of the soul, but subsisting in itself, it is shared in
by just spirits by means of a participation of itself. These
shares are the individual justices of spirits which are accidental to them.

   God is able to fill all things, and he can be participated in
by his own natural gift, and from that gift can be enjoyed. He
is participated in by all things on the level of essence, and in
accordance with essence on the level of the proper form, and
in accordance with both on the level of appropriate enjoyment. All things exist, because it is clear that being is first
and foremost in everything. For what does not exist is nothing at all. When a thing does exist, it is maintained in being
by some shape, or image, or form through which it is distinguished from everything else, and has some gift naturally
in itself. For nothing is given for nothing. Plainly, these three
are in every existing thing as a certain vestige as it were of the
highest essence and form and gift, that is, of the Father and
the Son and Holy Spirit. Eternity is in the Father, form in
the Image and enjoyment in the Gift.[35]

   21. Since God can fill all things as has been said, whatever
subsists in number, measure, or weight is able to receive
divinity. Nevertheless, in diverse ways and gradually this
participation rises from inanimate beings, through animation
and the power of sensation and of rationality, to its image
and likeness which shine forth in the higher part of the soul.
The soul can receive all things as God can fill all things. The

---

35. This triad is originally found in Hilary of Poitiers, *De Trinitate* 2, 1 and was
developed by Augustine in *De Trinitate* 6, 10(11).

soul can receive the universe through those five frequently named steps which proceed from its power of rationality to knowledge and from its positive appetite to love.

Therefore whatever things it perceives by any power of knowledge it immediately dips as it were in the seasoning of the positive appetite, so that it may taste of it and through the flavor be pleased or displeased. The natural power of knowledge, knowing all things and discerning among them, and the natural power of desire by which, in their order and degree, it loves all things, are in the soul and are what the soul is. It has, however, from nature faculties and instruments as it were of knowing and loving; nevertheless, it cannot possess the knowledge of truth and the right order of love save from grace. The rational mind was made by God, and just as it receives his image first and alone, in like manner it is able to receive knowledge and love. The vessels then that creating grace forms so that they can exist, assisting grace fills that they be not empty. Just as the fleshy eye, though it have the faculty of seeing from nature, and the ear the faculty of hearing, never achieve vision or hearing of themselves without the aid of exterior light and sound, so too the rational spirit fit to know the truth and love the good from the gift of creation, never attains the effect of wisdom and love unless it is filled with the ray of interior light and ignited with its heat. As the eye cannot see the sun except in the sun's light, the understanding is not able to behold the true divine light outside its light. "In your light we see light," says the Prophet.[36] Finally, as what enables the sun to be seen comes from the sun, but remains in the sun, since coming forth from it it still manifests it; similarly, the light which departs from God illumines the mind, though remaining in God, so that the mind may see first of all that very blazing forth of light without which nothing can be seen, and in that may see other things. On this account the soul, stretching out the understanding to the very source of light, itself finds and beholds it through light's own being.

36. Ps 35:10

22. So just as phantasms rise up from below into the imagination, so theophanies descend from above into the understanding. Just as soul is not sufficient of itself to animate its body, so it is not able of itself to produce wisdom. Therefore sense knowledge helps from the outside; imagination from below; reason, the gift of creating grace, from within (by it every man coming into the world is enlightened);[37] and discernment and understanding help from above.

23. Therefore the understanding is that power of the soul which is closest to God, just as the imaginative faculty of the soul is to the body, and the faculty of sensation of the flesh to the lowest point of the soul. Although in God, to whom by its knowing the understanding is closest, there are different properties, still nothing is inferior, nothing unequal.

No one knows the Father except through the Son and in the Holy Spirit.[38] The Father makes all things, gives all things, and forgives all things through the Son and in the Spirit. And so although all three persons are coeternal with each other and are coequal in that ineffable nature of theirs, nevertheless the Holy Spirit seems to be closer to the creature in some sense as the one who, proceeding from both, is Gift and Power. Every enjoyment of the Divinity we have is from this Gift, for he is the natural gift existing in God, by means of which God can be given to and enjoyed by every nature, as it was said above.

Corporeal light because it is light shines naturally, that is, unbegotten itself it begets light (for the term "light" signifies existing and unbegotten light, but the term "shines," light going forth and begotten). Because it shines, it illuminates, that is, it gives light. In the same way, there is a light in God in whom there is no darkness.[39] Rather, he is the light that is inaccessible[40] unless he himself draw near to someone by his natural gift, that is, by his illumination. Since he is light, he indeed shines, that is, sends forth brightness from himself;

37. Jn 1:9
38. Cf. Mt 11:27
39. 1 Jn 1:5
40. 1 Tim 6:16

and because light shines, that is, from itself sends forth brightness, it gives light, that is, it illuminates.[41] Therefore the light sending forth brightness from itself without losing it illuminates the understanding to acknowledge truth. The fire which it retains in itself, sending forth heat from itself, enflames the power of desire to love virtue. And therefore although the coequal nature of the Trinity is without distinction, just as divine gifts descend to us from the Father through the Son and the Spirit, or in the Spirit, according to the passage; "Baptizing them in the name of the Father, and of the Son, and of the Holy Spirit;"[42] so through the Spirit to the Son, and through the Son to the Father human gifts ascend. For upon the departure of the Son the Paraclete Spirit is sent that he might unite the body to the head, that is, to Christ, and Christ to God; as it is written: "Man is the head of woman, Christ of man, and God of Christ."[43] Therefore the Spirit rules, consoles, instructs, and leads the Church to Christ. And Christ at the same time offers it, without spot or blemish[44] as a kingdom to his God and Father.[45] May the glorious Trinity deign to fulfill this in us. Amen.

24. Amidst innumerable difficulties we have written these things to you, brother, lest we be disobedient. For the evils of plague and famine have descended on our regions this year, such as, it is thought, no past century has seen. Last year we saw and noted the signs of this, knowing that all events have causes from which they come, and preparations of a sort, and signs when they will happen, and ultimate benefits for which they take place. For nothing is done by Wisdom that is not wise, and by the highest Good that is not good, and well done, and for a good purpose. Farewell and pray for us, loving us, because we love you.

41. The three properties of light as a trinitarian analogy are taken from Augustine, *Soliloquiae* 1, 8 (15).
42. Mt 28:19
43. 1 Cor 11:3
44. Eph 5:27
45. 1 Cor 15:24

TREATISE ON THE SPIRIT AND THE SOUL

INTRODUCTION

BECAUSE I HAVE BEEN TOLD that I should know myself, I cannot bear being a stranger to myself.[1] It is very neglectful not to know that by which we consider heavenly things in depth, and investigate natural things by subtle searchings, and even yearn after knowledge about our Maker. It is not an extraordinary thing, nor one to be sought far from us; for it is the intellectual soul which makes it possible for us to experience these things.

The intellectual soul is always at work within us, speaking to us or considering things inwardly. It is given to it to know the secrets of such tremendous things and yet it often remains ignorant of itself. Indeed, it is granted only to a few to gaze at the intellectual soul by means of that soul, that is, to have the intellectual soul consider itself. But divine Providence has seen to it that the power of finding should not be beyond the reach of devoted persons who seek themselves and their God with uprightness, purity of intention, and fervor. I shall therefore turn to myself and to my God, in whose debt I am above all for my person, and I will consider what the intellectual soul is and what its native dwelling place might be.

1. This introduction is dependent on Augustine's *De quantitate animae* (hereafter cited as DQA), 14 and 28.

INTELLECTUAL SOUL–REASON–RATIOCINATION[2]

1. The intellectual soul is a certain substance which partakes of reason and is suited to ruling the body. When the intellectual soul is enlightened by wisdom it can see its source and know itself, and it can understand how wrong it is to seek outside itself what can only be found within. Lulled to a deep trance by the bodily passions and lured outside itself by sensible forms, it forgets what it has been. And because the spirit cannot in this state remember that it had been something else, it does not believe itself to be anything except what it sees. It is only taken up with sense knowledge of bodies and the imagination of likenesses of bodies and places, and is distracted with these whether awake or asleep. But when the intellectual soul raises itself from such distraction by the power of the understanding and is able to unify its attention, then it can be called rational. Reason, in fact, is one aspect of the intellectual soul, by which through itself it apprehends the truth. Ratiocination, however, is a seeking on the part of reason. The proper function of reason is to intuit, that of ratiocination to inquire.

THE INTELLECTUAL SOUL UNDERSTANDS ITSELF[3]

2. The intellectual soul is invisible. Otherwise, how could it discern other invisible things? It sees visible things through the body, but invisible thing of itself. In this process it realizes its own invisibility. Nevertheless, it can be seen in the body through the body, just as there is meaning in the letter and the meaning can be seen through the letter. As lord, ruler, and indweller of the body, the intellectual soul can see itself only through itself. I repeat: it sees itself through itself. It does not seek the aid of physical eyes. Rather, the intellectual soul must free itself of the clutter and noise of all bodily senses and turn to itself if it is to see itself in itself, if it is to know itself as it is. If, further, the intellectual soul wishes to

2. Dependent on DQA 13 and 27; Hugh of St Victor's *Didascalicon* 1, 2; and Isaac of Stella, *Ep an* 9.
3. Dependent on Augustine, *Enarratio in psalmum* 47, 7; Letter 14; and possibly William of St Thierry, *Phys an* 11.

know God, it must raise itself above itself by the penetrating power of the mind. And although God is not of the same nature as the intellectual soul, yet he cannot be seen other than by the intellectual soul even though never as the intellectual soul itself may be seen.

God is unchanging Truth without the imperfection that is substance. Not so the intellectual soul. It can both be deficient and excel, know and ignore, remember and forget. It can now desire and immediately not desire. Engaged in divergent thoughts and musings, it wanders all about. It has to consider and ponder over everything. It can see things that are far away, desire those abroad and even visit them "by vision." It can scrutinize whatever is hidden. In a second the intellectual soul can send its senses throughout creation and all its secrets. It can go down to hell and then soar up to heaven, it can cling to Christ and be united to God. For God is its proper element and dwelling place, deriving from the fact that it was made in God's likeness. Whoever, then, wishes to restore that image as it was made by God, that is, like unto God, should first return to himself and remain there in a searching attitude, trying to perceive man's makeup and to determine which of his parts has been made in God's image.

MAN'S MAKEUP[4]

3. Man is made up of two substances, the soul and the flesh. The soul possesses reason and the flesh senses. Only in close co-operation with the soul may the flesh stimulate the senses. The soul, however, exercises its power of reasoning quite independently of the flesh.

THE SOUL'S POWERS—THE FOUR POWERS OF DESIRE—THE FOUR VIRTUES—THE FIVE POWERS OF THE INTELLECTUAL SOUL[5]

4. The soul is rational, positively appetitive, and negatively appetitive. Because of its rationality it can be enlightened so

---

4. Dependent on Gennadius of Marseilles, *Liber de dogmatibus ecclesiasticis* (hereafter cited as LDE).

5. Much of this chap. is verbatim from *Ep an* 5 and 8.

as to know things which are below, above, within, or beside itself. The soul can, for example, know God, who is above itself; it can know itself, which is nowhere else than within itself; it can know an angel, which is beside itself or on its own level; and, finally, it can know all creatures under heaven which are inferior to itself.

By its positive appetite the soul can be led to attach itself to something it yearns for and love it. By its negative appetite, on the other hand, it can be turned from the undesirable and hate it. Every power of knowledge of the soul, then, arises from its rationality, while the power of desire comes from the other two.

We recognize four powers of desire. If we love something, we can be either enjoying its possession at present or hoping for that enjoyment in the future. If, on the contrary, we hate something, we may already be suffering from it or we may fear the future suffering it can cause us. Thus the two modes of positive appetite are joy and hope, and the two modes of negative appetite are pain and fear. These four powers of desire of the soul may be considered the principles or common matter of all vices and virtues.

The powers of desire indeed give a name to the actions which they provoke. And since a virtue is a habit of a well-formed mind, the powers of desire of the intellectual soul should be formed, instructed, and ordained toward their proper objects and in the proper way so that they can grow into virtues. Otherwise they easily slip into vice. It follows that when love and hate are prudently and humbly, forcefully and justly taught, they will necessarily grow into the virtues of prudence, temperance, fortitude, and justice: these are like the sources and hinges of all the other virtues. When these have been lovingly and rightfully implanted, the soul through hating the world and itself makes progress in loving God and neighbor. By scorning the lower, temporal goods it grows to desire the higher, eternal goods.

Now the power of knowledge is one thing in the soul and one with it. And although it is not a body yet it is termed bodily because it does not transcend the body and because it is exercised through the body's instrumentality. Although the power of knowledge is undivided in itself, yet from the number of instruments it uses we classify it under five headings. According to its various functions it varies and is severally named. The divisions are: sense knowledge, imagination, reason, discernment, and understanding. In the soul these five are nothing other than the soul itself, divided and subdivided into properties according to its exercises. But there always remains but one rational essence and one soul. The properties may be varied, but the essence is one. According to its functions there are many, but according to its essence all of these are but one in the soul and, indeed, the same thing as the soul.

The visible world is divided into five parts, namely: earth, water, air ether or firmament, and the highest heaven or "empyrean." Likewise the pilgrim soul, while in the world of its body, has five modes of advancing toward wisdom. These, as had been stated, are sense knowledge, imagination, reason, discernment, and understanding. Rationality then, strives toward wisdom in five different ways and toward charity with four different powers of desire. Making progress through this ninefold division by the power of knowledge and the power of desire, the soul advances as if on four feet. Since it lives by the spirit, let it also walk by the spirit even as far as the cherubim and the seraphim, that is, to the fullness of knowledge and the reign of charity; and let it through practice acquire the virtues for which it has faculties through nature.

THE SOUL'S POWERS COMPARED WITH THE CHOIRS OF ANGELS[6]

5. I invite the intelligent reader to compare these modes of advancing of the soul with the names and orders of the angels. It is easy if he can equate sense knowledge, which is the soul's first "messenger," with those angels called messengers. The imagination would then be the archangelic order,

6. Dependent on *Ep an* 8 where the comparison with the orders of angels is suggested.

since it perceives more than does sense knowledge. Fear
would be the equivalent of the virtues and pain that of the
powers; for the person who, terrified by the fear of punishment and made contrite by the pain of his sins, scorns the
world and himself—that person works miracles in the company of the virtues and routs demons along with the powers.
Let me say in passing that it is better to sneer at oneself than
at the world, for many have sneered at the world out of vanity.

We assign reason to the principalities, since reason rules the
senses and desires, much as the principalities are in charge of
the spirits below themselves. Love of neighbor, which is joy
itself, is comparable to the dominations, for those who love
unconditionally rule others well and rejoice in the general
good. Discernment is the counterpart of the thrones. The
thrones are called seats because God sits upon them. In such
a way, too, should you discern, since God dwells in our
hearts through faith, [7] through holiness, through peace,
through love, because he is a God of peace and love. [8] The
understanding would be represented by the cherubim. For
the knowledge of these spirits is proportionate to their more
intimate contemplation of God's divinity. Understanding, for
its part, is that power of the soul which is closest to God, for
it can discern him and those things which are in him. The
seraphim stand for love of God, for hope or desire for God.
God, as we know, is the hope of all the ends of the earth. [9]
The whole earth yearns after his countenance. Our entire
hope and greatest longing are centered precisely on the One
whom the seraphim desire to look upon.

Contempt for the world is similar to the virtues and self-
contempt to the powers. Reason is equatable with the principalities, love of neighbor with the dominations, discernment
with the thrones, understanding with the cherubim and love
of God with the seraphim. To such an extent do fear of
punishment and sorrow for one's sins result in contempt of

7. Eph 3:17
8. 2 Cor 13:11
9. Ps 64:6 (all Psalm quotations are from the Vulgate).

self and of the world, that these two—fear and sorrow—can perform miracles along with the virtues, and drive out devils with the powers. Hope in promised things and rejoicing in rewards attained produces love of God and neighbor.

TRACES OF THE TRINITY IN THE SOUL [10]

6. Made to the likeness of all wisdom, the soul bears within itself the likeness of all things. This is why a philosopher called it "the likeness of all things." It possesses certain powers by which it may apprehend all things. It may, further, inquire into all things. In this way it stands as a reflection of all these things by virtue of its oneness.

The soul resembles the earth in its sense knowledge. It resembles water in its imagination, air in its reason, the firmament in its discernment, and the highest heaven in its power of understanding. In essence it is like stones, like trees in its vitality, like animals in its sense knowledge and imagination. Still further, it reminds us of men because of its reason, of angels because of its discernment and of God because of its power of understanding.

Just as God may be received and participated in by all, so too the soul can receive all things. God is accessible to all and able to be shared in by all. Let us explain this. By God's natural gift, the Holy Spirit, and by its enjoyment through the gift of grace, all things may participate in God. This participation is by the essence which gives them existence, and according to this essence, by their form by which they differ from others, and according to both, by the proper enjoyment by which they make progress. These three— essence, form, and gift (or enjoyment)—are present in every living man as traces of the divine essence, form, and gift, that is as traces of the Trinity, Father, Son and Holy Spirit. Eternity is in the Father, form in the Image, enjoyment in the Gift.[11]

Eternity is the Father's because the Father himself has no

---

10. Dependent on *Ep an* 19-21, 23. Cf. the Pseudo-Augustine, *Manual* 26.
11. Cf. Augustine, *De Trinitate* 6, 11.

father. The son receives his nature from the Father and is coeternal with him. If an image is a perfect replica of that of which it is a reflection, then it must necessarily be equal to its source. Form is in the image, that is, in the beauty, the proportionality, the equality, the first and highest likeness, the first and highest life, the first and highest discernment. Enjoyment is in the gift. The gift of the Father and the Son is the Holy Spirit. Enjoyment, therefore, is in the gift, that is, in delight, joy, happiness, gaiety and sweetness.

The indescribable embrace between the Father and the Father's Image is not without perfection, without charity, without delight. Thus in the supreme Trinity we find the original source of all things, the most complete beauty and the most blissful kind of love. We men, however, can share in this enjoyment of the Trinity only by pure gift.

As the gift of the Father and the Son, the Holy Spirit seems somehow to be closer to us. Through grace he is the source of our enjoyment of the Father and the Son. The Spirit directs, instructs, consoles, and finally leads us, who constitute the Church, to Christ, who will himself in the end present us free of spots and wrinkles[12] to God the Father as his Kingdom.[13] The things which are proper only to God have thus come down to us from the Father through the Son and the Holy Spirit, or rather in the Spirit. The Father handed over his Son so as to redeem us who were enslaved. He then sent the Holy Spirit as the means of adopting slaves as his own sons. He gave his natural Son as the price of our redemption, the Holy Spirit in the privilege of our adoption, and kept himself in his fullness as the inheritance of those he had adopted. For this reason no one's faith in God's fidelity should waver, because his mercy exceeds our misery. Whoever cries out to him with his whole heart will be heard, because God is merciful. He is swifter in offering forgiveness to a sinner than the sinner is in accepting it. God so hastens to deliver the guilty man from the torture caused by his conscience that we would think God suffers more from his compassion for a wretched man

12. Eph 5:27
13. 1 Cor 15:24

than does the wretched man himself from the burden of his conscience.

THE SOUL CAN RECEIVE ALL THAT EXISTS[14]

7. The soul can receive all that is, because through its rationality it can come to universal knowledge and through its positive appetite to universal love. These, then, are two faculties of the soul, and they are identical with the soul: a natural power to know and judge things and a natural power of desire by which it can love things according to their kind and rank. Now the faculties, the instruments one may say, of knowing and loving are naturally inherent in the soul. But the recognition of truth and the gradation of love are possible to the soul only through grace. Since the rational mind has been made by God, along with his image it has received the power to know and to love. Provided that energetic cooperation be found, assisting grace will do its part in seeing to it that the vessels fashioned by creating wisdom do not remain empty.

THE SOUL IS AGAIN EXAMINED[15]

8. The soul is a rational and intellectual substance, made spiritual by God. It is not of the same nature as God, but rather a creature made out of nothing and able to follow either the path of good or evil. The soul, therefore, is to a certain extent mortal and to a certain extent immortal. It is mortal insofar as it can change for the worse and be alienated from participation in God's will, source of its goodness. And it is immortal insofar as it can never lose its power of knowledge, which after this life will be for it a source of either well-being or calamity.

We do not here mean, as some do, that the soul merited to take on flesh because of acts done before it had become incarnate. But neither then can a soul which is in a man be uncontaminated by sin unless it has been delivered by Christ.

14. *Ep an* 21.
15. Dependent on Cassiodorus, *De anima* 4. Cf. *Phys an* 1.

The soul comes to the body only at God's instance. If its actions then are in harmony with God's command, it will receive eternal life and the fellowship of the angels as its reward. If on the contrary, the soul spurns God's will, it will suffer the punishment of a very bitter and yet a very just sentence, that of uninterrupted pain and unending fire.

MAN'S SENSIBILITY IS TWOFOLD[16]

9. The soul receives its name from its function of animating or enlivening the body. The soul gives life to the body. The spirit is the soul considered in its spiritual nature, or derives its name from the fact that it may be regarded as the body's breath. Now, although "spirit" designates one aspect of the enlivening principle and "soul" another, yet the spirit and the soul of a man are in reality identical. Spirit refers to the substance and soul to the life-giving function. The essence is the same for both, but not the property. One and the same thing is called spirit when considered in itself and soul when considered in its relation to the body. It is spirit insofar as it is a rational substance, endowed with reason, and soul insofar as it is the life of the body, about which it has been said that "whoever shall lose his life for me shall save it."[17] Which means that whoever gladly and for God's sake looks down upon the perishable life which his body receives from his soul for a limited span, will in future times receive that same life, body and soul, in return, but with the difference that it will be unending instead of momentary, and imperishable instead of mortal.

Because the human soul can be both in the body and outside of it, it is simultaneously called soul and spirit. We disagree with those who posit two souls, a sensual one which would be the source of animation for man and a rational one,

16. Dependent on LDE 19 and Hugh of St Victor, *Commentarius in Lucam* 1, 47. It should be kept in mind here that the Latin word for "soul" is *anima*, from which "animate" is derived; and that the Latin *spiritus* can mean either "spirit" or "breath."

17. Lk 9:24

the supposed source of knowledge. We assert that the same indivisible soul at once exists of itself through discernment and endows the body with animation through the senses. The human body can neither live nor be born without the presence of a rational soul. Before it receives such a soul it merely vegetates, moves, and grows into a human shape in the womb, much like grass can move and grow without having a rational soul.

Now the life of the soul is twofold, for it lives in the flesh and in God. There are consequently two kinds of sense knowledge in man, an interior and an exterior one, each one having its own proper object which is its means of being renewed. The interior faculty is renewed in the contemplation of divine things and the exterior in the contemplation of things human. God became man, then, in order that the total man might find happiness in him. And indeed, if man's carnal senses should perceive a man in God, then man's whole concern and capacity to love would hopefully be spent on God.

It had really been a bliss for man to find nourishment in his Maker whether he went in within himself or out into the world of things: nourishment without in the flesh of the Savior and sustenance within in the divinity of the Creator. But this great blissfulness went the way of evil. After losing the treasure which was within, the soul sought foreign goods outside itself. The soul struck a pact with the pleasures of the world and found its rest among them without being troubled by the absence of its own interior good. This tragedy unfolded from the soul's finding its consolation in things which were not its proper end. While the exterior or carnal senses are occupied with their own object, the interior senses of the mind fall into a sort of slumber. The person who is taken up with frolicking about among exterior goods cannot know the goods of the interior sense. It is a truth that the man who lives carnally will only feel for carnal things. He will try to flee from the pains of the flesh insofar as he is able, but he will pay no attention to the sores on his soul nor procure any ointment for them.

Once the carnal senses of the soul are dead, however, then

the soul's spiritual senses by which it experienced itself will start coming back to life. Then it will know its sorrows, and the pains of its dormant wounds will indeed be felt, all the more intensely as they are its own. For the nearer an evil, the more it makes itself felt, just as the more interior good is the more beneficial.

THE SPIRIT[18]

10. The term "spirit" may be applied in many ways. For example, we call God a spirit. Also the air and the breath of air which, once received by the heart, is diffused throughout the body that it may distribute an element necessary to mortal life. Rightly, this type of spirit cannot be called "soul" since it changes with the changing air. The soul is also called spirit, whether it be that of man or that of the dumb animals. The rational mind is called spirit, since it possesses a spark which may be regarded as the soul's "eye" and whose property it is to reflect God and to know him.

The soul's eye is the mind, exempt from all bodily stain. The gaze of the mind is called reason, its discernment, vision. These three, then, are essential to every soul: wholesome eyes, the power to gaze and the power to see. A soul may be said to have wholesome eyes when it has been cleansed from mortal longings to the extent that these are foreign to it. A soul gazes when it fixes upon the divine light its eyes of contemplation. And finally, a soul is actually said to see when, engaged in the act of contemplative gazing, it discerns the indescribable extent of the joy and happiness, freedom from care, sereneness and cheerfulness to be had in the realm of the divine Light. The wholesomeness it enjoys makes it carefree; its gaze insures its being undivided in its purpose; and actual vision procures its bliss. Once freed from all impurities and washed of all stains, the soul will finally be at home with itself, fearing nothing from within and being the source

18. Dependent on Augustine, *De genesi ad litteram* 12, 7 and 23; DQA 33; and *Soliloquiae* 6 (12-13). This chap. also makes use of Hugh of St Victor's *De sacramentis* I, 6, 2.

of no distress. Only then does the soul, with unbelievably great confidence, strive on toward God, that is, toward the contemplation of Truth itself. The outcome of the undivided contemplative gaze is the vision of God, who is the end of contemplation. The soul is first made whole, then initiated into the divine knowledge, and, finally renewed by the divine Wisdom.

Spirit is a certain power of the soul, inferior to the mind, where the likenesses of corporeal things are expressed. The spirit itself is not a body, but may be said to be analogous to the body. The things seen by the spirit are not corporeal, only similar to corporeal realities. For example, the face of a man is to us externally visible, but it is also visible to our memory, where its image is preserved, an image which in itself is incorporeal but undeniably body-like.

The wonderful beauty of the world, too, is available to us exteriorly, and it also has its image in our memory—again an incorporeal image but body-like in appearance. We have recourse to it when we think about the beauty of the world with shut eyes. What a corporeal object in space is to the bodily senses, that the object's likeness in the memory is to the penetrating power of the soul. Likewise, just as the will must have an intention of uniting the object seen and the sight of it, so too the same willed intention is active in uniting the object's likeness, which is in the memory, and the vision of the thinker.

We say that this spirit is an image and likeness of God insofar as it can know the truth and love virtue. The image is in the knowing and the likeness in the loving. We speak of an image because knowing is a rational function, and we speak of a likeness because loving is spiritual. There is no intervening substance between the truth and the spirit. Therefore, we call "spirit" the rational faculty by which we reason, understand, and know. The Apostle calls this spirit "mind" when he says: "Renew yourselves in your mind's spirit,"[19] which is simply to say "your mind," for the spirit of one's

19. Eph 4:23

mind is nothing but the mind itself, just as when he says "the body of flesh" he simply means "the flesh."[20]

THE ORIGIN OF THE NAME "MIND"—THE SENSES AND THE IMAGINATION ARE DIFFERENT THINGS—THE EXTENT OF THE SOUL—WISDOM PRUDENCE[21]

11. The mind is called *mene* in Greek, which in Latin is rendered *luna* (moon). Just as the moon increases and decreases and changes at various times, restoring its form to what it had been and yet ever remaining new, so too the mind is capable of elevating our thoughts to sublime things and of lowering them to the least objects. The mind can also retreat within itself so as to refute error with the strength of truth. It can at one moment be occupied with governing bodily faculties and at the next concern itself with contemplating and consulting of an eternal nature.

Reason is a gaze of the mind whereby good and evil are distinguished, the virtues are chosen, and God is loved. The mind, which is capable of receiving all things since it bears a likeness to all things, is said to be all things on account of a natural power and a natural dignity it bears. By this we mean that it can grasp the invisible causes of things through understanding and gather the visible forms of physical things through the reception of the senses. Whether it goes out to sensible things through the senses or rises to invisible things through the understanding, the mind draws to itself the likenesses of things. It knows things present, understands those that are absent, probes into things it does not know, and abides with whatever it discovers.

We call "mind" the rational and intellectual light by which we reason, understand and know. The mind is so made in the image of God that it is formed by truth itself without the necessity of any intervening nature. The mind receives its name from its prominent position in the soul. For it is the pre-eminent power of the soul from which understanding de-

---

20. Col 1:22

21. Dependent on Cassiodorus, *De anima* 1 and 7; *Ep an* 10-11, 15, 17-18, 23; and Hugh of St Victor, *Miscellanea* I, 159, and *De unione corporis et spiritus* (hereafter cited as DUCS).

rives. Through its understanding the soul understands truth, and through its wisdom it comes to love truth. Wisdom is love of the good or a tasting of the good. The mind's vision is called understanding, and its taste goes by the name of wisdom. The former considers truth and the latter enjoys its possession. When we wish to ascend from lower objects to higher ones, we must first engage sense knowledge, then the imagination, then reason, discernment, understanding, and at the peak of the process, wisdom. The highest wisdom is God himself. Man's wisdom consists in devotion, which is exercised in the worship of God.[22]

Sense knowledge is that power of the soul by which it perceives as present the corporeal forms of bodily things. The imagination is that power of the soul which perceives the corporeal form of bodily things, but as absent. Sense knowledge perceives forms as they are found in matter; the imagination perceives them as found outside matter. So, then, when the power which is formed outside the individual—that is, sense knowledge—is brought within the mind, it is called imagination. We can readily see that the imagination has its origin in sense knowledge, and that its variations correspond to the multiplicity of sense-impressions.

The soul sees many things with its bodily eyes, but it also conceives many things with its phantasmal imagination. It pours itself out, as it were, over all things: it moves, swells and generally seems to behave in the manner of waves. Yet the soul never goes outside itself, but rather moves about within itself, as if in an enormous arena. It does not go out to exterior things, but rather pictures them within itself by its reflexive activity. We could almost say that the soul has width, length and height. Through charity the soul embraces God and all his faithful. Through meditation it can mull over all the things which God has wrought for our salvation from the beginning to the end of the world. Through contemplation, finally, the soul considers the heavenly things which are above.

---

22. This idea comes from Augustine, *De Trinitate* 12, 14.

Reason is that power of the soul which perceives the natures, forms, differences, properties, and accidents of corporeal things: in a word, all those incorporeal attributes which are not found apart from bodies, and subsist only in reason. By reflection—not by action—reason abstracts from bodies those things which are grounded in bodies. The nature of bodies, for example, according to which every body is a body, is not itself a body.

The discernment is that power of the soul which perceives invisible things, such as angels, demons, souls and every created spirit. The understanding is the soul's power which immediately contacts God. It looks upon the one who is highest truth and truly unchanging. Thus the soul perceives bodies with sense knowledge, the likenesses of bodies with the imagination, the natures of bodies with reason, created spirits with discernment and the uncreated spirit with understanding. Whatever is perceived by sense knowledge is represented by the imagination, formed by thought, probed by the soul's forethought, judged by insight, preserved by the memory, defined by discernment, and, finally, comprehended by understanding and led to meditation and contemplation.

Forethought is that power or inclination of the soul by which it reaches out and grasps the unknown. Thus forethought seeks out the unknown and insight defines what is found, while memory stores away those things which have been judged and brings them to light again for further judgment. This is how the ascent is made from lower to higher things, those at the bottom depending on those at the top.

Discernment is somehow an image and likeness of understanding, reason an image of discernment, and the imaginative faculty an image of reason. Fire, the highest of all bodies, is in turn joined by a certain likeness to reason, and air to fire, and water to air, and the earth to water. Sense knowledge informs the imagination, the imagination informs reason and reason results in knowledge and prudence. Again, by coming to its aid, divine prudence informs reason and produces understanding or wisdom. Thus in reason there is something which tends toward the heavenly things which are above. This tendency we call wisdom. And there is something else which concerns itself with passing and perishable things. This we call prudence. These two tendencies derive from reason and have their seat in reason. Thus reason tends to go in two directions: upwards, the way of wisdom, and downwards, the way of prudence. This division is like that of human beings into men and women. Man is superior and rules, while woman is inferior and is ruled. Whence the saying: "Better a man's wrong-doing than a woman's goodness."[23] It is, indeed, better to be fired up by heavenly desires and mortify the flesh even to the point of depriving it of necessities, than to be enervated by carnal desire in seeking to satisfy the flesh with every pleasure.

THE ROLE OF THE SENSES[24]

12. The senses operate outwardly. A bodily eye, even though endowed by its nature with the power of sight, will nevertheless not attain to seeing, nor an ear to hearing, unless an external light or sound be present. The imagination operates from below[25] since it arises from sense-perception. Reason operates inwardly. Although it is a rational spirit endowed by its Maker with the ability to understand the true and love the good, yet reason will never attain to the knowledge of wisdom and to the desire of charity unless it is suffused by the rays of an inward light and kindled by its warmth.

Discernment and understanding operate on a higher level, because God is fire and light.[26] This light sends out from itself that splendor which it yet retains within itself and illumines a man's understanding that he might acknowledge truth. This fire sends out from itself a warmth without losing any of its warmth and kindles a man's power of desire that he

23. Eccles 42:14

24. Dependent on *Ep an* 16, 21-22; and Hugh of St Victor, *Commentarium in Lucam* 1, 47. Cf. *Phys an* 3 and 14.

25. In place of the *exterius* of the PL text, we follow the reading suggested in the note there which is that found also in *Ep an* 22; *inferius*: from below.

26. Deut 4:24; Heb 12:29; 1 Jn 1:5

might love virtue. And just as the eye cannot see the sun except in the sun's light, so too understanding cannot see the true and divine light except in its light. That is why the Prophet says: "in your light, O Lord, we shall see light."[27] When this mortal body puts on immortality and this perishable body puts on incorruptibility,[28] then we will be made spiritual both in mind and in body. Through our minds' enlightening we will know all things in the measure proper to us, and through the mobility of an imperishable body we will be able to be everywhere at once. We will fly in mind through contemplation and we will fly in body because of our incorruptibility. We will discern things with our mind, but also with our body, since our bodily senses will be transformed into reason, and reason itself into discernment, discernment into understanding, understanding into God.

Visible things are perceived by sense knowledge. The images and likenesses of visible things are found in the imagination. The causes and definitions of visible things and the seeking out of invisible things are proper to reason. The comprehension and contemplation of spiritual and divine things belong to discernment and understanding. Now sense knowledge and imagination cannot rise to the level of reason, but rather remaining below they can lead it in a certain sense and from afar indicate certain things to which they cannot attain. In a similar manner reason can aid discernment and understanding, but cannot itself rise to their level, since it has its own goals and ends which it cannot go beyond.

We have sense knowledge and imagination in common with the other animals. They, too, see visible things and remember what they have seen. They even surpass us in certain senses.[29] It was only just that dumb animals should receive something extra by way of senses since they were to receive no discernment. On the other hand, man is made all the more aware of his need to use his reason as he realizes the greater deficiency of his senses.

27. Ps 35:10
28. 1 Cor 15:54
29. Cf. *Phys an* 3.

Reason begins at the point where something exists which we do not have in common with animals. Some things are below reason, some things are at reason's own level, and still other things are above it. Below reason are the things we perceive by sense knowledge, such as hard and soft, hot and cold, white and black, sweet and bitter. On reason's own level, and accessible to reason, are the things we grasp by reason, such as the favorable and the unfavorable, the true and the false, the just and the unjust. Thus reason is a certain movement of the intellectual soul which whets the mind's sight by distinguishing between true and false things. Above reason are found those things which are neither taught by sense knowledge nor inculcated by reason, but rather are grasped from divine revelation, or believed on the authority of Sacred Scripture. Such is the truth of God's being three in one substance and substantially one in three persons. We say that God is the whole of things and no one thing in particular. This is why he is not subject to the workings of reason, since reason can only deal with particular things.

THE DEFINITION OF THE SOUL—ITS ACTS, SIMPLICITY, POTENCIES AND POWERS[30]

13. The soul is a spirit which is intellectual, rational, always living, always in motion, and capable of willing both the good and the bad. According to its Maker's kindness and the exercise of its role, the soul is called by various names. It is called "soul" when it enlivens, "spirit" when it contemplates, "sense" when it feels, "intellectual soul" when it knows. Furthermore, the soul is termed "mind" when it understands, "reason" when it distinguishes, "memory" when it remembers, and "will" when it consents. Although all of these differ in name, yet they are but one substance, since all of these aspects are really but one soul. The properties are diverse, but the essence one. There is a difference, however, between the concepts "spirit" and "soul." Every soul is a spirit, but not every spirit is a soul.

30. Dependent on Alcuin, *De ratione animae* 10-11; Hugh of St Victor, *Didascalicon, II, 4; Ep an* 3-4.

The soul engages in two types of acts. On the one hand it rises toward God; on the other it leans toward the flesh. And this is the manner of its leaning: being subtle and invisible, the soul cannot be seen, but through its powers it operates and makes its presence known. Through its positive appetite it desires; through its negative appetite it rejects; and through its rationality it distinguishes between the two. The soul's whole essence consists in these powers, nor is it divided into parts since it is simple and undivided. If at times the soul is said to have parts, we must understand this is said because of certain likenesses, rather than as the actual statement of its makeup.

The soul is a simple substance. Likewise reason is in substance neither more nor less than the soul itself. So, too, the positive and negative appetites are neither more nor less than the soul itself. But we assign different names to one and the same substance according to its diverse powers. The soul has these powers even before it unites with the body. They are natural to it and are nothing other than the soul itself. The whole substance of the soul is perfect and complete when it has these three faculties: rationality, the positive appetite, and the negative appetite. We may even speak of these as the soul's "trinity." This trinity is the very unity of the soul and the soul itself.

God is *all* that he has; the soul is *some* of the things it has. It has certain things naturally and it is itself all these things. For the powers and potencies of the soul are the same thing as the soul. It also has accidentals which are not the same as the soul. The soul is the same as its own powers, but not the same as its virtues. For the soul is not its own prudence, nor its temperance, nor its fortitude, nor its justice. The powers of the soul are: rationality, the positive appetite, and the negative appetite. The potencies of the soul are: sense knowledge, imagination, reason, memory, discernment and understanding. Now the powers may interchangeably be termed potencies and vice versa.

FRIENDSHIP BETWEEN BODY AND SOUL—THREE ADMIRABLE UNIONS
—THE PROPER GOOD OF THE BODY AND OF THE SOUL[31]

14. Our soul is joined to our body by certain desires and a certain friendship which keep us from hating our own flesh. Even though the soul is at times oppressed by its relationship to the body, it nevertheless loves the body in an ineffable way. It loves its prison and cannot therefore be liberated. The soul is greatly affected by the body's sufferings. Unable itself to die, still the soul fears annihilation. Although its nature keeps it from being defective, yet the soul fears defectiveness. It is nourished by the eyes' sight; it delights at hearing euphonious sounds; it is gladdened by exquisite odors; it is refreshed by generous banquets. And even though the soul itself does not directly participate in these activities, yet it is afflicted with a heavy melancholy if they should be lacking. Because of this the soul is at times infiltrated by vices contrary to reason. For as the soul mercifully loosens the controls on its beloved body, it is unaware that an occasion is being prepared for sin.

Through the senses the soul proceeds to move and enliven the body. There are nine openings in the human body through which, in a natural way, enters and exits everything by which the body is enlivened and ruled. Now the highest part of the body and the lowest part of the spirit have much in common, which makes it possible for them to be easily joined in a personal union without a confusion of natures. For similar things find joy in similar objects. Thus the soul, which is truly a spirit, and the flesh, which is truly a body, easily and fittingly meet at their extremes. The extremes are the imaginative faculty—which is not a body, but similar to a body—and the faculty of sensation in the flesh—which is

---

31. Dependent on Cassiodorus, *De anima* 4-5; *Ep an* 11; and Hugh of St Victor, *Didascalicon* II, 5; *De sacramentis* I, 6, 3, 5-6; *Miscellanea* I, 120, 122; *De vanitate mundi* 2; and the *De substantia dilectionis* 6. The last two sentences are quoted from Gregory of Nazianzen, *Oratio* II, 7.

almost a spirit, since it cannot exist without the soul. The
highest part of the soul, understanding or the mind, bears the
image and likeness of that which is higher than it, which is
God; whence the soul can be receptive of God and, at his
willing it, can be taken up to a personal union with him
without any violation to its nature. Likewise the highest part
of the flesh, the faculty of sensation, which bears a likeness
to the soul, can receive the soul's essence that the two may
come to a personal union. We should not marvel at this, since
even in the sense knowledge and memory of an animal there
is a certain imitation of rationality, also an imitation of will
in the animal's desire and of disapproval in the things which
it refuses. For a corporeal spirit, which is a body, truly distinguishes between many things with its natural power of
knowledge, chooses with its positive appetite and rejects
because of its natural negative appetite.

Corporeal life has certain levels which signal its growth
toward being an image of the highest life. The first level is
that of sensation. The second is imagination operating
through the senses. The third is the memory of things
conceived through the imagination. The fourth is a certain
foreknowledge coming from sense perception which lacks the
discretion of understanding. It is not reason, but contains a
certain image of reason. In all of these instances corporeal life
imitates spiritual life. Firstly, because it senses. Secondly,
because it conceives sense knowledge. Thirdly, because it
retains the things conceived. Fourthly, because it is inclined
either to desire or to flee from certain things in a way similar
to reason's, whether it be with respect to things imagined or
to things sensed. There are two faculties, then, which very
fittingly signal the meeting of the flesh and of the soul. These
are the faculty of sensation in the flesh, which is mostly fire,
and the imaginative faculty, which is termed "a fiery
strength." This is why someone, speaking of souls, once said:
"Their strength is fiery and their origin is heaven."[32]

32. Virgil, *Aeneid* 6:730.

This fellowship between the flesh and the soul is indeed admirable; the breath of life is joined to the slime of the earth. Thus it was written: "God made man out of the slime of the earth, and he breathed the breath of life into man's face."[33] God gave man sense knowledge and discernment that he might through sense knowledge give life to the mire he had joined to himself and rule it through discernment. Through discernment man was to go inside himself and contemplate God's wisdom; through sense knowledge man was to go outside himself and contemplate the works of wisdom. God enlightened man inwardly with discernment and beautified him outwardly with sense knowledge, so that man might find refreshment in both instances, happiness within and rejoicing without.

Because exterior goods cannot last long, man has been told to return from exterior to interior things, and to ascend from interior things to those above. Such is the dignity of the human condition that none but the highest good can suffice for it. Awesome indeed it is that things so radically different from one another could be so intimately conjoined. And it is no less awesome that God united himself to the slime of our flesh so that God and slime should be joined, such sublimeness with such baseness. For there is nothing more sublime than God, nothing baser than slime. If the first conjunction, that of body and soul, had been a subject of marvel, so was the second, nor will the third be any less so, when man, the angels and God will be one spirit.

Man is good by the same goodness that angels are good, and they will both be blessed on account of the same goodness, if only they desire the same thing with the same will and spirit. If God could conjoin in one association and friendship the very disparate natures of flesh and soul, then it will not be impossible for God to exalt the rational spirit, which had been humiliated to sharing fellowship with an earthly body, raising it to the participation of his glory, along with its

33. Gen 2:7

glorified body. Now that same body will be for the spirit reason for glory. This fellowship will be with those blessed spirits who remained constant in all their purity. The Most High created the spirit out of pure love, not out of necessity, so that he could make it a participant in his own beatitude.

If there is, then, such joy and happiness in this temporal life, which consists in the presence of the spirit in a perishable body, what will be the happiness and joy in eternal life which comes from the presence of the Deity in a rational spirit? If the body is subject to the intellectual soul and the intellectual soul to God, then the spirit shall be one with God. And so indeed it will be if the spirit remains humble and acknowledges its Maker's graciousness, through which it will be exalted and glorified.

Man is made up of flesh and an intellectual soul, and each of these has its own proper good which is the source of its gladness and joy. God and his overflowing sweetness are the soul's proper good. The world and its abundant joy are the proper good of the flesh. Now while this world is external to man, God is interior to him. For nothing is more inward and more present than God. He is inside everything because all things are in him; he is outside everything because he is above all things. Returning to God from the world around us, then, we should go upwards from lower to higher things by passing through ourselves. Ascending to God means, first of all, going into oneself; but it further entails a going beyond oneself, at one's deepest being, which cannot be put into words. A man may truly be said to have ascended to God when, going inside himself even to his deepest being, he transcends himself.[34] We should, therefore, recollect our heart from the distractions of this world and invite it to partake of interior joys. And if we are unable to keep a constant check on our heart, we should at least refrain from forbidden and vain thoughts, so that we might at times fix our hearts on the light of divine contemplation. Our heart finds its rest in its desire to abide in God's

34. This basic insight has been shared by Cistercians of all times; it was central in the theology of prayer of Thomas Merton. See John Higgins, *Merton's Theology of Prayer*, CS 18 (Spencer, Mass., Cistercian Publications, 1971), pp. 25ff.

love. And the life of our heart is this: contemplating its God and being sweetly refreshed by its contemplation. It is always sweet for our heart to consider that in whose love and praise it always delights. Nothing, then, seems more beneficial to a happy life than that a man should turn into himself, having closed his carnal senses and having placed himself outside of the flesh and of the world. Estranged from the lust of perishable things, he will speak only to himself and to God.[35]

HOW THE BODY IS RULED BY THE SOUL—THE BODY'S MAKEUP— THE CONSEQUENCES OF ITS HARMONY OR DISHARMONY [36]

15. Since the soul is incorporeal it rules its body through the two finest substances, which are fire and air. Fire and air are the foremost bodies in this world, and thus most like spirits. These two are the first to receive the commands of the life-giving soul, since they are closer to being incorporeal substances than are moisture and earth, so that the whole mass of the body is directed by the immediate instrumentality of fire and air. Without them there would be no senses in the body and no spontaneous moving of the body on the part of the soul. Fire and air, being light in weight, move water and earth, which are heavy. This is why we see bodies move even after the soul has left them. For fire and air are held together in an earthly, humid body by the presence of the soul, so that a harmony of fire, air, earth and moisture results. But after the soul's departure from the body, they escape to higher things and free themselves.

Now this is the body's makeup. The body consists, first of all, of organs with a specific function. But all of these are in turn made up of similar cells, the cells from humors, the humors from consumed food, and the food from the elements. None of these, of course, is the soul. But the soul plays upon them as upon an instrument, and through them

35. As noted above (n.31) the last two sentences are from Gregory of Nazianzen.

36. Dependent on Augustine, *De genesi ad litteram* 7, 15 and 20; DQA 31; and *Ep an* 13 and 18.

instructs the body in this life in which man becomes a living soul. When these constituent parts of the body are harmonious and well-ordered they work together in giving the body life, and the soul never departs. But if the parts should be unduly mingled and confused, then the soul must reluctantly withdraw, taking with it all its faculties: sense knowledge, imagination, reason, discernment, understanding, the positive appetite, and the negative appetite. And from these, according to its merits, the soul passes over to either joy or pain. While the body had previously been integrated like a well-tempered instrument, ever ready to produce music at the least touch, now, on the contrary, it lies broken and useless. With the elemental components of the body each gone to its own milieu, the soul no longer has an instrument upon which to exercise its faculties, and so it rests from the movements by which it moved the body through time and space. (The soul itself had moved through time, but not through space.) Even though the instrument had been destroyed, yet the melody has not ended, nor has the player perished.

Placed between God and the body, the soul moves through time by remembering the forgotten, by learning the unknown and by willing what had been denied. However, it does not move through space, since it is not extended over the space of places. God, for his part, does not need a body in order to exist, nor a place in order to be somewhere, nor a time in order to be at some time. Neither does he need a cause (for he is not originated), nor a form (for he is not one thing in particular), nor some kind of subject in which to subsist or to which to adhere.

THE EXCELLENCE OF A SOUL ENDOWED WITH CHARITY[37]

16. The soul has a certain natural property which is more excellent than the bulk of worldly elements. This property cannot be conceived in terms of the phantasmal, corporeal images which are perceived through the senses of the flesh.

37. Cf. Hugh of St Victor, *De laude caritatis* and the *Manuale* 21.

Rather must it be understood with the mind and experienced in one's very life. This property can be understood, but not felt. It is not a body, nor is it God, nor the non-sensory life of trees, nor the irrational life of animals. It is life, and life eternal.

In its present state this life is less than that of the angels.[38] But if it is lived in accordance with our Maker's precepts, it will one day be equal to that of angels. Now God's precept was that we should abide in his love. He said: "Abide in my love."[39] Through love he has united the rational creature to himself, so that these should always have him near and abide in him, delighting, rejoicing and exulting in him and because of him. Through love rational creatures have been united to their Maker and to one another. For only the bond of love has the power to unite two beings as if they were one. Through the love of God we all cling to him, and through the love of neighbor we are all made one. In this way the common good becomes the good of each individual and each one possesses in another what he does not have in himself. Charity is God's road to men and men's road to God. For through charity God came to men, he made himself present among them, he became man. Through charity men love God, choose God, run to God, arrive at God. Charity is such a personal thing with God that he refuses to make his dwelling where there is no charity. Therefore, if we have charity, we have God, for "God is charity."[40]

INCITEMENT TO THE LOVE OF GOD[41]

17. What a wretched man I am! What should be the extent of my love for God, who made me when I did not exist and redeemed me after I had perished? I did not exist and he made me out of nothing. He did not make me a stone, nor a

38. Ps 8:6
39. Jn 15:9
40. 1 Jn 4:8
41. Dependent on Hugh of St Victor, *De arrha animae* and *De modo orandi*. This chap. was later used in the seventh of the twelfth-century *Meditationes* ascribed to St Anselm.

tree, nor a bird, nor a dumb animal of any kind, but he wished me to be a man. He gave me life, feeling, the ability to discern. I had perished and he condescended to me, a mortal. He took on mortality, he endured suffering, conquered death, and in this way he restored me to what I had been. Sold for the price of my sins, I had been ruined and went into exile. And yet, he followed after me in order to buy me back. He so loved me that he put down his own blood as my price, and by means of this transaction he brought me back from my exile and bought me back from my slave's condition. He even called me by his own name, so that remembrance of him should never leave me. He anointed me with the same oil of gladness with which he was anointed,[42] so that anointed by the Anointed, I might henceforth be called Christian after the name of Christ.

In these various ways his grace and his mercy have always come to my rescue. For my liberator has often freed me from many dangers. When I have strayed, he has led me back. When I have been in ignorance, he has instructed me. When I have sinned, he has corrected me. When I have been sad, he has been my consolation. When I was in despair, he strengthened me. When I fell, he raised me up. When I stood up, he supported me. When I started to walk, he led me on. When I came to him, he received me. These and many other things has my God done for me, and I shall never tire of talking sweetly about them; by thinking about them and thanking him for them I will always have reason to praise and love him for all his benefits. God watches over all of us, filling each of us with his presence. Everywhere present, he takes care of all by providing for us both as individuals and as a group. He does it in such a way that I see him concerned about taking care of me personally, that it is as if I stood watch over myself. He seems to have forgotten all else and to be concerned about only me. He always manifests his presence, and there is no end to his offers of help, if only he finds me ready to co-operate. No matter where I might turn, he never

42. Ps 44:8

forsakes me if I do not first forsake him. Wherever I might be, he is not absent, because he is everywhere. And wherever I go, there do I find him ready to be my companion. He likewise aids me in whatever I do, being, as he is, the constant supervisor of all my thoughts, intents and actions.

When I ponder over these things, I am thrown into confusion by both great awe and great shame, because I realize that he is always present to me and that he sees all my hidden doings. There are many things in me which make me blush when I stand before him and which, I fear, make me very displeasing to him. And for all these things I have nothing with which to repay him except only that I love him. For there is no better nor more becoming way of repaying something given through love than by loving in return. These few thoughts may seem to be an irrelevant digression from my subject, but they are certainly not without their usefulness for me and for those who, with me, feel what I feel.

THE SOUL, LIFE OF THE BODY—HOW THE SOUL IS BOTH MORTAL AND IMMORTAL, CORPOREAL AND INCORPOREAL— HOW THE SOUL IS PRESENT IN THE BODY[43]

18. The soul enlivens the body by its presence. It is bound to the body in such a way that it cannot separate itself from the body at will, nor can it hold back when it hears its Maker's beckoning. The life of the body is grounded in the life of the soul, and the soul's death is derived from the body's death. For the soul vivifies the flesh by giving it of its own life; it animates it by watering it from the fount of its own nature. If, for its part, the flesh clings to forbidden lusts, it can in fact kill the soul through the corruptibility of its own matter. When one of the two natures conquers, the other is conquered and both take on the nature of whichever is the victor, that is, either the soul makes the flesh spiritual by adorning it with virtues, or the flesh makes the soul carnal by conquering it.

43. Dependent on Cassiodorus, *De anima* 6-8; LDE 11-12; Hugh of St Victor, *De sacramentis* I, 3, 18; *Ep an* 14.

The soul can have no part in death unless death is ministered to it by the vices, nor can the flesh retain any life within itself unless it be watered by the soul. Neither can one nature be transformed into the other unless the soul is infected by vices or unless the flesh is abandoned by the virtues. The soul is stamped with the seal of reason. Reason teaches the soul most excellent skills and instructs it with select disciplines, so that it can taste of the divine and deal with the human. This is the way the soul, a rational substance, rightly surpasses the other animals. The soul, properly speaking, is a rational substance and a rational spirit. The soul is immortal because it does not differ from the likeness of its Maker. It could not be an image and likeness of God if it had death as its confining goal. We thus see that according to a certain manner of life which it cannot lose the soul is immortal; but according to a certain changeableness by which it can become better or worse, it is mortal. It is corporeal in comparison with the incorporeal God, just as it is mortal when it ceases to live in happiness, though it cannot cease to live even though it is in misery. Only God—Father, Son and Holy Spirit—can be believed to be invisible and incorporeal by nature.

We say that God is incorporeal and invisible because he is infinite, boundless, simple, self-sufficient, and self-sustaining in every way. Because he is everywhere in himself, God is discerned to be invisible and incorporeal. Every rational creature on the other hand is corporeal. The angels and all the virtues are corporeal even though they do not subsist in flesh. We say that intellectual natures are corporeal because they are bound by a place. The human soul, for instance, is shut in by the flesh; for this reason the soul can be said both to be in a place and to be localized. The soul is said to be in a place because it can be present either here or at any other one place. And it is said to be localized since the whole of it can only be in one place at a time.

Not having bodily bulk, neither does the soul have bodily dimensions or boundaries. Yet it is said to be localized because through its presence and its operation it is limited to a definite place. But it is not localized in the same way a body is localized, having a beginning, a middle and an end. By comparison with God's incorporeal nature, which is everywhere supremely unchanging, the soul is corporeal (for the soul is not the same as God.) But neither can the soul be said to be situated in or to move through the space of a given place, occupying a greater area with its bigger parts and a smaller area with its lesser parts, and to be smaller in a part than in the whole. In actual fact the soul is wholly present in even the smallest parts of the body. It is erroneous to say that in the smaller parts of the body there is a smaller part of the soul, and in the greater parts a greater. More attentive in one part and more negligent in another, the soul is completely present in all the parts and completely present in each part. We say that God is wholly present everywhere in the entire world and in each of his creatures. In the same way we can say that the soul is wholly present everywhere in its entire body, which is the soul's own world, as it were, yet more intensely present in the heart and in the brain, just as God is said to be present especially in heaven.

WHEN THE SOUL ACTS, THE WHOLE OF IT ACTS[44]

19. The soul is invisible and incorporeal. If it were visible, it would also be corporeal. And if it were corporeal, it would have parts and would also be divisible. In that case it could not be wholly present in one place at the same time. No body can be totally affected at the same time, or at the same time totally make its own impression. As it is, however, the soul is wholly present at the same time in all of its movements and actions. The whole of it sees and remembers what it has seen. The whole of it hears and recalls the heard sounds. The whole of it smells and evokes the smelt odors. The whole of it tastes through the tongue and palate and distinguishes between flavors. It is the whole soul which touches hard and soft things, and the whole soul which either approves or rejects

44. Dependent on *Phys an* 10.

things. If we sense something to be hot or cold with our fingertips, it is the whole soul which does the sensing. The whole soul is sight, the whole soul is hearing. The whole soul remembers, and since all of it remembers, all of it is memory. Since all of it wills, all of it is will. Since all of it thinks, all of it is thought. Since all of it loves, all of it is love. The soul can, however, think in part and love in part.

THE SOUL'S POWERS IN BEHALF OF VIRTUES—AND AGAINST VICES—THE SACRAMENTAL VIRTUES—BY WHAT MEANS THE SOUL ADHERES TO GOD, AND BY WHAT MEANS TO THE BODY—THE SOUL'S NATURAL POWER[45]

20. The soul has affections which incite it toward the virtues. Such are sorrow for sins, fear of punishment, desire of things promised, and joy in rewards: they are incitements of virtues. The soul also has virtues which instruct it and arm it against the vices. Because of its prudence, for example, the soul knows what it should do. Its temperance counteracts prosperity, its fortitude counteracts adversity. Its justice tells it what is due to each person. Prudence consists in knowing one's capabilities, fortitude in doing what one can do, temperance in not presuming to do what one cannot do, justice in not wanting to do more than one is capable. Prudence is exercised in one's choices, temperance is exercised in the things one uses, fortitude in the things that must be borne, justice when one apportions. Prudence is not desiring anything which will be regretted and not wishing to do anything but what is just. Temperance is fearing only base things and guiding by reason all our actions and thoughts. Fortitude is not only curbing worldly lusts, but forgetting them inwardly. Justice is directing every thought of the intellectual soul to God alone and gazing on him with all the penetrating power of the mind as if nothing else existed.

The soul also has sacramental virtues to which it is initiated. Such are faith, hope, the sacrament of baptism, anointing, confirmation and the other virtues which conse-

45. Dependent on William of St Thierry's *Phys corp* 5.

crate the soul to God. The soul has other virtues which make it progress and which unite it to God; such are humility, purity and charity. Humility subjects the soul to God, purity joins the soul to God and charity unites the soul with God.

The soul has certain powers by which it is mixed with the body. We designate the first of these as the natural power, the second as the vital power, and the third as the animal power. Just as God, who is one and three, true and perfect, holds, fills, sustains, surpasses and embraces all things, so too, the soul is diffused throughout the whole body on account of the three above-mentioned impulses. This diffusion does not result from spatial expansion, but from vital intention.

The natural power produces blood and other humors in the liver, which it then conveys through the veins to all the bodily members that these may be nourished and grow. This power has four aspects: the appetitive, the retentive, the expulsive, and the distributive. In its appetitive aspect the natural power seeks the things that are necessary for the body. In its retentive aspect the natural power retains what has been eaten until it is duly disgested. In its expulsive aspect it expels from the body whatever is harmful or useless. Finally, in its distributive aspect the natural power distributes to the different bodily members the healthy humors of beneficial foods, in the measure needed by each member. Now all animals possess these powers and thus they are seen to be proper to the body and not the soul.

THE VITAL POWER[46]

21. The vital power is found in the heart. It regulates the heart's heat by the inhaling and exhaling of air. In this way it provides life and health for the whole body. The vital power drives the blood, which has been purified by fresh air, throughout the body by means of pulsing veins, called arteries. Physicians are able to tell from the movement of these arteries whether or not the heart is functioning well.

46. Cf. *Phys corp* 5.

THE THREEFOLD ANIMAL POWER[47]

22. The animal power is found in the brain, and from there it gives rise to the body's five senses. This power elicits sounds to come forth and commands the movement of the bodily members. Now the brain has three lobes. The first of these is the anterior lobe from which the senses are derived. The second is the posterior lobe, from which movement takes its origin. The third is located between the other two and is called the medial or rational lobe.

This is how the body's senses are formed. Light is the finest substance in the body, and for this reason it is most like the soul and closest to it. This light is first diffused throughout the eyes themselves, flashing in the eyes' beams so that objects may be seen. Then by some mixture, first with pure air, secondly with misty and foggy air, thirdly with more fleshy humor, fourthly with the density of the soil, it perfects the five senses with the eyes' sight, where light alone prevails. I think that, because these senses are located in the face, it has been written that God "breathed the breath of life into man's face, and man was made a living soul." [48]

The anterior part of the brain is rightly placed before the posterior, because the anterior leads while the posterior follows. The former gives us the senses, while the latter is responsible for movement, just as thought precedes action. These powers can be said to belong both to the soul and to the body, because they are operated in the body by the soul and cannot come to be without the action of both. In the first or anterior part of the brain the animal power is called phantasmal or imaginary, because in this part are contained the likenesses and images of corporeal things, and hence it is spoken of as the imaginative faculty. In the medial part of the brain the power is termed rational, since there it probes and makes judgments upon the things that are represented through the imagination. In the third or posterior part of the brain the animal power is termed memorial, because there it entrusts to memory whatever reason has judged.

47. Cf. *Phys corp* 5-7 and *De genesi ad litteram* 7, 18; 12, 16.
48. Gen 2:7

HOW MANY POWERS OF THE SOUL THERE ARE–SEXUAL DREAMS[49]

23. We have one faculty by which we sense bodies. This we do with the body's five senses. We have another faculty by which we discern those things which are not bodies, but similar to bodies. Thus we see ourselves as being similar to bodies. There is still a third and different faculty in us by which we perceive those things which are neither bodies nor likenesses of bodies, and which have no images similar to themselves, such as God, the rational mind itself, understanding and reason. Such, too, are the virtues—prudence, justice, chastity, charity, piety—and all the other things which we enumerate, discern and define by understanding them and thinking about them.

Now the soul is not a body, since not every likeness of a body is a body. When you sleep something like a body may appear which is not your body, but your soul. Nor is it a true body, rather the likeness of your body. While your body is reclining that likeness can be walking about. Your bodily tongue may be silent, the likeness will speak. Even if your eyes are shut, the likeness has vision. And so in that likeness you can recognize a detailed replica of your flesh. In that likeness your soul can wander over familiar or unknown places, capable of feeling joy or sadness. In the likeness of its body the soul of a dead man, like that of a sleeping man, can experience good and bad things. The things to which souls deprived of bodies become attached, for better or for worse, are not corporeal, but similar to corporeal things. These souls appear to themselves to be similar to their own bodies. But the joy and the annoyance experienced by these souls are, nevertheless, true joy and true annoyance, made from a spiritual substance in a spiritual substance.

It is certain that there is in us some spiritual nature where either the likenesses of corporeal things are formed or where these likenesses are imprinted ready-formed. This happens when we perceive present objects by one of the body's senses and the likeness of these objects is immediately formed in the

49. Dependent on *De genesi ad litteram* 12, 20, 32, 23, 12, 15.

spirit and stored in the memory. This also happens when we think of known or unknown objects which are absent, and a spiritual discernment is formed as a result. Instead of forming judgments and opinions, we contrive innumerable things in our mind which either do not exist at all or which at least are not known to exist. Many times, too, the forms of innumerable things wander about in our mind while we are engaged in doing something or in planning to get something done. Some spirit is then snatching up our soul and the soul is distracted to the consideration of the intruding forms, which may be good or bad. The images of corporeal things can be so firmly impressed upon the spirit that we would think it was the body's senses perceiving other bodies, rather than images of bodies. This phenomenon takes place as a result of either an intense concentration of thought or the violence of an illness (such as occurs to delirious persons who are running a high fever) or by the influence of some other spirit either good or evil. In either instance things that are far-removed are perceived as present, and things which do not even exist come to life in the mind.

Sleeping persons often see things which may have much meaning or none at all. The images of corporeal things can at times be seen so vividly by sleepers that there seems to be no difference between the images seen in sleep and the actual things seen in a waking state. Thus, one can hardly distinguish between the things sleepers see and the true activities of persons who are awake. This immediately effects movements of the flesh in sleeping persons. Against their intention and the norms of right behavior they take positions proper to sexual intercourse and the fluid which nature collects in their bodies is emitted through the genital passages. Waking persons who are chaste can control such movement of the flesh. Sleeping persons, however, cannot because they are not empowered in their state of repressed corporeal images, which are the natural source of the flesh's movements. The flesh's movement is followed for sleepers by what is to be expected, something which waking persons cannot engage in without sin.

We see then how the images of corporeal things appear in the spirit and how many things are contrived in place of sound judgment or even contrary to sound judgment. The soul itself is always in movement by its own motion. But sometimes, because the body does not allow the soul to perceive corporeal things fully or to direct to corporeal things the full drive of the soul's exertion, the soul waits for the body to be deep in slumber and proceeds on its own either to produce likenesses of corporeal things just as it is accustomed to think about the images of bodies on its own, or to consider the objects which are offered to it by some spirit or other.

WHAT THE SOUL IS AND WHAT IT IS NOT—THREE TYPES OF VISION—WHICH OF THESE ARE LIABLE TO BE FALSE—ECSTASY—OTHER TYPES OF VISIONS[50]

24. The soul is a spiritual substance. It is simple indestructible, invisible, incorporeal, passible, changeable, lacking weight, shape or color. We should not believe it to be a part of God nor of the same substance as God, nor yet made out of some elemental matter. Rather, it is a creature of God, created out of nothing. If God had made the soul out of himself, it would surely not be prone to vice or changeable or at times in a pitiable state. If, on the other hand, the soul had been fashioned out of the elements it would perforce be corporeal. Being incorporeal, the soul has an unknown origin. It does have a beginning, however, but no end. Since it has a spiritual nature, the soul is unalloyed, having no earthy consistency or anything in common with water, air or fire. It has no color, it is not contained in any place; it is not outlined by specific members as is the body, nor is it defined by a given space. We must think of the soul and understand it to be like wisdom, justice and the other virtues created by the Almighty. The soul is invisible by nature. Thus, it remains invisible while it is in the body and it is invisible when it leaves the body.

50. Dependent on Isidore of Seville, *De differentiis* 2, 26, 23 and *De genesi ad litteram* 12, chaps, 11, 14, 18-26, 30;

The soul sees other bodies through the body in which it is. In this way it sees the heavens, the earth and whatever is in them which is attainable by our eyes. In the spirit the soul sees bodies' likenesses. Now whatever is not a body, but is something nevertheless, is rightly called a spirit. Resultannly, the soul can at times be taken up by a certain hidden spiritual power so that instead of seeing bodies it sees in the spirit the distinct likenesses of corporeal things. But by discernment the soul perceives those things which neither are bodies nor have the form of bodies. Such are justice, wisdom, the mind itself and every good sentiment of the soul.

There are, then, three manifest types of vision: the first is corporeal and involves the perception of bodies through the body's senses; the second is spiritual, consisting in the vision of bodily likenesses in the spirit, not in the mind; the third type of vision is the intellectual. Intellectual vision is perceiving those things which have neither bodies nor bodily shapes.

In intellectual vision the soul never makes a mistake. If the soul understands something it is true. If it is not true, it is not understood. In corporeal vision, however, the soul can often be mistaken, as when it attributes to actual bodies what it perceives only in the senses of the body. Those at sea, for instance, may see objects on the land as moving, whereas actually they are still. Likewise those who gaze at the stars may think that stars are stationary, whereas in fact they are moving. When the beams of the eyes are refracted, one single object can appear to have two shapes, one man with two heads, an oar in the water can seem broken, and so forth.

Even in spiritual vision the soul can be mistaken and misled. The things it sees can at times be true, at times false, at times troubled, and at times tranquil. True things which are seen are sometimes extremely similar to future events, and those which are openly uttered are sometimes wrought with obscure meanings and figurative pronouncements. In ecstacy, for example, when the soul is far-removed from all the body's senses, more than when the body is asleep but less than in death, the soul cannot be mistaken. Supported by God or with someone supplying it with what it sees, the soul receives a great revelation as happened to John in the *Book of Revelation*. When the soul is taken up by a good spirit, it cannot be mistaken, because the holy angels in a marvelous manner are able to communicate to us the things which they themselves see by means of a powerful union and relationship which they establish with us. They convey their vision to our spirit in an ineffable way. Angels are in charge of judging and ministering to corporeal things. They can so grasp in their spirit the significant likenesses of corporeal things and they can probe them with such accuracy that they are able to convey them to men's spirits through revelation. The Lord's angel thus appeared to Joseph in dreams and said: "Do not be afraid to take Mary as your wife."[51] And at another time he said: "Take the child and his mother and flee into Egypt."[52] God also says through the prophet: "I will pour out my spirit over all flesh. Your young men shall see visions and your old men shall dream dreams."[53]

There are other more common ways of seeing on the human level. These can either arise in various ways from our own spirit or they can be suggested to our spirit by the intellectual soul, according as we are affected by the body or the mind. Waking men are not the only ones who mull over their concerns by thinking with corporeal images; sleeping men often dream about the things they need. They carry on business from avarice; or they partake of food and drink to their soul's content if they happen to be hungry or thirsty while they sleep. When waking men prophesy we know that the thoughts they utter are given them in some hidden manner. This was the case with Caiaphas the high priest, who prophesied when he had no intention of doing so.[54]

The soul sees many things, and the nature of all its visions is the same whether they be in waking, sleeping or in sick persons. The things seen are of the same nature as the spirit, since it is from the spirit that the likenesses of bodies proceed and in the

51. Mt 1:20
52. Mt 2:13
53. Joel 2:28
54. Jn 11:51

spirit that they are seen. The visions of delirious persons are similar to those of sleepers, for their normal channels of perception are obstructed so that they see what sleeping persons see. And the visions of sleeping persons are similar to the thoughts of waking men. The channel of perception in the brain of sleepers is in a state of slumber and it is this channel which gives to the eyes the intention of seeing. The intention, therefore, turned in another direction, beholds the things seen by sleeping men as corporeal forms. Thus sleepers seem to themselves to be in a waking state, and they are not aware that they are seeing things similar to bodies and not bodies themselves.

For my part, I much more admire the speed and ease with which the soul constructs in itself the images of bodies seen with the body's eyes, than I do the visions of delirious or sleeping persons, or even the visions of ecstatics. Be of whatever nature they might, the things seen by these three latter groups are certainly not true bodies. It is not the bodies seen which form images in the spirit, nor do they have power to form anything spiritual. It is rather the spirit which with admirable speed forms images in itself, as an intellectual and rational spirit.

THE FIVE TYPES OF DREAMS—WHY DREAMS DIFFER[55]

25. The dreams which sleeping persons experience may be classified in five types. These are: the oracular dream, the prophetic vision, the enigmatic dream, the nightmare and the apparition. We speak of an oracular dream when in a dream one of our parents or some other holy and respectable person, or a priest, or God himself, announces openly that something is to take place or is not to take place, that something is

---

55. The five types of dreams in this chap. are taken from Macrobius, *Commentarius in Somnium Scipionis* 1, 3(1-11). The translation of the terms is that of William Harris Stahl in his version, *Macrobius' Commentary on the Dream of Scipio* (New York, 1952), p. 88.

to be done or is to be avoided. We have a prophetic vision when something occurs exactly as it had appeared in a dream. An enigmatic dream is enveloped in figures and cannot be understood without interpretation. When the things which worried and concerned a waking man return to him when he is asleep, we call this dream a nightmare. The subject of a nightmare can be food, drink, some project, one's profession or even one's infirmities. A person can dream of the projects he is undertaking in waking life; or the events of one's profession, implanted in the mind, can return to one while asleep. According to one's different infirmities, different dreams can take shape. Dreams also vary according to the diversity of one's customs and humors. For example, the sanguine have certain dreams which differ from those of the choleric; phlegmatics and melancholics have still other dreams. The sanguine and the choleric see red and mottled dreams, while phlegmatics and melancholics dream in shades of black and white. We speak of an apparition when one who has barely begun to sleep, and still thinks he is awake, seems to see men rushing down upon him or sees variously differing shapes floating about, which shapes may be either placid or tumultous. To this class belongs *ephialtes*,[56] which is popularly said to attack the slumbering and burden them with the full brunt of its oppressiveness. *Ephialtes* is simply the result of a certain gaseousness which rises to the brain from the stomach or the heart and there oppresses the animal powers.

THE CAUSE OF SPECTERS

26. Popular stories have it that, under the spell of certain women's crafts and by the power of demons, men can be turned into wolves and beasts of burden. In that state men can play the part of beasts, carrying loads, and after the spell is over they again return to their previous forms. The whole time they retain their human reason, not taking on a beast's

56. In Greek mythology Ephialtes, the son of Aloeus and brother of Otus, was one of the giants who stormed Olympus. He was slain by Apollo.

mind. These stories are to be understood as follows. Since demons cannot create natures, what happens is that they do something which makes certain things seem to be what they are not. The intellectual soul and the body could not possibly be truly turned into the form and shape of a beast by any art or power. But man's imaginative faculty can take innumerable shapes through thought and through dreams, and although this faculty is not itself a body, it can take on with amazing speed forms similar to bodies. When man's bodily senses are in a state of slumber or of suppression the imaginative faculty can be diverted to the corporeal shapes of other perceptions. Thus the living body of a man can be lying somewhere, with its senses more intensely suppressed than occurs during sleep. In such a case that imaginative faculty, formed as if in the shape of some animal, may appear to the senses of others. The man will appear to himself just as he appears in dreams—in this case carrying burdens like a beast. If these burdens are true bodies, it is the demons who carry them so that they can deceive the men who are seeing partly the true bodies of men and partly the false ones of beasts of burden.

WHAT IS WROUGHT BY ANGELIC SPIRITS UPON HUMAN SPIRITS[57]

27. The human spirit is at times taken up by a good spirit and at times by an evil spirit. It is not easy to discern at a given moment which of the two spirits is involved, except that a good spirit instructs, while an evil spirit deceives. But the evil spirit will often deceive under the guise of good things, so that when he has proved convincing he can then lead his victim astray. The evil spirit has been known to snatch up the human spirit in such a way that by some obscure mixture he seems at once to be a suffering spirit and the very spirit of agitation, as is the case with demoniacs. We know, however, that no creature can substantially fill the soul and mind of man; only the Trinity can. When we say that

57. Dependent on *De genesi ad litteram* 12, chaps. 13, 14 and Bede, *Commentarium in Actuum Apostolorum* 5.

Satan fills the mind and heart of someone, we do not mean that he enters inside a man and his senses. Rather, we mean that Satan, luring the man with deceit and evil and every wickedness and seducing him by the desire of evil, draws him on with debased thoughts and the incentive to vice of which he himself is full as the false, vile, and fraudulent deceiver of souls. The devil does not fill a man and dwell within him through a participation of that man's nature or substance, as some think. The devil inhabits a man through fraudulence, deceit and malice. Only the Trinity can enter a man and fill the nature and the substance which it has created.

THE DEMONS' SKILL AND EXPERIENCE AT DELUDING MEN[58]

28. In the keenness of their perception and in the swifness of their airy bodies' movements demons easily surpass the senses of earthly bodies. They can utter thoughts which men marvel at because of the slowness of the latters' earthly bodies. Demons have a far wider experience of things than do men on account of the great expanse of time that their lives span. Demons are wont to lure and seduce men by making pronouncements about the future and by generally performing what to men appear to be marvels. We know especially of certain girls, who, having gone over to Satan, are seduced by the delusions and apparitions of demons. They believe themselves and announce themselves to be the submissive riding partners during night hours of Diana, pagan goddess, and of Herodias, Minerva, and many other women. After Satan has transformed himself into an angel of light[59] and has seized the mind of some weak girl, subjecting her to himself through her unfaithfulness, then he changes himself on the spot into the appearance and likeness of different persons. He continues to lead the captive mind astray, through devious paths deluding it with dreams and parading before it a multitude of cheerful and morose things, of known and unknown

58. Dependent on Augustine, *Liber de divinatione daemonum* and the *Capitula concilii Ancyrani.*
59. 2 Cor 11:14

persons. Since only an unfaithful spirit can undergo such corruption, it thinks that the things are happening to it in the body rather than in the intellectual soul. But it is a stupid and blunted person who can believe that the things happening to him in the spirit are also happening in the body. He forgets that Ezechiel and the other prophets, as well as John the Evangelist and the other apostles, all saw visions in the spirit and not in the body.

APPARITIONS OF THE DEAD—THE IGNORANCE OF THE DEAD
CONCERNING EARTHLY AFFAIRS—HOW THE DEAD
COMMUNICATE WITH THE LIVING[60]

29. When dead or living persons appear to sleeping or waking men, they do not appear in the actual circumstances in which they really are, but in certain likenesses of those circumstances. We are of the opinion that this occurs through the operation of angels. God's providential dispensation arranges for these apparitions, since it is God who makes good use of both the good and the evil according to the inscrutable depth of his judgments. Whether mortal minds are instructed or deceived in this, whether they are consoled or alarmed, he whom the Church wisely praises for both his mercy and his justice is the one who determines where mercy is to granted and where justice is to be exacted.[61]

The spirits of the dead are in a place where they can neither see nor hear the things which are done by men or which happen to men in this life. But even though the dead are completely unaware of living men's actions, yet they are concerned about them, just as we, the living, are also in our ignorance concerned about what happens to the dead. The dead are indeed ignorant of what happens in our world; but only while it is happening. After the happenings have occurred they can learn them from those whom death takes from our world to theirs. Even then they do not learn everything absolutely, but only in the measure granted to the messengers and to their listeners. The angels, who are in charge of us, the

60. Dependent on Augustine, *De cura pro mortuis gerenda* 12-16.
61. Cf. Ps 100:1

living, and who bear our souls to the other world when we die, are another source of information for the dead. God's spirit can also reveal to the dead the things that happen in the world of the living which they ought to know.

A dead man can also be whisked away to the world of the living through divine power rather than through the nature of the dead person. However, I do not dare to assert whether these things happen through their actual presence or through angels taking on their person. In any event, it is God almighty who, being present everywhere, uses the widely-diffused services of the angels to provide the living with the consolations which he deems they need in this life's tribulations.

HOW THE SOUL DOES NOT GROW—WHERE THE SOUL IS AND WHAT IT DOES ONCE DEPRIVED OF ITS BODY[62]

30. The powers and virtues of the soul grow as a result of long practice and the passage of time. The soul itself, however, neither grows nor diminishes. What happens is that, because of the unevenness of the body's members, and because of the varying density of the humors and the restricting effect of their decay, the soul cannot at times exercise its powers. The soul deprived of the body lives, sees, hears, and retains all of its senses and genius, since it is pure, keen, swift and eternal. Just as God is everywhere in himself, so too the soul in some manner is everywhere in itself. Because of this, the bodiless soul is present where it had been while acting through the body. God is now present where he had been present before the world was made, where he would also be present if the world should cease to be.

As it has often been said, the soul is incorporeal. Nevertheless, after it leaves the body, the soul can retain a likeness of the body and of all the bodily members, a likeness which would not itself be corporeal, but similar to a body. The soul goes either to spiritual realms as a reward for its merits, or to places of punishment which resemble corporeal

62. Dependent on *Ep an* 14 and *De genesi ad litteram* 12, 32-33.

places. This has often been shown in persons whose senses are
momentarily snatched from them. Their body lies as if dead,
but they effect in themselves a certain likeness of their body
by which they can be carried to those places of punishment
or of reward and to experience visions as if with their senses.
If souls become fondly attached to the corporeal images of
visible things while they live in their earthly body, these
souls will suffer torments through these same images
once they have left their bodies. These souls can be held fast
there by corporeal sufferings because they have not been
cleansed in this life from the corruption of corporeal attachments. They had acquired these attachments through the
body's pleasure. Some souls are punished in the same places
in which they committed their sin. Others are kept in hidden
retreats until the last resurrection, according as each deserves
rest or misery.

MAN'S MORTALITY—HOW THE SENSES KEEP
MAN FROM KNOWING HIMSELF[63]

31. I have said many things about the soul, but I have not
yet told the time of its creation or the time of its exit from
the body. I will discuss later the time of its creation; as for
the time of its exit from the body, that I cannot tell, for I do
not know when my end will come. One thing I am certain of:
that we are mortal, and that whether we want it or not, we
shall all die. Nothing is more certain than death, and nothing
is more uncertain than death's hour. We do not know when,
how, or where we will die, for death is everywhere awaiting
us. For this reason we should always be ready for death, so
that when the body returns to the earth from which it was
taken, the spirit too may return to him who had given it.
Above all else we should be stirred by the ancient sages'
definition of man' "Man is a rational and mortal animal."[64]
The genus "animal" being established, two differences are

63. Dependent on Augustine, *De ordine* 2, 11(31). This section is also repeated
in the Pseudo-Anselmian, *Meditatio* 7.

64. This definition is frequently repeated by Augustine, e.g., *De ordine*
2,11(31); and *DQA* 1,25(47).

added which should serve as a warning to man. The first tells man how he is to return to himself; the second what is to be avoided. Just as the soul's progress had reverted to a state of mortality, so should its reinstatement be based on reason by which the soul is capable of resisting the attacks of vices, so that the soul may live according to its nature and seek to be subordinated to him by whom it should be ruled, while at the same time itself ruling those things which it should. The attribute "rational" separates man from the animals, while "mortal" distinguishes him from God. Unless man remains rational, he becomes an animal; unless man fully accepts his status of mortal he shall never attain to God.

In order that man, who is a stranger to himself, might come to know himself, it is most important for him to withdraw habitually from the senses and to recollect his intellectual soul. In this way he can remain within himself. Man's senses keep his soul from looking at itself and at its Maker, whom the soul should gaze at in solitude and simplicity without the aid of earthly eyes.

HOW THE MIND KNOWS ITSELF BEST—THE UNITY OF SOUL AND BODY —HOW THE SOUL COMES DOWN INTO THE BODY—HOW THE SOUL RISES ABOVE THE BODY—MEDITATION—CONTEMPLATION [65]

32. The rational soul surpasses all the things God has created. It is close to God when it is pure, and God thoroughly illumines it with his intellectual light to the extent to which the soul clings to him through charity. In God are found the most perfect beauty and the most blessed vision, by which the soul itself becomes blessed. But the soul does not see God with the eyes of the body, but rather with its understanding, which is its principal part. Let the soul, then, put outside its area of concern all the concepts and notions which come to it through the external senses. Corporeal things and their likenesses, the senses and the images fixed in the memory—all of these belong to the exterior man, since they are messengers to the soul, so to speak, of the things that are outside it.

65. Dependent on Augustine, *De Trinitate* 10, 8-10; *De genesi ad litteram* 7, 21 and 14; *DQA* 33, which is quoted vebatim in *Phys an* 14, and *DUCS*.

Nothing is more present to the mind than the mind itself. The mind sees itself in itself through a certain interior presence which is genuine and not an imitation. The mind knows best what is closest to it, and there is nothing closer to the mind than the mind itself. The mind knows itself to live, to remember, to understand, to will, think, know and judge. The mind knows these things in itself; it does not imagine them as if they were corporeal things outside itself which had to be reached by one of the senses. If the mind does not confuse its thoughts about corporeal things with thoughts about itself—in such a way that it comes to think of itself as corporeal—then whatever remains to it after corporeal things have been removed is the mind itself. There is nothing which is more in the mind than the mind itself, and there is nothing which knows the mind as it knows itself. When the mind seeks to know what it is, the mind actually knows that it is seeking itself and that it is itself which is doing the seeking. Nor does the mind seek itself starting from any place except the mind. When the mind knows itself to be seeking, it surely knows itself. And since the whole of it knows whatever it knows, thus the mind knows itself wholly. If in its search it finds but a part of itself, and not the whole, nevertheless the mind is fully present to itself because the whole of it is doing the searching.

Nothing can be more present to the mind than the mind itself. But the mind also seeks to know things about itself: its previous existence, its future existence, the mode of its being, its similarity and dissimilarity with respect to God, the degree of its humility, its devotion, purity, holiness. And because it exists in these corporeal matters which it thinks about with affection and with which it agrees in love, without such corporeal images the mind is incapable of seeing itself or even of being in itself. The bonds of affection which unite the mind with corporeal things are so strong that even when these are absent from the mind's ambit, still their images are present to the mind's thoughts. This is why the mind cannot detach itself from such images even when its purpose is to inspect and see itself alone. The mind's alternative, therefore, is to return to itself and remain there, not searching for itself as if it were somewhere else, but rather trying to see and recognize itself as being present. The mind must firmly direct the intention of the will, which at other times permits it to wander over many other things, to remain in itself and think about itself, with the final end of knowing and loving itself.

When the mind has reached a state of interiority it will at once realize that it has always loved and known itself. The difference is that it has loved other things along with itself and has confused itself with those other things, so that it cannot detach itself from other things without great toil. After all, it has been bound to them by its affection. But such attachment to the phantasms of corporeal images has had the effect of deforming the mind, and they are so firmly imprinted in it that it cannot rid itself of them even after it is deprived of the body. If the mind is not purged of the corruption of corporeal attachments in this world, it will still be subject to the body's passions even after it is separated from the body. Let the mind, then, consider how it will purge itself of such filth in this life, so that when it leaves this world it will carry nothing corporeal with it and be free of all bodily attachments.

The soul comes down into the body through vivification and sensation. By its presence the soul enlivens or vivifies the body, gives unity to the body, and preserves that unity. The soul does not allow the body to deteriorate or to waste away gradually; it insures the body's harmony and safeguards the proper balancing of its elements, not only in what pertains to the body's beauty, but also to its growth and reproduction. For example, by safeguarding the sense of touch the soul can feel and distinguish between hot and cold, rough and smooth, hard and soft, heavy and light. Likewise, by tasting, smelling, hearing, and seeing the soul can distinguish an innumerable variety of flavors, odors, sounds and shapes. In all these activities the soul seeks the things which are conformable to its body's nature and shuns those which are in opposition to it.

At certain intervals of time the soul withdraws from the body's senses and renews their operations by giving the senses a holiday, as it were. At those times the soul considers within itself the images of things which it has taken in through the senses. These images are examined both in groups and singly. Thus, when it wishes to consider divine things, or God, or itself and its virtues, the soul removes itself from the body's senses which are an aid only in sensing corporeal shapes and colors. Then it glances at itself through the spirit and reason, and ascends to God through meditation and contemplation. God descends to the soul through revelation and divine inspiration. Meditation is a diligent inquiry into hidden truth. Contemplation is a joyful marveling at manifest truth. Divine revelation must enlighten the soul's meditation in order that it may come to know the truth; divine inspiration kindles the fire of contemplation in order that the soul may love truth. The body rises to the spirit through sense knowledge and imagination.

THE BODY'S MATTER–HOW SENSE KNOWLEDGE AND IMAGINATION ARE FORMED–WHAT THE IMAGINATION IS–THE CORPOREAL SPIRIT[66]

33. The human body is made up of four elements. In the flesh and in the bones, because of their earthy solidness, earth predominates. Water is mostly found in the humors and air in the lungs. The lungs are always in motion as the bellows of the heart. It is the lungs' function to keep the heart from being consumed and destroyed by an excess of heat. Fire makes its home in the heart, and this is why the heart resembles the shape of fire by being wider at the bottom and narrower at the top.

There is a certain fiery power which, after being tempered by air, rises from the heart to the brain—our brain being the heaven of the microcosm which is our body. In the brain the fiery power is cleansed and purified, and then it goes outside the body through the eyes, ears, nostrils and other sensory apparatus. The power is formed into a shape when it contacts things exterior to the body, and makes the body's five senses,

---

66. Dependent on *De genesi ad litteram* 7, 13 and *DUCS*.

that is sight, hearing, taste, smell and touch. The sense of touch passes from the anterior to the posterior part of the brain and from there it descends through the cervix and the spinal medulla and is diffused through the body.

The fiery power is formed into a shape on the outside through the sensory apparatus (through which it goes out and in which it is shaped) and itself takes on the name of "sense." Now this power is subsequently interiorized and brought back to the phantasmal chamber, where it becomes the imagination. The imagination moves from the anterior to the medial part of the head, thereby touching the very substance of the rational soul and occasioning the capacity for distinguishing. The imagination has by now been purified and made keen to such an extent that it is joined to the spirit with no other substance intervening, while all along it truly retains the nature and properties of a body. In dumb animals the imagination does not go beyond the phantasmal chamber; in rational animals the imagination is made purer until it is brought into contact with the rational and incorporeal substance of the soul. Seen thus, the imagination is a likeness of the body. It is formed externally when through the corporeal senses the fiery power contacts corporeal things. After being formed, the imagination is led back through those same senses to the purer part of the corporeal spirit and it is imprinted upon it. At its highest part the imagination is a corporeal spirit, and at its lowest something rational which informs bodily nature and is in contact with rational nature.

I call air a corporeal spirit. Fire merits this description even more so, since, because of its subtlety, it cannot be seen and it enlives bodies interiorly by animating them. Some bodies are animated but do not have senses, like trees, grass and all the things which sprout forth on earth. Some things have both animation and senses, such as the dumb animals. Still some of these have senses, but no imagination; others have both senses and imagination. Because it is a greater thing to have senses than to have only animation, it is obvious that this force is the most subtle of all, and the more subtle it is, the greater its share in spirit. It thus comes closer to having an incorporeal nature when it forms the imagination than when it bestows sense. There is nothing in a body which is more excellent or closer to having a spiritual nature than that part of the body where the power of imagining is born, resulting from sense knowledge but going beyond it. So lofty a thing is the imagination that the next above it is reason itself.

SENSE KNOWLEDGE AND MEMORY–THE MIND AND THE SPIRIT–HOW "INTELLECTUAL SOUL" IS THE SAME AS "SOUL IN GENERAL"– REASON–WHO IT IS THAT RISES TO GOD IN THE SOUL– AN ADMIRABLE WAY OF DIVIDING THE SOUL– THE MIND AS IMAGE OF GOD[67]

34. "Soul" is a term referring to the whole interior man, by which that clay-like mass moistened by vital juices is enlivened, governed, and held together lest it be destroyed through desiccation. The body's informing principle is properly called "soul" when it enlivens. When it wills, it is called "intellectual soul." When it knows it is termed "mind." When it remembers it is named "memory." When it judges, "reason." When it breathes or contemplates, "spirit." When it feels, it is designated "sense."

The soul is called "sense" from the fact that it feels things (by a way of thinking then it takes the name). The body is said to have five "senses." These faculties are each also called "sense" because through them the soul very subtly confers on the whole body the power of feeling. The different functions of the soul are so joined to it that the soul is but one thing, and not many things. Because of the variety of its efficacious causality, the soul receives a variety of names. Although simple in essence, the soul is multiple in its functions.

Since memory is mind we say that those who have lost their memory have also lost their mind. The memory is the treasury and guardian of all things, nor can it ever be completely unfurled, so great is its intricacy. The intellectual soul

---

67. Directly dependent on Isidore, *Etymologiae* 11, 1, 13 and *De differentiis* 2, 29, 97. Cf. also Pseudo-Ambrose, *De dignitate humanae conditionis* and Augustine, *De Trinitate* 10, 9. The second part of the compilation, which begins here, is sometimes provided with an introductory chapter, "On the sevenfold distinction of things". Norpoth has edited it in his study.

is the same thing as the memory. When I say "mind" I am likewise referring to the soul; but the same thing is called "soul" in one of its aspects and "mind" in another. For everything in man which is alive is man's soul. When the soul acts within itself, through itself and of its own motivation, then it is only called "mind." When the soul is fulfilling its functions it is more commonly referred to as "sense." There are two passages in St John's Gospel which show that "soul" is the same thing as "spirit." In the first of these the Evangelist writes: "I have the power of laying down my soul, and I have the power of taking it up again."[68] Later on, speaking about the Lord's soul at the time of his Passion, he writes: "Inclining his head he gave up the spirit."[69] What is the meaning of "to give up the spirit" if not "to lay down one's soul"? The same thing is called "soul" because it is alive and "spirit" either because of its spiritual nature or because it is the principle of breathing in the body.

Likewise we say that "intellectual soul" is the same as soul in general. "Soul" refers to the life-principle, while "intellectual soul" implies the principle of reflection. This is why the philosophers say that even without an intellectual soul life nevertheless remains in a person, and that, even without a mind the soul still subsists, as in the case of the insane. Knowing, therefore, is proper to the mind, while willing is proper to the intellectual soul. Nevertheless infants in the womb live without knowing or willing. The mind (*mens*) receives its name from the fact that it towers in the soul (*emineat*) and because it remembers (*meminerit*). The soul is not itself called mind, but, rather, what is highest in the soul is called mind, like the head or the eyes are said to be eminent parts of the body. It is because of his mind that man is said to bear God's image. The mind, thus named because it towers in the soul, is the most excellent of the soul's powers, since from it proceeds understanding. Reason is also a movement of the intellectual soul which sharpens the mind's eye and distinguishes true from false things.

68. Jn 10:18
69. Jn 19:30

Let the rational mind, then, return within itself and
become recollected interiorly, so that without corporeal
images it may study itself and the invisible nature of God
almighty. To this end the mind must block out the apparitions of earthly images and whatever else comes to it which
pertains to this earth. Then may the mind seek itself and see
itself as it is, without the aid of corporeal images. Seeing
itself thus, the mind realizes that it is God's creation, located
in rank below God but above the body. Following such a
realization the mind can rise above itself, forsaking itself, and
in some hidden manner it comes to forget itself, humbly and
devoutly giving itself over to the contemplation of its Maker.

When the mind begins going outside itself through pure
understanding and begins totally entering into the brightness
of God's incorporeal light, then it also begins to experience a
relish of intimate sweetness in the things it sees interiorly,
and from that to season its understanding and to turn to
wisdom. So great an ecstasy of the mind brings about that
peace which surpasses every sensation, so that the very heavens become hushed as it were for half an hour.[70] His intellectual soul is never disturbed during such contemplating by
the clamor of warring thoughts. Furthermore, it finds nothing which it either seeks through desire, rejects through aver-
sion or condemns out of hatred. The soul, rather, is completely recollected in the quiet of contemplation and it is
granted a very rare and precious interior sentiment which
consists of an indefinable sweetness, which, were it always
felt in this way, would be the source of the greatest bliss. In
this state of soul neither sensation nor the imagination is
active. Every one of the soul's lower powers is temporarily
deprived of its own function. The purer part of the soul, on
the other hand, to its great joy is initiated to a mystery of
intimate repose and is introduced into the sanctuary of the
highest tranquility. "God's word to us is something alive, full
of energy. It can penetrate deeper than any two-edged sword,

70. Rev 8:1

reaching the very division between soul and spirit."[71] There is nothing in creation which is more marvelous than this division. What is one in essence and indivisible becomes separated; and what is simple and lacks parts is divided by a certain partitioning.

It is clear that in the same man spirit and soul do not have different essences, but rather there is only the one substance which is proper to a simple nature. Because two words—soul and spirit—are employed, we are not to understand that there are two substances. The two powers of the one essence are distinguished by saying that one is superior and is "spirit," while the other is inferior and is "soul." In this division the soul and what is proper to animals remain below; the spirit, however, and whatever is spiritual, soar to the heights. Spirit is divided from lower things in order that it may be raised on high; it is separated from soul in order that it may be united to God, "because whoever clings to God is one spirit with him."[72] This is indeed a fortunate division and a marvelous separation: the body-like and impure parts of man's soul remain below, while its spiritual and more subtle parts are raised to the vision of divine glory and are transformed into that glory's image. The lower part is recollected in the greatest peace and tranquility, while the higher part is raised to glory and rejoicing.

Even though the human mind is not of the same nature as God, nevertheless it is the image of that nature and there is no nature better than it. In that image must be sought and found what is best in us. In order to do this the mind must first be studied in itself; only then will God's image be discovered in it. When the mind looks at itself through thought, it comes to understand and know itself. When, on the other hand, the mind by contemplation ascends to God in order to understand and love him, it is called the image of God. The Apostle says that the mind is manly when it thinks of eternal things: "A man should not cover up his head, since he is God's image and glory."[73] The more the mind goes out to the

71. Heb 4:12   73. 1 Cor 11:7
72. 1 Cor 6:17

eternal, the more does it become an image of God. It should not be hindered from going out to the eternal so that it may then contain itself and be moderate. But when the mind is engaged in thinking about temporal things, then it is called womanly. In this case it should not be called an image of God, and it should cover up its head lest it excessively descend to lower things; lest, while engaged in lawful activities, it may come to lust after the unlawful.

THE DIGNITY OF THE HUMAN CONDITION—THE EXTENT OF MAN'S BEING AN IMAGE OF GOD—HOW GOD'S IMAGE IS IN THE SOUL— THE EXTENT TO WHICH GOD'S LIKENESS IS IN MAN'S SPIRIT [74]

35. We base our convictions about the dignity of the human condition on the fact that man was created, not only by a word of command—as were the creatures of the other six days—but by the very deliberation of the Trinity and the work of divine majesty. From the honor of his original state man should realize how much he owes his Maker, who gave him the privilege of already being in such an exalted condition of dignity. Man's love for his Maker should thus flow from the realization of how wonderful the state is in which he has been created. Nor should the Holy Trinity's deliberative intervention in man's creation be the only motivation for man's love, but also because he has been created in the image and likeness of his Maker, a privilege which God has bestowed on no other creature.

This image of God in man should be carefully studied, considering the dignity and nobility of the inner man. The Apostle has said that "we live, move, and have our being" in God.[75] This is so because the one God is always wholly present everywhere, enlivening all things, moving and governing them. In much the same way the soul is wholly present everywhere in its body, enlivening it, moving and

---

74. Dependent on the Pseudo-Ambrose, *De dignitate humanae conditionis* (really a product of the circle of Alcuin) and the Commentary of Rabanus Maurus, *In Ecclesiastem*, 4, 5. Cf. cc 46-47 of the *De interiori domo (Domus haec)*.

75. Acts 18:28

governing it. Nor is a greater part of the soul present in the larger parts of the body and a lesser part in the smaller; on the contrary, the soul is wholly present in even the smallest parts and again wholly present in the largest. The soul has been infused into the body in such a way that it is not divided up among the different parts of the body. If a given part of the body is struck, it is the whole soul which feels the pain. Since the soul is not diversified in its nature, it cares for all the bodily members by one and the same enlivening function. Through the body's instrumentality, however, the soul effects varied actions. It is the soul which sees through the eyes, hears with the ears, smells through the nose, tastes by the mouth and touches things with the bodily members (distinguishing the smooth from the rough). Even though the soul itself is not divided into different parts, yet through the senses it does have a variety of operations. From this we can discern that the soul is in its body according to its own mode, just as God is in this world of his in his own manner. The soul is within and without, above and below the body: when it rules, it is above; when it supports, it is below; when it fills up, within; and when it surrounds, without. The soul is within in such a way that it is also without; it is around so that it also penetrates; it rules so that it also supports; it supports so that it also rules. Just as God does not grow along with his growing creatures and does not shrink with those that shrink, so neither does the soul diminish in order to be present in the smaller bodily members, nor increase to be present in the larger. Such is the image or likeness of almighty God which the soul bears within itself.

The soul also bears a certain image of the Holy Trinity. Just as God exists, lives and knows, so too the soul exists, lives and knows after its own manner. But there is also another trinity in the soul, deriving from its having been made in the image of the perfect and most exalted Trinity which is in the Father, the Son and the Holy Spirit. Having but one nature, the soul nevertheless has three faculties. These are the intellect, the will and the memory. This threefold distinction is already found in other words in the Gospel, where it says: "You shall love the Lord your God with your whole heart,

and with your whole soul, and with your whole mind."[76]
Which means that you shall love God with your whole intellect, your whole will and your whole memory. For just as the
Father begets the Son, and the Holy Spirit proceeds from the
Father and the Son; so too does the intellect beget the will,
and from these two proceeds the memory—as any wise man
can tell you. The soul cannot be perfect without these three,
nor can any one of the three be complete without the other
two, especially in what concerns it happiness.[77] And just as
God the Father, God the Son and God the Holy Spirit are
not three gods, but one God and three persons; so too the
soul-as-intellect, the soul-as-will and the soul-as-memory are
not three souls in one body, but one soul with three powers.
The interior man wonderfuly bears the divine image in these
three, and from these as it were more excellent powers of the
soul, we are commanded to love our Maker so that he is loved
to the extent to which he is known, and he is remembered to
the extent that he is loved. But knowing God is not enough if
his will is not accomplished by our loving him in return. And
even knowledge and love are not enough, unless memory
also comes into play so that God may always be present to
the person who knows and loves him. Just as there cannot be
a moment in which man does not use and enjoy God's goodness and mercy, so too there should not be any moment in
which God is not present in man's memory. For these reasons
I think it accurate to say that the interior man is an image of
God.

Let us now say a few things about likeness. God, the Maker
who has created man in his image, is charity, goodness,
justice, patience, meekness, purity, mercy and the other
eminent and holy virtues which are attributed to him. Deriving from this model, man himself has been created that he
may have charity, that he may be good, just, patient, meek,
pure and merciful. The greater a man's virtues, the closer he
is to God, since his likeness to his Maker is all the more exact.

76. Mt 22:37
77. Reading *beatitudo* as suggested in the note in the PL edition rather than
habitudo in the text.

But if (God forbid!) a man should become a degenerate by departing from that very noble likeness of his Maker through vice and general evil-doing, then the Scripture is fulfilled in him which says: "When man enjoyed greater honor he did not realize it."[78] What could be a greater honor for man than to have been made in the very likeness of his Maker, and to have been adorned with the very same virtues which are proper to his Maker? We read that "the Lord reigns as king, robed in majesty."[79] This means that God is adorned with the splendor of all the virtues and the beauty of goodness itself. And what could be a greater disgrace and a more wretched fate for man than to lose the glory of being like his Maker and thereby to descend to the misery of bearing the deformed and irrational likeness of brute beasts? Let every man, therefore, attentively realize the excellence of his first state, and let every man acknowledge within himself the awe-inspiring image of the Holy Trinity. Let every man strive to do honor to the divine likeness in which he has been created by living nobly, by practicing the virtues and by storing up worthy merits. If a man does this, then when he appears as he truly is, he will be found to be similar to God, who wonderfully made man in his own image in the first man, and who still more wonderfully re-created man in the second man, that is, in himself.

A COMPARISON OF THE SOUL WITH GOD[80]

36. There is a great similarity between God and the soul. For God is life, spirit, wisdom and love. The soul likewise is life and spirit, and has within it wisdom and love. God is life and the soul is life, but in a different manner. They are alike because the life which the soul has in itself is not only living but life-giving as well, just as God is all these things; they are unlike, because one is the Creator, and the other is created. If the soul

---

78. Ps 48:13
79. Ps 92:1
80. Dependent on Augustine's *Confessiones* 10, 6 and Bernard of Clairvaux, *Sermones in Cantica* 80-82.

had not been created by God it would not have existed; if he had
not given it life, it would not live. The soul lives by this natural
life even if it is not spiritually alive (but such life is death rather
than life: "For grievous is the death of sinners.")[81] The soul
that lives according to the flesh is dead while it is alive; it
would be better for it not to live than to live in this way. Life
is the soul, living indeed but from no other source than itself;
so it is not so much living as life. The soul lives by being
breathed into the body so that from the presence of life the
body is not life itself but is living. The soul is created by God,
alive from life, simple from simplicity, immortal from immortality, and so that it might not be far from its Creator, it
seems to come near him by the simplicity of its essence and
its immortality. For even if it is not alive spiritually, it must
live immortally. The soul is created great by greatness, right
from uprightness. It is great because it is capable of eternity;
it is right, because it has a desire for heaven; it is blessed
because it is one with God. The soul that beholds the goodness of God is subject to him in humility, led back to him by
repentance, led on to him by righteousness, conformed to
him by obedience, reaches him by perseverance, enters into
him by devotion, is joined to him by purity and united to
him by charity.

The soul has love within itself by which it can always either
be with God, or, if it has been moved by desires or even
defects to go away from him, it can return to him. Among all
the powers of desire and knowledge of the soul, it is only by
love that the soul can make its response to its Creator and
pay him in similar kind, though not according to equality
with him. If it loves little, it will be little, and if it loves with
the whole of itself, where the whole is, nothing can be
lacking. So renouncing all other desires, it relies entirely and
solely on love, pours itself wholly into love, responding to
God by a return of love. God loves to be loved and when he
loves he wants nothing other than to be loved, for he knows
that it is by love that those who love him will be blessed. By
love he comes to men, he comes into men, he was made man

81. Ps 33:22

and "his delight is to be with the sons of men."[82] Our
delight is to come to him, to see him as he is, and "then we
shall be like him."[83] Then there will be open vision, full
knowledge, true delight, firm conjunction, the unity of each
with all, perfect likeness, and the life of blessedness in eternity and on into ages of ages. Just as in its resurrection the
body will receive its life and sense, so in its resurrection the
soul will receive its life and sense, which is the knowledge and
love of God. This knowledge will be life eternal, as Truth
himself affirmed saying, "This is eternal life, that they might
know you the true God, and Jesus Christ whom you have
sent."[84]

Love is a power of knowledge. Just as in this life the exterior
man knows the temporal things around him by the five
senses, that is, sight, hearing, taste, smell and touch: so in the
life of blessedness, the interior man will know the five ineffable aspects of God by love in five ineffable ways. For when
he will love his God he will love a kind of light, sound, smell,
food and interior embrace. A shining is there which belongs
to no place, a sound which no time takes away, a smell which
no wind disperses, a taste which does not cloy with eating, an
embrace is there which satiety does not destroy. There God is
seen without intermission, known without error, loved
without offence and praised without wearying.

THE SOUL IS THE CITY OF GOD—ABOUT THE CITIZENS—THE LEADERS,
THE SOLDIERS, THE COMMON PEOPLE—THE THREE POWERS OF THE
SOUL ACCORDING TO PLATO AND THE DOCTORS—REASON,
UNDERSTANDING, MEMORY AND APPETITE[85]

37. The soul is a noble creation. It is the city of God of
which "such glorious things are spoken,"[86] and it is made in

82. Prov 8:31
83. 1 Jn 3:2
84. Jn 17:3
85. Cf. Bernard's *Sermo in dedicatione* 5, 9. The concept of the *partes virtuales*
(virtual parts) of the soul also appears in *Ep an* 3. The source for much of the
other material in this chap., such as the comparison of the son and its powers to
the ideal city, and its three classes of citizens which go back to Plato's *Republic*,
is probably, Chalcidius *Commentarium in Timaeum*, chaps. 233-34. The division of
the powers of the soul into intellectual, rational and animal is Origenist.
86. Ps 86:3

the image and likeness of God. The city merits its name of Jerusalem for it is created to enjoy the full vision of peace "which makes both one."[87] Its mind is a paradise and it meditates on celestial things as if delighting in the joys of paradise. Because of the unity of its walls, the soul is the house of the Father; by love, it is the spouse of Christ; by sanctification, the temple of the Holy Spirit; because of its peace and civic concord, it is the city of the eternal King. Because a city is nothing apart from its citizens, our Maker has put in it three grades of population, that is, the wise ones who rule, the soldiers who fight and the builders who serve. The citizens of this city are the natural and inborn powers of the soul, as if native to it, and of these there are distinct grades: some are higher, some lower and some in the middle. The higher ones are the intellectual powers of knowledge: the ones in the middle, rational power; the lower, what ever belongs to the animal life. Among them there is this distinction: the animal or sensual part strives for what can be seen; the rational part sees with the eye of discretion what to reject; the intellectual part draws the soul to divine things. As rulers of the soul, the intellectual powers say to it, "Fear God and keep his commandments: this is the whole law for man."[88] The rational parts are like soldiers who strive for purity and fight the enemy with arms of righteousness; the animal or sensual parts are like rustics or craftsmen who follow the laws of the body and minister necessities to the body. These three powers of the soul, that is, the sensual, rational and intellectual powers, are called by philosophers not integral but virtual powers, for they are faculties of the soul.

Sensuality is the power of the soul which makes the body grow, and by the bodily senses it knows and discerns what is outside itself. For all the senses, whether exterior or interior, have reference to the soul inasmuch as they proceed from it. In order to sense they all depend on the soul. Reason is a power of the soul higher than the bodily powers but below

87. Eph 2:14
88. Eccles 12:13

the spiritual powers. It can discern truth from falsehood, which is logic. It knows virtue from vice, which is ethics. By experiment it explores the nature of things, which is physics. In these three the whole of philosophy consists. Thus reason comprehends all philosophy. Discernment or understanding is that power of the soul by which it knows God, as far as that is possible for man. Reason on its own cannot penetrate the mysteries of heaven, unless it is aided by God. If it does well, it achieves its goal, when after seeking for a long time, it arrives at the knowledge of mysteries, and this is termed discernment or understanding. Boethius says that understanding belongs only to God and is, after a manner, given to a few men,[89] but it is often given to these for others. Memory aids and co-operates with reason, for without it reason can neither explore what is unknown nor retain what is known. Memory is the power of the soul that retains what it has, recalls what is past and remembers what has been forgotten. Human appetite is placed between the higher and the lower parts of man, and since it is frequently divided between the two, it experiences contradictions within itself. It takes its name from that part into which it passes as a whole. If it feeds on the pleasures of the flesh, it is called animal or carnal; if it delights in the desires of the spirit, it is called spiritual. Appetite is a natural power in the living being to move the senses vehemently.

DEFINITIONS OF THE POWERS OF THE SOUL[90]

38. I have said a great deal about the powers of the soul and so I ought to define them, so that what has been or will be said about the soul can be more clearly understood. Sensuality, sense knowledge, and imagination are said to belong as much to the body as to the soul. Sensuality is a kind of

---

89. The observation is not from Boethius but from Plato's *Timaeus* 51e which in the trans. of Chalcidius reads: "*Intellectus* vero dei proprius et paucorum admodum lectorum hominum" (ed. Waszink, p. 50). The substitution of *intelligentia* for *intellectus* found here was common to texts connected with the School of Chartres.

90. Dependent on Hugh of St Victor, *Didascalicon* 2, 6; 3, 8, 11; and DUCS.

fiery power in the body. The sensuality, or animality of the soul is its lower energy which draws with it the sensuality of the flesh as an obedient servant; it makes sense impressions and imaginings and places them in the treasury of the memory. Sensuality is the instrument of sense knowledge and is the origin of imagination. When this fiery power is connected with external things it is called sense knowledge; when it shapes these into forms within, it is called imagination. Sense knowledge prepares the way for imagination, imagination for thought, thought for meditation. Forethought is excited by meditation, reason by forethought. Reason leads on to discernment, discernment to understanding; in contemplation understanding marvels at the truth itself and by charity takes pleasure in it. Sense knowledge is a passion of the soul in the body arising from accidental qualities that come to it from without. Imagination is a power of the soul which can discern the form of bodily things that are absent from the body without exterior senses. Reflection is when the soul is occupied with anything. Consideration is an intense form of reflection. Meditation is frequent reflection, looking into the way and cause and reason of anything. Forethought is that power placed in the soul by nature that has power in itself. Reason is that power of the soul that discerns and judges all things, most of all when it is open to spiritual things and preserves in itself the image of God. Discernment is to perceive the true nature of creation. Understanding is to have a true and sure knowledge of the true principle of things, that is, of God, ideas, matter, incorporeal substances. Contemplation is to perceive the truth and rejoice at the wonder of it. Charity is unity of mind, the society of the elect, the life of the blessed saints and angels, for neither the soul nor angels live except through charity.

WHY THE SOUL IS IN THE IMAGE AND LIKENESS OF GOD[91]

39. The rational and intellectual soul is made in the image and likeness of God, so that by the image it may know its

---

91. Dependent on Hugh, *De sacramentis* 1, 6, 3.

Creator and by the likeness love him. Because it is in the image of God, the soul has reason; because it is in the likeness, it has charity; indeed, charity in itself represents the Trinity. Reason understands this and peacefully seeks it; charity finds it and when it has seen blessedness it rests in it. In this world, faith follows after, hope accompanies it as far as heaven, charity embraces the Trinity forever. The spiritual mind, or the rational understanding, first beholds its Creator; then it sees his creation and because of free will it refers itself and all things to him who made them. Thus the Trinity, which shows forth charity, appears in man so that man, who is adorned with the image of the Trinity, may always show forth charity and always look to him. Thus man will preserve the likeness of him whose image is his by nature. The image of God appears in the rational understanding, in the spiritual mind, in the dignity of free will. The likeness of God appears in behavior for the sake of nature, in works for justice, in virtue for grace, for behavior completes nature, justice is shown by good works and grace is fulfilled in virtues; thus the Lord is always present. The soul entirely animates the whole body of man. God breathed life into man not from previously existing material, but he made him out of nothing. Of other living things Scripture says, "Let the waters bring forth living creatures," "Let the earth bring forth living creatures."[92] Neither earth nor water produced a soul, but God breathed it in, not as alive or life-giving, but as the breath of life [93] —rational because it was in the image of God and created in his likeness.

THE WRETCHED SOUL IS FAR AWAY FROM GOD—FAR FROM HIS LIKENESS NOT FROM HIS IMAGE—THE SOUL IS NOT BEGOTTEN

40. The soul is not part of God. This is proved by the changeableness which occurs. For God is unchanging; the soul changes often. Sometimes it is condemned for a fault, and sometimes it is made miserable by punishment. But

92. Gen 1:20, 24
93. Gen 2:7

nothing can harm the soul unless it goes away from God. It
goes from him when it sins. When the soul is tormented by its
wretchedness, it flies back to God. When it loses its hold on
the One, it is scattered among the many, and because of its
intemperance it is sick and hurt. Because the senses of the
body are troubled, the memory is disturbed and becomes
blunted, wasted and dulled. So the flesh suffers, begins to be
sick, and is heading for violent death. The man who is against
God and turns away from him by sinning, is apart from God
and so he is estranged from himself and bears within himself
his own punishment. The soul was not formed out of unformed matter but in its creation received the form by which
it was the image and likeness of God. If it turns away from
this, it becomes unformed, because it is guilty and not like
God, but it does not become irrational, because it keeps the
image of God from which it can be formed again. Although
man for his foolishness is compared to an animal,[94] it is not
as if the whole soul were included under sin, and therefore
became the soul of an animal or of another body.

The soul dwells in the body now and it will in the end,
since they are made one person, but it does not become a
body, even if it is completely dulled. The soul is not distributed among the parts of the body, nor located in one
place. There is not more life in the greater parts of the body
and less life in the smaller parts. The rational soul is a spirit,
however bruised by evil, and is whole in every part.

The soul is not transmitted from father to son, lest there be
one soul for two people. The Lord says: "The soul of the
father is mine, and the soul of the son is mine."[95] No part of
the soul of the father is passed on to the son he begets. It is not
distributed or divided, increased or diminished, because of
its substance the spirit knows nothing of this. The soul cannot be greater, but better. If it was transferred in any way, it
would prove to be of the body. Some say erroneously that
the seed of the body has in it the seed of the soul and it is
passed on in the act of procreation, but this can lead to many

94. Ps 48:13, 21
95. Ezek 18:4

shameful and impossible effects that ought not to be said or thought about a rational spirit. It is not decent to probe into the private parts and examine the seed of the flesh that is wickedly emitted.

THE SOUL WAS CREATED IN TIME—THE MATERIAL OF THE FIRST CREATION WILL NOT BECOME THE MATERIAL OF THE NEW CREATION—ORIGINAL SIN IS CONTRACTED THROUGH THE FLESH—THE NECESSITY OF BAPTISM

41. We say that in their essence rational souls are made new daily from nothing, but in their nature which is in the likeness of God, they are not new. Souls of the same sort as he made on the sixth day of creation, male and female,[96] God now breathes into each daily, not a new type but a new creation from nothing. The Lord said, "My Father works and I work."[97] The Father and the Son work in this way, new in operation but not new in institution; acting in the case of the operation, resting in the case of the institution. After the first act of creation, no new bodily materials were created, but all created at one time, bodies are propagated by formation in time. Souls were not essentially all made together in this way, but they were made in a like nature, in the image and likeness of God. Thus they are thought to have been made together but judged not to have been sent out together; not sent out together for the sake of the essence, but made together for the sake of the form that is like to the image and likeness of God. Flesh is passed on to flesh in the act of procreation, but the spirit is in no way begotten by the spirit.

We hold as certain the doctrine that when flesh is drawn from flesh by the law of concupiscence, as soon as it is vivified, it is bound by the chain of original sin, and the soul which vivifies the flesh is weighed down by its affections. Children who die without the remedy of baptism are held fast by this chain of sin. They contract original sin not through the soul but through the flesh. It is that which infects the soul. For the flesh is so united to the soul that

96. Gen 1:27
97. Jn 5:17

they form one person. By the creative act of God, the soul and the flesh are one man, single and undivided, so that, saving what is proper to each nature, what is of the soul is added to the flesh, and what is of the flesh is added to the soul—for the unity of the person, not for the diversity of the nature. What there is then proper to each, becomes common to both; proper by nature, common by person. So the soul received the wound of original sin which was contracted by the flesh and passed into the soul to which the flesh is united in person although divided in nature. So it is essential that each child while he is alive should be renewed by the sacrament of Christ, lest the soul be harmed by companionship with the sinful flesh. For it weighs the soul down even when the soul goes forth from the body, if the soul does not receive the saving remedy of expiation while alive in the body. Adults who run, run on their own behalf. Let them apply the sacrament of faith to children. Let them receive the faith of Christ with the sacraments, so that the faith of the Church may protect these little ones reborn and works of faith may be united with the sacraments in the adults. This grace of new birth will ultimately be fulfilled in the general resurrection. The flesh itself will ultimately rise in glory and be restored to its soul, living and eternal, happy and blessed.

WHY THE SOUL IS GIVEN TO THE NON-BAPTIZED—WHAT NATURE IS—THE BREATH OF LIFE[98]

42. If you ask why God gives souls to those he knows will die without the remedy of salvation, we reply that it is because the divine institution by which all things were made, is not taken away by sin nor shackled by violence. For this reason the law of fleshy copulation is not deprived of its effect even in the evil. Adulterers, fornicators and profane persons beget children; in these, the natural process has not been lost. For nature, as God instituted it, accomplishes its

---

98. The doctrine here and in the preceding chap. is generally Augustinian, particularly on the fate of unbaptized infants.

own. Nature is an energy and power divinely implanted within created things which gives to each thing its being. Whoever uses good things wrongly is judged to be evil. Justly are they punished who abuse things that are permitted. Justly indeed are they punished who try to snatch incessantly at what is forbidden. Thus Satan lost heaven, and thus Adam (the first created) lost paradise. They abuse things that are permitted who disgrace the good things of God with forbidden uses. They likewise soil the good gifts of God, who exercise the act of carnal intercourse with ardor of lust. From these are born children, with bodies formed as creatures to serve their Creator, and God gives them life by breathing into them the breath of life. Understand the breath of life as the human soul, not produced by earth or water, but breathed in by God. By this he makes the senses of the body alive, and man is made a living soul.

In these and in other ways, the Almighty has done nothing to help the good or hinder evil, in that which he instituted. He advances the good by his grace, and the wicked he terrifies by his justice. And we his servants, find ourselves equally accused and wretched when we misuse the good gifts of the Lord. But the Lord, holy and almighty, is to be adored, who uses the evil of his servants for good. He has ordained that he will breath the soul into the earthly body propagated from the transmission of sin, turning to good our inbred wickedness which if it were natural to us could be imputed to the Creator. But our Creator has at all times prepared sacraments and proposed loving commands to obedience so that the sacraments should be a remedy of sin and the observance of passing commandments would offer the reward of eternal gifts. So if any child born under sin dies without the remedy of salvation, let him fear the justice of God, who ought to do no other than condemn in each the evil which he has not created in them. When children are redeemed by the sacrament, the mercy of God should be admired. For just as they know nothing of the guilt with which they are born from the flesh, so they know nothing of the grace by which they are reborn through Christ. Children are not exempt from guilt because they know nothing about it, nor are they excluded from grace because they know nothing about it. Do you ask in what their guilt consists? You will find that it is passed on to them by the flesh. Do you ask about their grace? You will find it comes from God. Because of the one, they deserve to be condemned; by the other they are saved without deserving it. One proclaims justice, the other shows forth mercy. In both God is known, whose mercy and justice is sung with perpetual praise.[99] But when we consider such matters our mind, feeble and blunted by sin, quickly returns to itself and seeks a remedy for itself so that what fell in Adam may rise again in Christ.

THE NATURE OF THE SOUL—THE DEATH OF MAN[100]

43. It is known that the ancients have said many things about the nature of the soul, but there is still something left to say. I have put their words together as carefully as I can, briefly and surely reducing them to one study which can be committed to memory. The memory of man is dull and rejoices in brevity; if it is divided among many things, it remembers less of each.

Man consists of body and soul. Whatever is seen with the eyes of the body is for the sake of the body, the body is for the sake of the soul and the soul for God. The life of the body is the soul; the life of the soul is God. The soul is immortal, because it lacks flesh, nor can it fall so that it needs to be restored after ruin, unless it falls into sin. So in death we do not lose our life, but the body is abandoned. The soul does not lose its power, but what it vivified it leaves, and, insofar as it pertains to it, it causes the death of the other which it itself does not experience. This, I say, it does by not vivifying what it leaves, not by losing its own life. So the death of man is none other than the destruction of the flesh. When the energy of the living power has been taken

99. Ps 100:1
100. Dependent on Hugh of St Victor, *Didascalicon* 2, 11; 4, 12.

away, it returns to the earth from which it was taken, losing the senses which it did not have on its own. The soul gives life to the flesh just as the sun gives light to the day when it comes; and it causes death when it departs. So death does not complete the union, but divides man, so that each part returns to its source. Lest anyone should think that the soul is involved in the death of the body, hear what the Lord said in the Gospel, "Do not fear those who kill the body but cannot kill the soul."[101] The body is wearied by the thoughts of the mind, and the mind while in the body is afflicted by the sorrows of the body.

THE SOUL IS INVISIBLE–REASON IS THE MIRROR IN WHICH IT SEES GOD[102]

44. The body is made up of four elements. The soul is neither an element nor from the elements but was made from nothing and is known to its Creator alone. It sees that it neither is nor can be any of the visible things that it sees in the body. It separates and divides itself from all that it sees visibly and it sees that it is entirely invisible in that it sees itself and nonetheless sees that it cannot be seen. So it raises itself above itself and sees the invisible God in that first and foremost mirror for beholding God, the mirror made more in his image and likeness by nearneis and knowledge. This mirror is reason itself, and by using reason the mind, which was made the first likeness of God, is able through itself to find him who made it and rest gently in his love and contemplation. Those who are most like their Creator manifest him more perfectly. This is so of the rational creature which more quickly knows and loves its Creator whom it has not seen when it knows itself to be in his image.

The rational mind is that which understands itself by thinking and from its birth has its image which is its word. The word of a thing is the knowledge of it formed from memory

101. Mt 10:28
102. Dependent on Hugh of St Victor, *De sacramentis* 1, 3, 6-7.

into its likeness. In this way it is manifest that the highest Wisdom begot a likeness of one substance with himself, that is, his Word, when he understood himself in his act of speaking. Because the rational mind is not always thinking about itself the way it always remembers itself, it is clear that when it reflects on itself, its word is born from memory. Whence it is clear that if it always thought about itself, the word would always be born from the memory. And this is so of the highest Wisdom, which always utters itself just as it always remembers itself. It is clear that the Word is born coeternally from the eternal memory. Just as the highest Wisdom is eternal, so his memory is eternal and he eternally understands himself, and eternally utters himself, when he speaks that which he understands. Since he utters himself eternally, his Word is eternally with him. The rational mind alone among all creation is able to rise up to look into the highest Wisdom, and to go forward in that discovery. It must always be diligent to remember him, to understand him and to love him. It was made for this, so that it might live foreever, if it always loves the highest Life, the highest Wisdom, the highest Essence, to whom it owes the fact of its existence. Man cannot love unless he remembers and takes care to understand. Therefore let him do that for which he was made, so that he may live well.

THREE KINDS OF REASON–THREE POWERS OF THE SOUL–WHAT LOVE IS[103]

45. The beatitude of almighty God cannot be increased because he is perfect nor diminished because he is eternal. He created rational spirits not out of any need of his, but only out of love, so that they might have a share in his beatitude. Some spirits he confirmed in his purity in heaven; other he cast into hell because of their pride; other, to test their humility and obedience, he joined to earthly bodies to live on the earth so that they might animate earthly matter. They

---

103. Dependent on Hugh of St Victor, *De sacramentis* 1, 6, 1; *De substantia dilectionis* 2 and *DUCS*.

have in their nature a certain mutability, since they have undertaken to give life to the body; in this they lay aside something of their purity. They are affected by preference for the body which drags them down like a weight and corrupts their purer nature. And while they are in these bodies, the more they cling to this vice, the more difficult it is for them to leave it when they depart from them. For they cannot do away with passion, even when they do away with the cause of passion, unless they have taken care in this life to cleanse themselves from this filth. So we who find ourselves in the midst of good and evil, ought often to consider the joy of the angels and the suffering of the devils and our own wretchedness. Our soul is rational and we can discern between good and evil. By the positive appetite and the negative appetite we can love good and hate evil. From the positive appetite love is born, and from love, desire and joy. Love is a delighting of any heart in another for his own sake, running there with desire and resting there with joy; desire is in the longing, joy in the fulfillment. If the human heart is good at all it is good for no other reason than that it loves well that which is good. If it is bad at all, it is bad because it loves badly that which is good. For everything that is, is good: but in that it is loved badly it is evil. From the negative appetite is born hatred, for from wrath comes hatred. And from hatred comes sorrow and fear. When we have a negative feeling toward our sins and begin to hate them, we sorrow because we have sinned and we fear the punishments for sins.

THE DIVERSE FATES OF RATIONAL CREATURES—THE FUNCTION OF THE FOUR POWERS OF DESIRE OF THE SOUL— THE FUNCTION OF REASON[104]

46. God the creator of all things deigned to crown the rational nature beyond all the rest of creation; he set on it the seal of his likeness and willed that it should be partaker

---

104. Concerning Stoic doctrine of the fourfold power of desire see the remarks on the treatises of William of St Thierry and Isaac of Stella in the Introduction, above, pp. .

of his bliss. But although rational creatures seem to have had the same origin, they were made for different states: some were established in eternal felicity; others were pulled down by the bonds of hell and committed to the pit of nether gloom to await their sentence in pain;[105] and a third part were joined to earthly bodies and given a middle place. At first this middle state was among the pleasures of paradise, near heaven; now because of the guilt of disobedience, it is nearer to hell and is humbled to a place of affliction. The highest of these places has the fullness of joy: the lowest, only sadness. In the one place there is complete happiness; in the other there is only the greatest misery. In the middle place, there is hope for heaven, but fear of hell. We have more cause to fear than to hope; for we are nearer to hell, and pass our time cast down under the shadow of death.

Since God knows that the human soul can, in virtue of the quality of its merits, partake of bliss or eternal damnation, he has put four natural powers of desire in man, so that he can choose the good and rejoice in it, and he can fear evil and grieve over it with perpetual sorrow. Our present condition is more serious when it does not show its grief and present harm. But fear has its punishment and hope which, deferred, afflicts the soul.[106] Our loving Father and terrible Judge has prepared at the end true and perpetual joys for his sons and unending sorrows for the guilty, but in this present state he wills us to have some experience of both joy and sorrow, so that these matters may not only more surely be believed, but also more lovingly hoped for and feared. Present joys cannot be compared to those joys, nor can present sorrow be compared to that sorrow. That man is foolish who prefers in all that he does to avoid the troubles of this life and lay hold of its joys, rather than to desire those joys and dread those sorrows. In this life we have to discover the kind of joy that can profit us and the kind of sorrow that will be for our healing. If anyone thanks God for his benefits and rejoices in them, he is both lifted up by devotion and also deplores the

105. 2 Pet 2:4
106. Prov 13:12

sins of himself and his neighbors. For this reason, Divine Providence has placed reason in the midst of the powers of desire in the heart of man, so that he can discern and judge in what to rejoice and in what to sorrow, what to desire and what to fear. We are taught that there are three powers of the soul: reason, and near to it, positive and negative appetite. The different powers of desire are joined to them by a certain relationship. Fear and sorrow seem to be included under the negative appetite, desire and joy under the positive.

MAN IS BETWEEN THE WORLD AND GOD[107]

47. During the interim the human soul fluctuates among different emotions, but finally it must accept an established place either in the depths or in the heights, to continue there henceforth in either total joy or complete sorrow. God is above, the world is below. God remains always in his same eternal state. The world fluctuated and is always unstable in its changing course. The human intellectual soul is as it were placed in between them. By excellence of its condition it rises above the mutability which is below, it yet does not reach to the true immutability of God. If anyone is immersed by his own desires into the passing things of the lower realm, he is at once caught in infinite distractions and in some way he is divided from himself. If he rises up from the infinite distractions below and leaves these weaknesses, and gradually collects himself into one, he has learned to be with himself. The more he rises up by thought and desire, the more he is unified until at length he will be wholly immutable and come to that true and unique unchangeableness which is with God, where he will rest forever without the vicissitudes of change.

THE ORIGIN OF SOULS—FREE WILL—ELECTION[108]

48. We believe that souls were not created in the beginning with the angels, as Origen taught. Nor were they begotten by

107. Dependent on Hugh of St Victor, *De vanitate mundi* 2.
108. Dependent on LDE 14-18 where this information on ancient theories of the soul is found.

the intercourse of bodies, as the Luciferians, Cyril and other Latins presume to affirm. We say that their creation is known solely to the Creator of all things. The body is begotten by intercourse, by the judgment of God it is solidified in the womb, put together and formed. When the body is formed, the soul is created and infused into it. So man lives in the womb, formed of body and soul, and he comes forth alive from the womb as a fully human person. Nor do we believe that there are two souls in man, as many have written—an animal soul which animates the body and is part of the blood, and a spiritual soul which is part of reason. We say it is one and the same soul in man, which vivifies the body by its companionship and disposes itself by its own reason having in itself free will, so that knowing itself it chooses what it wants. Free will was committed to man. After Eve was seduced by the serpent and fell,[109] man lost the goodness of his nature and the vigor of his judgment but not the power of choice, lest he not have the means to emend his sin. It remained to him to seek salvation by free will, that is by rational choice; but first he had to be helped and inspired by God to seek salvation. That we accept the inspiration to salvation is within our power; that we attain what we desire to attain is a divine gift. It is due to our concern and also heaven's assistance that we do not waver once we have received the gift of salvation. If we do waver it is because of our weakness and laziness. We believe that only man has a substantial soul which lives on when it has put off the body and which keeps a lively hold on its powers of knowledge and genius.

The soul does not die with the body as Aratus asserts; nor after it is buried, as Aeno said; it lives substantially. The souls of animals are not alive substantially, but the animation of their bodies is born with their flesh and ends with the death of the flesh. So they are not ruled by reason, as Plato and Alexander thought, but they are led by all natural attractions.

The human soul does not die with the flesh, because, as we said above, it is not begotten with the flesh, but formed in

109. Gen 3:6

the bodily womb of the mother. We say it was created and infused by the judgment of God, so that man lives in the womb and thus at his birth enters into the world. The soul has its beginning from its Creator, from whom it is, and it is perfect in its kind. He knows all that man can know, except the burden of the flesh. The first man, before his humanity was corrupted, knew from whence he was, because he had perfect human knowledge. But this was corrupted by the corruption of mankind, which joined it to corruption. Nor could man exercise his properties until he had learned discernment by practice and experience and the teaching he was given. Just as if someone with keen eye-sight went into a dark place; he would not be able to see there until he became accustomed to the darkness or lit a light. As Vergil says: "How greatly are they held back by the evil of the body."[110] Some actions belong to the body, others to the soul, but the vices and virtues of the body belong properly to the soul. For this is the purpose of the soul, that it might correct the unlawful motions of the flesh, and restrain its ignorance or negligence. If the disciple of a teacher or the servant of a master sins by negligence, the teacher or master is not without blame: so the soul is not without blame for what happens in the body. The soul ought to rule and the body to obey.

THE INTERIOR SENSES OF MAN—THE NEED FOR MEDITATION[111]

49. Man is formed of two substances, soul and flesh: the soul with its reason, the flesh with its senses. The senses without being joined to the soul would not move the flesh, but the soul retains its reasoning faculty apart from the flesh. It should be noticed that those very senses which we have described in the exterior man in a similar way are manifested in the interior man in their own manner; for spiritual things are not understood by the corporeal senses but by the spiritual

110. *Aeneid* 6:731
111. Dependent on LDE 19-20 and Hugh of St Victor, *De modo orandi* 1. This chap. also influenced the seventh of the Pseudo-Anselmian *Meditationes*.

ones. So it is that the Divine Voice says in Deuteronomy: "See, I am God and there is none else beside me,"[112] and in Revelation: "Those who have ears to hear let them hear what the Spirit says to the churches,"[113] and in the Psalter: "Taste and see how gracious the Lord is." [114] The Apostle also says: "Christ is to us a sweet savor, to those who are perishing and to those who are saved;"[115] and in the Gospel the Lord showed that the woman touched him by faith rather than by the body when he said: "Someone touched me, for I felt power go out of me."[116] So we should notice very carefully just what pertains to the senses of the body and what to the dignity of the soul, lest perhaps because of a confused order and an irrational statement it seem to someone to be contrary to the truth. There is no third spirit in man's make-up, as Didymus contended, but the soul itself is the spirit; it is called "spirit" either because of its spiritual nature or because it is breathed into the body. The soul is so called because it animates the body making it live and give life. The third spirit which the apostle mentions together with the soul and the body,[117] we understand to be the grace of the Holy Spirit which the Apostle prays may be preserved whole in us, so that our vices will not lessen it or make it flee from us for "the Holy Spirit will flee deceit, and go away from thoughts that are without discernment."[118]

When we engage in meditation we stir up the intellectual soul and consider our miseries and necessities, our labor and our sorrow. For we come into this life sorrowing, we live in it by labor, and we go out of it with grief and fear. We know how short our life is, how slippery the way, how certain is death, and how uncertain the hour of death. We reflect that when anyone enjoys any sweet or happy event, there is much bitterness mixed in with it; we think how false and suspect, unstable and transitory, is whatever is born of love of this world, whatever it promises of fairness or temporal beauty. We should consider the beauty, sweetness and goodness of the heavenly country. We should direct our attention and

112. Deut 32:39
113. Rev 2:29
114. Ps 33:6
115. 2 Cor 11:15
116. Lk 8:46
117. 1 Thess 5:23
118. Wis 1:5

ourselves to the place whence we have fallen, and see where we find ourselves, understand what we have lost and what we have found, so that from both we may understand how much we should grieve because of our exile. As Solomon says: "He who increases in wisdom, increases in sorrow."[119] Because the more a man understands his evils, the more he sighs and groans.

WHAT MEDITATION IS—KNOWLEDGE—COMPUNCTION—DEVOTION— PRAYER—DESIRE—THAT KNOWLEDGE SHOULD GOVERN ALL THESE[120]

50. Meditation leads to knowledge, knowledge to compunction, compunction to devotion, and devotion is completed in prayer. To meditate is to look into things continually and investigate mysteries with interest and wisdom, bringing what is hidden to light. Knowledge is when a man attains through careful meditation knowledge of himself. Compunction is when his heart is touched by inner grief from considering his sins. Devotion is a pious and humble desire for God, humble because we know our own weakness, pious in consideration of the mercy of God. Prayer is devotion of the mind, that is, conversion to God through a pious and humble desire. Desire is a spontaneous and sweet turning of the soul toward God. Nothing so moves God to love and mercy as the pure desire of the mind.

Men are accustomed to praise and love the knowledge of heavenly and earthly things: but it is much better for a man to know himself. That intellectual soul is more praiseworthy that knows its own wretchedness than he who disregards it and examines the stars and the nature of things. Anyone who truly watches unto the Lord, the Holy Spirit stirs up with warmth, and in his love he knows himself to be vile. He longs to come to God, but he cannot. He attends to the light that is within him, and finds himself, and realizes that his own illness cannot be mingled with God's purity. Then he weeps

---

119. Eccles 1:18
120. This chap. is found in the Pseudo-Bernard, *De interiori domo (Domus haec)* 29; it also influenced the seventh of the Pseudo-Anselmian *Meditationes*.

for love, and prays God to have mercy upon him, and deliver him out of all his miseries. And so knowledge does not puff up this needy and sorrowful man, because charity builds him up.[121] He prefers one kind of knowledge to another, that is, to know himself and his weakness, rather than to know the virtues of plants and the nature of animals. And by learning this knowledge he learns sorrow, the sorrow of a pilgrimage and the desire of his homeland and the vision of God whom he sees as the goal, to whom is glory forever and ever. Amen. He grieves over his exile, for he is far from the kingdom. He grieves also to realize what evil he has done, how great it is, and how intolerable are the punishments he will have to suffer.

EXAMINING AND CONSIDERING OUR STATE—A CONSIDERATION OF THE VICES[122]

51. Since no knowledge is better than that by which a man knows himself, let us consider our thoughts, words and deeds. Of what profit is it to us if we subtly explore the natures of all created things and effectively comprehend them and yet do not know ourselves. Let us look at what we have done, and see if it was what we ought to have done, and consider whether what we do in the futue is going to be according to the will of God. It is very necessary to examine ourselves carefully, so that we may learn from what we have done to act more cautiously in the future. Often we find that the work we believed we had begun with good intentions, has thrown us into a snare of deception, and that to the degree in which, secure in the goodness of our intention, we did not look carefully to the end of the action. We are imprudent and run straight into the pit; we see what we are doing, but we pay no attention to what the result will be. In this way the desire of the soul is ambiguous, for we can discern the quality of the intention only from the end of the work. So it is necessary every day that we judge our loves and examine ourselves

---

121. 1 Cor 8:1

122. This chap. is found in the *De interiori domo* 43. It depends on Hugh of St Victor, *De institutione novitiarum* 9. Chaps. 51-65 constitute a separate work. L. Norpoth, according to D. Aschoff, *op. cit.*, 293, holds that they are of a thirteenth-century origin.

about what we have done, by day and night. How eager have we have to do good, how constant in avoiding evil? In any work of ours have we been misled by the snares of the enemy? Has past deception made us aware of the possibilities of future fraud? Then, may we be neither unprepared for temptation and fall into evil deeds, nor fall into negligence by undertaking good works without discretion.

Whoever submits his heart to this kind of scrutiny is listening to what the wise man said: "Know yourself."[123] Know whence you came and whither you are going; how you live, how much you are progressing or losing ground; how far you are from God or how near, not by space, but by likeness or unlikeness of character. Know what it is to be a man, conceived in sin, born in misery, living in punishment, dying of necessity. It is certain that you will die, but it is not certain how or when or where. For death everywhere awaits you and if you are wise you will expect it everywhere. Take heed and be careful what you do, or what you ought to do. If you do what you ought to have done, if you have not mingled evil with your good deeds, if what you have done is good, it should fill you with devotion. Consider if you love the good of another as your own, and if you reprove evil in yourself as you would in another; if you are turning away from evil to do good. There are those who fuss a great deal about avoiding evil; these are fainthearted, and it keeps them from doing good lest they be surprised by evil. There are others who attend only to the good they do, they so please and flatter themselves by their good works, that they are not the least afraid of their being mixed with evil. There are some wise to do evil but ignorant of how to do good. These are the worst of all, for they rejoice when they do evil and exult in the worst deeds. There are those who seek God through external things leaving aside the interior ways by which God is within.

123. Socrates claims to have received this precept from the Delphic oracle: Xenophon, *Memorabilia* 4, 2, 24-25. It was inscribed on one of the columns of the peristyle in the front of the temple: Plato, *Charmides* 164d. *Phys corp* opens with this, see above, p.

THREE STAGES OF THOUGHT–THE MIND IS EXTENDED–THE MIND IS
LIFTED UP–THE MIND IS OUTSIDE ITSELF–THE MIND OF MAN IS A
MIRROR BUT IT IS DARKENED BY SIN–HOW IT IS CLEANSED[124]

52. Let us return to ourselves, so that we can ascend to
ourselves. The ascent we must make is threefold: first we go
up from exterior and inferior things to ourselves; then we go
into the depths of the heart, and the further we go, the
higher we ascend. He who does not go up, goes down, and he
who does not go forward goes back. In the third ascent we go
up to God. The first part of the ascent is made by considering
the world and despising it. We consider how perishable and
transitory are earthly things in order to condemn them and
return to ourselves. The second part of the ascent is made by
knowing and despising ourselves. When we realize how prone
we are to evil, and how weak we are for good, we despise
ourselves and go beyond ourselves. The third part of the
ascent is made by knowledge and love of God. This third
ascent is made by expanding the mind, raising the mind and
going beyond the mind. The mind is expanded when we hold
many things in one insight whether it be about the wisdom of
God, or his power or his goodness. We have to consider how
God mightily created everything from nothing, wisely gov-
erns it and benignly provides for it. He made the whole beautiful world for the sake of the body, the body for the soul
and the soul for himself. We should care for our souls dil-
igently, so that we may be able to give them back, cleansed
and sanctified, to God from whom we have received such
great goods for them.

The mind is raised up when we rise from things visible to
things invisible. When we consider the dignity of man, we are
in wonder at the honor of God, who has so marvellously
created the rational spirit in his own image and likeness. The
mind goes beyond itself when it is taken up above itself. No
man can be taught anything about this going beyond the

124. Dependent on Hugh of St Victor, *De arca Noe morali* 3, 6. The three stages
of mystical ascent *(dilatatio, sublevatio, alienatio)* are found in Richard of St
Victor, *Benjamin maior* 5, 2-5.

mind because there is nothing that is his own. He can be taught about expanding and raising the mind, for he has something there. It is taught sometimes by human effort, sometimes by divine revelation or inspiration. Sometimes in the mirror of his heart, that is, the rational mind, a man can see himself and God. The heart of man is so made that the Lord should dwell in it as in his temple and be reflected in it as in a mirror; so that he who cannot be seen in himself may appear in his image. Great is the dignity of man, to bear the image of God and always to see his face in himself, always having his presence there through contemplation. After we had sinned, we scattered our delight upon the earth, and by sin our heart was covered with dust. We fell from the inner mirror of contemplation to wander among the wretched shadows of this life, where we cannot worthily serve God because of the filth of our iniquity. We wander about in the darkness of ignorance, and for the most part we do not see either what we should do or what we should avoid. Let us cleanse our mirror from the love of vanity and from the love of iniquity, that is from dust and from filth, so that we may see in it ourselves, and our Creator, whom we cast behind our back when we sin. We are the adversaries of God, our sin separates us from him. So we say with the prophet, "Turn us, O God of our salvation."[125] If a woman loses the mirror in which she looks at herself she eagerly searches for it and carefully cleans it from dust and filth. How much more ought we to seek and cleanse and look into the interior mirror of man, so that we may see in it the whole of our shamefulness and thus through knowledge of ourselves come to the knowledge of God.

TWO THINGS ARE NECESSARY FOR SELF-KNOWLEDGE—MAN IS DUST AND ASHES—HOW MUCH WE OWE TO THE GRACE OF GOD—THIS KNOWLEDGE GIVES BIRTH TO HUMILITY, CHARITY AND SO ON[126]

53. Two things are necessary that we may know ourselves, namely, in what way we are evil and in what way we are

125. Ps 84:5
126. Dependent on Augustine, *Confessiones* 2, 7. Cf. also *Manuale* 25.

good. We are prone to evil and if the mercy of God were not holding us back, we could fall into every kind of vice and not rise up again unless the mercy of God were to follow us and lift us up. This the Prophet knew well when he said, "Lord, your mercy is ever before my eyes"[127] which has care of me, and "your mercy shall follow me"[128] to set me right. We are incapable of good and without the grace of God we cannot do good or persevere in it. This the Apostle realized when he said: "By the grace of God, I am what I am, and his grace has not been in vain in me, but is ever with me."[129] Both these thoughts were known to Abraham when he said, "I speak to my Lord, I who am but dust and ashes."[130] Man is indeed a thing of dust. Just as dust is blown by the wind in every direction, and cast into some place and remains there, so man can fall into every vice, and he cannot rise unless the mercy of God helps him. Man is ashes. Just as ashes bring forth no life of themselves nor foster the life of any seed they receive so neither can man do good nor persevere in any good without the grace of God. So we should give the greatest thanks to God who has given us so much good and forgiven so much evil that we have done and delivered us from many sins which we were as able to commit as the many we actually did. Whatever evil we have not done, it is of his mercy that we have not done it. If he had permitted it, we would have done it, either in deed or in desire. Therefore, I do not know if we should love him more for the evil which he forgave us, or for the evil from which he preserved us. Perhaps we should think of those things which we have not done as if we had done them and he had forgiven them, since we would have done them at least in will if he had allowed it. Whoever in truth so knows himself is humble before God and men. He loves God for the sake of God, and all men also for God's sake. If he has perfect charity, he judges no one, accuses no one and condemns no one; he is not angry nor does he cause

127. Ps 25:3
128. Ps 22:6
129. 1 Cor 15:10
130. Gen 18:27

quarrels; he does not sow discord nor increase harm; he does not persecute the innocent nor hate those who are against him. He does nothing underhand, gives no false evidence, is not a perjurer; he runs no one down, hurts no one, hates no one, but loves all men. As Scripture says: "You ought not to owe any man anything except that you love one another."[131] Charity is so dear to God that he will not dwell in him who has not charity. Whoever has charity, has God; for God is charity.[132] And whoever hates any man, loses God and all the good he has done. So let each man take care lest for hatred of one person, he lose God and all good.

THE DOUBLE GOOD IN MAN—THE TWOFOLD SENSES—THE INTENTION OF AN ACTION—REASON LEADS TO KNOWLEDGE OF THE TRINITY[133]

54. Now let us turn back to our mirror and see how we can ascend from knowledge of ourselves to knowledge of God himself. The nature of man is twofold. There is an interior man, which is the essential man, since each man is his mind;[134] and another exterior man which is his body. Man is compacted of this twofold nature, and so that the whole might come to bliss God has from the beginning prepared a double good, one visible, the other invisible, one corporeal, the other incorporeal, that in the one the senses of the flesh might find enjoyment and in the other the mind's power of knowing might be happily fulfilled. The rational soul is taught by both these, taking in what is visible by the bodily senses, and what is invisible by the mind's power of knowledge, so that by both visible and invisible things it is stirred up to knowledge and love of the Creator. All human actions should be directed to the end either of restoring the likeness

131. Rom 13:8

132. 1 Jn 4:16

133. Dependent on Hugh's *De sacramentis* 1, 6, 5-6; 3, 21 and *Didascalicon* 7, 21, 23. This chap. also appears in *Manuale* 26.

134. " ... *quoniam mens uniuscuiusque est ipse.*" This quotation from Cicero's *Somnium Scipionis* was know to the Middle Ages through the *Commentary* of Macrobius (ed. Willis, p. 162.).

of the image of God in man, or of seeing to the necessities of life. The divine likeness is restored in us in two ways, by seeing truth and by exercising virtue, for in this man is like God who is wise and just. Those things more perfectly manifest their Creator which are most like him. This is especially true of the rational mind which was made excellently and properly in his likeness. It then quickly knows its Creator whom it has not seen when it understands that it is made in his likeness.

In this the mind first discovered traces of the Trinity when it began to know what it was in itself and from that considered what was above itself. It sees that the wisdom which is in it comes from itself and it loves that wisdom; and love proceeds from it and its wisdom, by which it loves what is born of it, and what remains undivided from it. So there is here three in one: mind, wisdom, and love. Wisdom is from the mind, and love proceeds from the mind and wisdom. This is a trinity in which the unity is not lost; they are at once both three and one. Thus it is in us. It is even more so in God. For God is the origin of all wisdom and he always has wisdom and always loves it; because he always loves it, he always has love. He begets the wisdom he has, yet it is always with him, because the begotten does not separate itself from the begettor. It is being begotten because it is always eternal; always having been begotten because it is perfect. It does not begin when begotten nor cease after having been begotten. He who begets is the Father, he who is begotten is the Son, and he who proceeds from both is the Holy Spirit. The Father proceeds from no one, the Son from the father alone, the Holy Spirit equally from the Father and the Son. We confess that these three must be substantially one in God. Because he who is begotten cannot be he from whom he has been begotten, nor can he who proceeds from begettor and begotten be either he who begets or he who is begotten, by an incontrovertibly true argument we are compelled to recognize that in God there are three persons, one in substance and equal in majesty. So the Father and the Son and the Love of the father and the Son are one God, and by one love they love themselves because they are one, nor do they love anything in each other except what each loves in himself. No one of them is anything but what the others are, so that each must love himself and one another. God our Father manifested this charity and this trinity to us when for the overwhelming love whereby he loved us[135] he sent his Son in the likeness of sinful flesh[136] for our salvation and he sent the Holy Spirit to bring us the adoption of sons. He gave the Son as the price of redemption and the Holy Spirit as the privilege of love and himself he saves as an inheritance for the adopted sons.

THE NAMES OF THE TRINITY—THE LIFE OF ETERNAL HAPPINESS[137]

55. Father, Son and Holy Spirit are names of goodness, names of gentleness, sweetness and love. Who is more gentle than the Father, who so great, kind and merciful? Who is dearer than Jesus Christ? Our savior is all healing, all goodness, gentleness, sweetness. Who is more loving, dear and holy than the Holy Spirit? He is the love of the Father and the Son, and by him all who are made holy receive sanctification. Let us consider how great will be the glory, how ineffable the joy when we come to God the Father and he places us in his kingdom as sons and heirs; when Jesus Christ treats us as brothers and co-heirs; when the Holy Spirit makes us to be one spirit with them. He is the indissoluble bond of love and of the Trinity. Then we shall enter into the power of the Lord,[138] and we shall see that city of which such glorious things are spoken.[139] In that city life is calm, there is tranquil peace, perpetual happiness, beauty to be wondered at, sights to be praised, joys to be longed for, glory to be desired, joy ever-new, festivity without end, the sweetest of songs. There all hearts are turned to a kind of ineffable gentleness and

135. Eph 11:4
136. Rom 8:3
137. Dependent on Hugh of St Victor, *De arrha animae* and *Didascalicon* 7, 21. This chapter is very similar to the Pseudo-Hugh, *De diligendo Deo* 2 and the Pseudo-Bernard, *De cognitione humanae conditionis* 3.
138. Ps 70:16
139. Ps 86:3

rejoicing. Eternal joys are there which fill those who partake of them with sweetness and lead to no corruption; always renewed, never failing, they give nourishment and remain whole; they come to fruition and are forever incorrupt. In that city delight flows into enjoyment, beauty into rejoicing, vision into delight. There all beauty is, for there is the height of all beauty. How great must be that beauty, where all loveliness flourishes without defect, abides without passing away, continues without corruption and is eternally unchanged?

If there is so much that is beautiful that is not true beauty, what is beauty? O holy city, beautiful city, whatever is in you is entirely beautiful, gracious, joyous—it is one single good and all goods are in it. For whatever good I can name is entirely there, for all goods are in one good and are one good. The love and desire for such great good touches me at times and affects me greatly and sweetly, and takes me out of myself, I know not how. Suddenly. I am changed and altered, caught up by desire, drawn on by longing, and it begins to be well with me, beyond anything I am able to say. Awareness is heightened, the memory of passing sorrows is forgotten, the intellectual soul rises up, the discernment is clear, the powers of desire turn towards things above, the heart is illuminated, longings rejoice. I seem to be elsewhere, I know not where. For I see, but still as if far off, choirs of angels and archangels praising and lauding God. It is all one there, to contemplate the wonders of God and to praise him in all his works. There everything is seen, praised and enjoyed in God whose countenance is love, whose face is beautiful and whose words are sweet. He is delightful to see, gentle to possess, sweet to enjoy. There one always sees him, always possesses him, always enjoys his possession and delights in him. He is pleasing himself and because of himself. This is merit enough, reward enough. Nothing outside him is sought there, because everything that is desired is found in him, and everything that is loved. There is one good, and all good is in it. Only the good see and have this good; they love it and praise it with unending praise.

THE INTELLECTUAL SPIRIT—THE LIFE AND DEATH OF THE SOUL—THE WEIGHT OF ETERNAL PUNISHMENT—THE CHIEF PUNISHMENTS[140]

56. When I consider the nature of the soul, I see that it can give life to the flesh but it cannot recollect itself in good thoughts as it desires. So it seems to me that it is an intellectual spirit, living by the power of its Creator and keeping the body alive, but under the control of vanity and subject to change for it is often lifted up by joy, afflicted by fear, dead because of sin and alive because of righteousness. God is the life of the soul; sin is the death of the soul. "The soul that sins shall die"[141] but he who does what is right and just shall live and not die. So the soul is immortal and yet can die and it is mortal yet it cannot die. Mortal by immortality and immortal by mortality. For to the miserable death is without death, end without end, weakness without weakness, for death lives on, the end is always beginning, and weakness knows no expiration. Death will bring it to an end, but it will not extinguish it; sorrow will torture it, and dread will not leave it; the flames will burn it but not banish the darkness. In the fire there will be darkness, in the darkness, fear, in the fear, burning. So the reprobate will be dragged into the flames of hell, to feel the pain of torment and in sorrow and anguish they will tremble. They will suffer always and they will always be in fear, because they live without end, always in agony, with no hope of pardon or mercy, which is misery beyond misery. For if after as many thousand years as there are hairs on the heads of all who have ever lived or will live, they could hope that their punishment would end, they would bear it much more lightly. But because they have not and will not have any such hope, they fall into despair, and cannot bear the torment. Of these Isaiah has written, "Their worm dies not and their fire is not extinguished"[142] because they are not consumed. Worms gnaw the conscience, fire burns the flesh, for whoever sins against the Maker in his

---

140. Dependent on Hugh, *De sacramentis* 2, 18, 4. This chap. is also very close to the Pseudo-Bernard, *De cognitione humanae conditionis* 3.
141. Ezek 18:20
142. Is 66:24

heart and body is punished in heart and in body. When the soul is cut off from the life of bliss and the body cast into eternal torment, there is fear and anguish, struggle and grief. Then one will in truth only groan in sorrow because repentance then will be of no avail. The cruel tormentor will be there, the gnawing worms, the consuming fire. Sins will be exposed, the guilt will be punished, and this will be forever. Whoever goes into that torment will not get out again. The pain of burning will torment from without, the punishment of blindness will obscure from within. They will see the torments of hell, and in those torments they will see those whom they have loved with inordinate love contrary to the commandments of God, so that the ruin of these latter will afflict them, increasing their damnation. God they see not, which is the misery of all miseries. Who can say how great the punishment is of not seeing the Creator and Maker of all things, the Son, the Redeemer and Savior, the King of heaven and earth, the Lord of all, "by whom we live and move and have our being."[143]

OF THE PRUDENCE OF FOLLOWING AFTER GOOD AND AVOIDING EVIL—A MEDITATION ON ETERNAL JOY—THE JOYS SHARED BY THE BLESSED—PERFECT HAPPINESS—OCCUPATION AND GIFTS[144]

57. Therefore we must always be watchful and careful not to do what is wrong, or to fail to do the right that is laid upon us. We must not be puffed up by the thought of the good that we have done. Many have fallen into hell because they were proud of their virtue. Let us seek after good and desire it, and be alert to avoid evil, lest under the appearance of good we do evil because often the vices deceive us by seeming to be virtues. Whoever calls to mind the evil he has done, takes care to abstain even from what is licit; and he who has done what is forbidden, deprives himself even of what is allowed. He who truly laments his sin, fears to commit evil; and reprimands himself for small things, when he remembers the wrong he has done in great things. No matter

143. Acts 17:28
144. Dependent on *DQA* 34.

how serious the mind becomes and increases in virtue, yet the fleshly senses have to root out a certain external childishness; and unless they are bridled in their youthful heat, they draw a weak mind to inconstancy and levity. If this goes on for long, when the mind wishes to rise above it, it cannot, but is held down by the weight of bad habits. "So let whosoever stands take heed lest he fall;"[145] and if anyone should fall, let him rise up quickly in compunction of heart, by the confession of his lips and the works of sanctification. Let him be more humble in his own conscience, more fervent and prompt to do penance and more cautious to be on guard.

He who desires only the bliss of heaven despises temporal things and loves nothing that is worldly, but strives only toward that eternal country; he cherishes a great tranquility of mind by which man discerns more clearly how great God is when he finds himself alone with him alone. Nothing is more present than God, nothing more hidden. Let us seek to cut off from our minds the crowd of earthly desires, and expel from the hidden depths of the heart the tumult of unlawful thoughts. Let us sigh for the heavenly country in the love of inner quiet and rise up to the height of the contemplation of God. Let us contemplate the choir of angels, the company of blessed spirits, the majesty of the vision of God and see how God refreshes his saints by the sweetness of his eternal vision. No one in this life is able to understand the happiness of seeing God face to face, the sweetness of hearing the music of the angels; the joy of the companionship of the saints. Each one will rejoice in the bliss of the other, as much as he does for his own unspeakable joy, and he will have as many joys as he has companions. In that glory I look upon nothing more readily, I find nothing more delightful to contemplate than that movement of inner love by which each one will love the other as much as he loves himself and God more than himself and all others with God. And God will love them more than they love themselves in this perpetual joy. We shall see nothing there extraneous; we shall love nothing unworthy, we shall hear nothing that would offend

145. 1 Cor 10:12

our ears. Everything there is agreeable, everything joyful, everything peaceful. All are at one, because all are safe under the rule of heaven. All happiness is there, all sweetness, all joy, all pleasantness, all beauty and all gentleness.

Whatever is free and pleasant is there; there is all that is rich and delightful, all rest, all consolation. There is continual tranquility, pleasant serenity, eternal rejoicing, joyful and beautiful praise and full knowledge of all that is good. What can be lacking there where God is in whom nothing is lacking? However many are there they are gods, nor is it necessary for anyone to say to another, "Know the Lord."[146] All know him and see him; all praise him and love him. They know without error, see without ending, praise without wearying, love without tiring. They always behold and always desire to behold, so desireable is it to behold him. They always love and always desire to love, so sweet he is to love. And as much as they love, so much more they want to love; so delightful he is to enjoy. They rest in this delight in the fullness of God, full of blessing and holiness. Always cleaving to beatitude, they are blessed; always contemplating eternity, they are eternal; joined to the true light, they are made light; always gazing at what does not change they are changed into unchangeableness. With as much freedom as sweetness they gaze at his loving appearance, his gentle face, his sweet words. O the blessed vision, to see the King of Angels in his beauty,[147] to behold the Holy of holies, through which all are holy! To see him is the height of happiness, the sum of rejoicing, eternal and blessed life.

CONGRATULATIONS TO THE DEVOUT WHO ENJOY GOD—TO THOSE WHO HAVE NOT EXPERIENCED THEY CANNOT DESCRIBE THEIR JOY

58. O you righteous, rejoice and exult, because you see him whom you love, you have him whom you have long desired, you hold him whom you never fear to lose. Therefore, sing and exult in him, for he is the Lord your God, glorious and beautiful, he is salvation and life, honor and glory, peace and

146. Jer 31:34
147. Is 33:17

all good things. How great a peace is there, where nothing annoys you whether from others or from yourselves, but the Lord is your shepherd and you lack nothing.[148] He has prepared for you a kingdom, that you may eat and drink at his table in his kingdom.[149] "Taste then and see how sweet the Lord is."[150] It is sweet to see, sweet is the Lord. It is sweet to live, it is sweet to taste. I cannot say how great is the pleasure of that taste, how great the savor of that joy, how delectable that scent. You who have known by experience cannot intimate to us who have never tasted it the greatness of that sweetness. Just as no one can explain in words the sweetness of honey to him who has never tasted anything sweet, since he will not grasp by hearing a savor which his mouth has not tasted, so no words can express the sweetness the righteous know by experience.

HE DEPLORES HIS WRETCHEDNESS AND INVOKES THE SAINTS— THE SOURCE OF THE CHANGEABLENESS OF THE MIND, AND WHAT IT TEACHES US [151]

59. Alas, miserable man that I am, I never experience what you experience, nor am I where you are. You are in that place of coolness, light and peace, where you will never taste death, where you know no error, where your love has no offence and your joy no concern. In this region of the shadow of death[152] I do not know my ultimate end,[153] I do not know if I will deserve love or hatred.[154] I know not when I shall go forth from the body. I shall go forth, I know not when, and perchance that day is very near, therefore, trembling and afraid, I look daily for death which threatens me on every side. I think that the devil is all around me to attack me

148. Ps 22:1
149. Lk 22:29f
150. Ps 33:9
151. Dependent on Hugh of St Victor, *De sacramentis*, 2, 18, 21. Much of this chap. is also in the Pseudo-Bernard, *De cognitione humane conditionis* 10.
152. Mt 4:16; Is 9:2
153. Cf. Ps 38:5
154. Eccles 9:1

on every side. I fear and tremble at the final judgment and the wrath of the stern judge, lest for my sins he send me into the fires of hell. And just as you cannot show to me your joy and gladness in the vision of God, so I cannot properly explain to you the needs and weaknesses that I endure, the sins and offences I have committed, the faults and infinite negligences that I have done and do daily without ceasing in heart and mouth and deed, in all the ways by which human frailty can offend God.

You who have deserved to be citizens of the eternal city and enjoy the glory of eternal light, pray for me to the Lord, that he may deliver me from this prison in which I am bound and held captive.[155] The mind is blind and wandering, it varies with the quality of the things it see; its thought and sense are changed with what it beholds; and when it tries to be stable, it is, in some way I know not how, divided from itself. When it is intent on anything, it is soon moved from it by boredom. When it strives eagerly in thought and suddenly is tired of thinking, it is taught that it depends on some other source and there where it was placed it will not find rest. It rests in God alone, who has formed it. But because everything it desires below is less, it follows that it cannot be satisfied by whatever is not God. So it is that here below it is distracted and drawn away by many things, seeking rest where there is none. It seeks places of delight where it may pause. But because it has left the one God who can satisfy it completely, it is led among many things, so that since it cannot be satisfied with the quality of them, it is at least satiated by the variety.

THE MIND MUST BE RECALLED TO HEAVENLY THINGS—
ASPIRATIONS FOR DOING THIS—THE GLORY OF
HEAVEN—THE JOY OF THE HEAVENLY CITY

60. Therefore we must recollect our scattered thoughts and draw ourselves together in the single longing for eternity. Let us accustom ourselves to contemplate the Creator always so as to enjoy stability of mind. We strive now with toil to do

155. Gen 40:14

this in imitation of that which later we will receive with rejoicing as a gift. Let us be solicitous to withdraw our years from earthly care, to withdraw them from evils, so that we may turn in thought and desire for an hour or a half to the city of the Lord of Hosts.[156] Let us consider and estimate as far as we can what that glory will be, how great that joy, that solemnity, that veneration, that dancing of the heavenly citizens, who have chosen assiduously to praise their Creator, to give him honor, offer him devotion, and sing the new song, that joyful song, with a tremendous voice, most fervent love, ineffable singing, wondrous desire, celestial jubilation and spiritual modulation. He indeed is their true food, full satisfaction, eternal rest, highest beatitude, eternal happiness, everlasting salvation, unchanging virtue and immortal life.

I often think upon these things and strive to rise up to them.
I sigh, I lament, I reach out thither by prayer and longing.
And I marvel at their ways there, how they circle round.
There the mind cleaves to Christ, the heart delights in him;
There it rests and rejoices, there it wonders and adores.

The more often, the sweeter; much desired, but never producing satiety; how rare the hour and short the stay. If only I might rest in peace in the self same,[157] and dwell in the house of the Lord all the days of my life.[158] If only I shall ever be able to see him—so desirable—upon whom the angels desire to look.[159] I could then say lo, I see him whom I have desired, I have him whom I have chosen. When shall I come and appear before the face of the Lord,[160] to see him in the goodness of his elect, to rejoice in the joy of his nation that he might be praised with his inheritance.[161] When shall I see that city of which it is said, "Your streets, O Jerusalem, shall be paved

156. Cf. Rev 8:1; Ps 23:10
157. Ps 4:9
158. Ps 26:4
159. 1 Pet 1:12
160. Ps 40:13
161. Ps 105:5

with pure gold, and in you they shall sing songs of joy, and in all your streets they shall say, alleluia"?[162]

O holy city, beautiful city, I hail you from afar. I cry out to you and seek you. I desire to see you and rest in you, but I cannot be there, held back as I am by the flesh. O city to be desired, the stones of your walls are one, your keeper is God. Your citizens are always glad, for they always enjoy the vision of God. In you there is nothing corrupt, nothing lacking, nothing old, nothing of anger, but perennial peace is there, solemn glory, eternal joy, continual festivity, true joy and exultation, the flower and beauty of youth and perfect health. There is in you no yesterday and no tomorrow but just today. Yesterday is your tomorrow, the day before is one and the same. Your health, your life and your peace are infinite, to you God is all. "Glorious things are spoken of you, city of God. All rejoicing dwells in you."[163] There is in you no fear, no sadness, all desire passes into joy since whatever is desired is at hand and whatever is wanted abounds. All your citizens receive joy in overflowing measure, all rejoice together and their rejoicing is without bounds. All their joys will be one when brethren live as one, where all agree in one.[164] All are made one, for he prayed for his family and because of his reverence he was worthy to obtain his prayer:[165] "As you, Father, are in me, and I in you, may they be one in us."[166] The whole city will rejoice, it will rejoice in its unity, it will rejoice as a city whose sharing is within itself. The spouse will rejoice in the kisses and embraces of the Bridegroom and will rejoice and exult with thanksgiving, praising him for ever and ever. As the bridegroom rejoices over the bride,[167] as the Lord rejoices in all his works,[168] seeing what he has made and that it is very good,[169] the

162. Tob 13:22
163. Ps 86:5, 7
164. Ps 132:1
165. Cf. Heb 5:7
166. Jn 17:21
167. Is 67:5
168. Ps 103:31
169. Gen 1:31

Father will rejoice that through the Only Begotten he has gained many sons by adoption. The Son will rejoice to be the first born of many brethren[170] whom he receives as worthy to be sharers in the inheritance of the Father. No less does the Holy Spirit take pleasure in them for by him they were adopted. New joys and ineffable prayers are sung by the neighboring angelic powers to the supreme Shepherd with the utmost gratitude for this good that he has found and in a wonderful way brought back the hundredth sheep.[171] In these is the Father's glory, in these the Spirit's delight, in these the Son exalts: heaven is filled with joy.[172] These indeed are those redeemed by the Lord, and they confess it with devotion, and say: "For he is good, for his mercy endures forever."[173] Eternal joy will be in them,[174] the praises of God in their mouths forever,[175] to ages of ages, in unending eternity.[176] Blessed are all that dwell in your house, O Lord. They will praise you forever.[177] They will be drunk with the riches of your house and you will give them to drink of the torrent of your pleasures, for with you is the well of life, and in your light shall we see light,[178] when we shall see you in yourself, and us in you, and you in us, in continual vision and perpetual happiness.

THE SEVEN DEGREES OF ACTION IN THE SOUL—THE CONTEMPLATION OF TRUTH—TRUE RELIGION[179]

61. The soul is simple in its essence; in its operations it is multiple. It has seven levels of acting, in which it shows its powers and potency. The first is giving life; the second is sense; the third, art; the fourth, correction; the fifth, tranquility or purity; the sixth, contemplation; the seventh, rest.

---

170. Rom 8:29
171. Cf. Lk 15:5-6
172. The last verse of a hymn used at the Divine Office on the feast of apostles.
173. Ps 106:1
174. Is 61:7
175. Ps 149:6
176. Dan 12:3
177. Ps 83:5
178. Ps 35:9-10
179. Dependent on *DQA* 33 and 36 and *Phys an* 14.

In the first stage or action, the presence of the soul makes the body come alive, gathers it into one and holds it together. In the second it goes out to make use of what is outside itself through the senses. In the third, it understands diverse arts. In the fourth, which is the beginning of all goodness and true praise, the soul cleanses itself from iniquity and prepares for purity. When it has cleansed itself from all dirt and washed off all stains, it keeps its purity. It is one thing to attain purity, another to keep it. Then with a certain innate and incredible confidence it enters into God, that is into contemplation of truth, and that is the sixth stage. In that vision or contemplation which is the seventh stage, which is rest or rather abiding, the soul stays there and rejoices; it is happy and takes delight. It is one thing to direct the eye of the mind toward what is to be seen, another to hold it there steadily.

The first stage we have in common with trees, the second with animals, the third with the learned and the unlearned. In the third stage, God binds the soul, that is he begins to lead it; in the fourth he purges it, in the fifth he confirms it, in the sixth he leads it home, in the seventh he feeds it. What can I say about the contemplation of truth? It is pleasure, it is celebration without end in the vision of God, the happiness of love without any lack. It is heat without suffering but rather with delight. What desire for vision with satiety and what satiety with desire! It is the fruit of the true and highest good, serenity, pleasantness and rejoicing. We believe what great and holy souls have said who have seen and see. If we ourselves undertake that course of life which God sets before us to hold to, if we hold on very constantly, through the grace of God we will come to that true and highest good. When we religiously, constantly, and vigilantly put into practice the commandments of God, we are pursuing the only way there is to flee from so much evil to so great a good. That religion is true in which the soul by reconciliation binds itself again to God from whom it has cut itself off by sin.

> The power of our soul lays claim to seven modes of action:
> It makes alive, it is aware, it follows various arts,
> Corrects excess, and makes for virtue,
> Directs all our gaze to God, rejoices in him.

The first is contained in seeds; brute animals share in the second.
There are two specific to our nature,
Bodies are made alive by the first act and grow;
Thence comes vigor, connections, complexity, movement,
And a particular state of being, a form, and a certain harmony.
From the next, we touch, see, hear, taste and smell,
Hate and love, seek what is good, avoid what is not;
This part of the soul is set free in sleep and wanders about in dreams.
It remembers things forgotten, looks ahead to what is to come,
And does many things which it learns from sense and not from reason.
The third mode does various clever things,
Carrying them out with ingenuity and discipline;
It gathers together and cleaves to ideas with various success.
In the fourth, the soul calls the man back from sin
And seeks to convince the mind of guilt and so a man
Begins to know himself, and learns to pass on to new beauty.
We learn in the fifth to hold to the natural law,
To avoid what is wrong by the love of virtue,
And to love what is right without making a test of it.
The sixth into the vision of the sun and the light of heaven
Snatches the cleansed soul almost equal to the angels.
The seventh binds the soul and is a pledge of stable love,
And joins it to God whom it now sees as its dowry.
What bridal chamber, what worship, what festivity shines there?
Who says, "Come, my bride? " It is said to blessed
And great souls, nor do they have that power
Nor that speech by which they can reveal these things
Which are beyond the power of knowledge and merit as a hidden reward.

WHAT THE NATURE OF THE SOUL SHOULD BE[180]

62. Hear now, O my soul, what you are and what you can be; I have heard of what kind you are and can be. You are

---

180. Dependent on Bernard of Clairvaux, *Sermones in Cantica* 83 and 85. This matter is also found in Pseudo-Bernard, *De cognitione humanae conditionis* 8.

burdened with sins, ensnared by vices, caught by allurements, captive in exile, emprisoned in a body, stuck in the mud, fixed in the mire, confined by your members, riddled with cares, dispersed in business, tensed by fears, afflicted with sorrows, wandering in error, uneasy with suspicion, anxious with trouble, a foreigner in the land of enemies, befouled with the dead, classed with those who go down into hell. If from such damnation and despair you wish to look for the hope of pardon and mercy, and take up the sweet yoke of love with the King of Angels, you must be modest, shy, truthful, timid, circumspect, admitting nothing that would take away the glory of your conscience.

Have nothing on your conscience for which you have to blush in the presence of truth, for which you would have to turn away your face from the light of God. And that this beauty may please God, go outside and pour it out through all the members and senses of the body, so that it may shine out in all actions, words, looks, in walking and laughing. Let mirth be mixed with gravity and full of honesty. Whatever movement, action or use of the whole body you make, let it be pure in act, modest, entirely without insolence or lust, levity or ignorance. Let your speech be sparing, your face happy, your appearance meek, your gait modest. Take care that beauty of soul and cleverness of mind go together with a good conscience to give you the reputation for integrity, so that, as the Apostle says, you may do good not only before God but also before men.[181] Such beauty leaves all other things and cleaves only to God, lives in God, loves nothing other than God and what is to be loved for the sake of God. Show yourself always careful to look for the Lord at his appearing,[182] that he may correct and illumine all your thought, that he may turn the virtue which he initiated in you into wisdom, and turn your beauty into rejoicing. Blessed is that soul to whom it is given here below to want the good and to know it and be capable of it, insofar as the will is present and ability is not lacking. Alas for me, that I should

181. 2 Cor 8:21
182. Ps 15:8

find all this in my memory and write it on the page, and yet not Lave it in my life. I have not written here what I am but what I wish to be, and I am ashamed not to be.

SEEKING GOD—WHAT GOD IS—THE IMAGE OF GOD IN OUR MINDS[183]

63. You have heard, my soul, what you should be. Go apart for a while from your usual concerns and leave aside for a space the tumult of your thoughts. Enter into the inner chamber of your mind and exclude everything except God and what will help you in seeking him; and when you have found him, rest a while in him. My soul, say to God: "Who are you, Lord, that I may know you? " You alone are what you are and who you are, that is, that than which nothing greater can be thought, nor anything better, nor more joyful. You are life, wisdom, light, truth, goodness, eternity, the highest good. You are complete fullness, lacking nothing, the one whom all need that they may exist and be happy. My soul, you have found what you were seeking; you were seeking God and you have found him to be the highest of all, that than which nothing greater can be thought, and this is life, wisdom, light, truth, goodness, eternal beatitude, blessed eternity and all that is good. God the Father, this good is you. And this good is also your Word, that is, your Son; for you are simple, and what is born of you is yourself. There is one love and communion between you and your Son which is the Holy Spirit who proceeds from you both. Nothing can proceed from that which is most simple other than itself. Thank you, Lord God, for giving me this grace, that I may seek you and find you. In my mind, which is your goodness which you have created in your image and likeness, I find a trinity, that is, memory, intelligence and love, by which I can remember you, understand you and love you. You remain in my memory, where I have known you; there I find you, when I remember you, and I delight in you. Remain there, most dear Lord, so that I may be able to find you there and

183. Dependent on Anselm's *Proslogion* 1, 22, 14, 23.

rest in you. This is my glory, here is my delight, here is the
joy of my heart, when I can be free for you and see what you
are. You are the highest essence, the highest life, the wisdom,
the highest salvation, the highest light, supreme greatness, the
highest beauty, the highest blessedness, the most perfect immortality, the ultimate in unchangeableness, the highest
unity, the supreme good in which is all goodness, even the
whole and one and total and only good.

AROUSING THE SOUL TO THINK OF THE HIGHEST GOOD, IN WHICH IS ALL GOOD[184]

64. Rouse yourself, my soul, and waken the whole of your
discernment; consider how great you can be, and the nature
and greatness of the goodness of God. If each single good is
delectable, consider how delectable is that good which contains the joy of all goods, not such as we are accustomed to
in created things, but as different as the Creator is from the
creature. If created life is good, how good will the Creator of
life be? If the fact of salvation is so joyous, how much more
joyous is the Salvation by which all are saved? If the wisdom
that knows created things is pleasant, how pleasant must be
that Wisdom which created all things out of nothing? Finally
if there are many and such great delights in delightful things,
how great and how many must be the delights in him who
made so much delight?

What will the man be like who enjoys this good and what
will he not be like? Surely he will be what he wants to be,
and he will not be what he does not want to be. In heaven
there are the goods of body and soul such as the eye has not
seen nor the ear heard, nor the heart of man thought.[185]
Little man, why do you wander about through many things,
seeking the good of your soul and body? Love the one good
in which are all goods and it suffices. Desire the simple good
which is all goods and it is enough. What do you love, my

184. Dependent on Anselm's *Proslogion* 24-25 and Augustine, *De civitate Dei*
22, 29-30. Some of this material appears in the Pseudo-Bernard, *De conscientia,*
14.
185. Is 64:6; 1 Cor 2:9

flesh? What, O my soul, do you desire? Whatever you have loved is there, whatever you have desired is there. If beauty delights you, "The just shall shine as the sun."[186] If you delight in swiftness, strength or a freedom of the body which nothing can hold back, "They are like the angels of God,"[187] "for that which was sown an animal body is raised a spiritual body,"[188] by power not by nature. If you take pleasure in a long life and good health, there is there a healthy eternity and eternal health, for "the righteous live forevermore,"[189] and "the salvation of the just is from God."[190] If you desire satiety, "they shall be satisfied when the glory of the Lord shall appear."[191] If you want to drink, "They shall drink of the riches of the house of God."[192] If what you love is song, the choir of angels sing together to God without end. If you long for any pleasure that is pure, "the Lord shall make them to drink of the torrent of the pleasures of God."[193] If it is wisdom you seek, "they shall all be taught of God."[194] Wisdom itself will show itself to them as it is. If you want friendship, they will love God there more than themselves and each other like themselves; and God will love them more than they love themselves because it is he that they love in themselves and in each other, and he loves them in himself. If what you seek is unity, they shall all have one will, for there will be nothing there except the sole will of God. If you want power, "they shall enter into the power of the Lord,"[195] and their wills will be all powerful like their God. For just as God can do what he wants through himself, they can do what they want through him. Just as they have no will apart from his, so whatever they will, he wills; and whatever he wills, cannot not be. If you long for honor and riches, "God

186. Mt 13:43
187. Mt 22:30
188. 1 Cor 15:44
189. Wis 5:16
190. Ps 36:39
191. Ps 16:15
192. Ps 35:9
193. Ibid.
194. Jn 6:45
195. Ps 70:16

will place his good and faithful servants over many things."[196]
Moreover, they will be called and will be gods, and sons of
God, for where the Son is they also will be,[197] heirs of God
and co-heirs with Christ.[198] If it is true security you want,
certainly there they can be sure that their good will never be
exhausted, and they can be equally sure that of their own
free will they will never depart from it, nor will God who
loves them take it away from his beloved ones against their
will.

What joys are these and how great are they. Where is such
and so great a good to be found? Heart of man, needy heart,
heart experienced in wretchedness, weighed down with
misery, how greatly would you rejoice if you abounded in all
these things? Ask your inner self if it is capable of the joy of
such great beautitude. If someone whom you love in every
way as yourself were to have the same beatitude, your joy
would be doubled, for you would rejoice no less for him than
for yourself. If two or three or many more have the same
bliss, you would rejoice for each one as for yourself, if you
love each one as yourself. So in that perfect charity of the
innumerable blessed angels and men, where no one loves
another less than himself, joy will be without number. If the
heart of man can scarcely contain his own joy in such a good
of his own, how can he hold so many and such great joys in
that perfect happiness? Where everyone loves God incom-
parably more than himself and all others along with him, he
will rejoice inestimably more for the happiness of God than
for his own and for all others. So they love God with their
whole heart and mind and soul, since the whole heart alone is
not sufficient for such loving. They rejoice with their whole
heart, but it is not sufficient for such fullness of joy, so great
it is. God of infinite mercy, fount of all goodness and piety,
make us partakers of such great joys. You are the fullness of
joy, the highest bliss; you are that than which nothing better
can be desired, nothing more blessed or more useful possessed.

196. Mt 25:23
197. Jn 17:24
198. Rom 8:17

THE THREEFOLD ENJOYMENT OF GOD BY THE BLESSED—THE THREE
POWERS OF THE SOUL IMPLANTED IN THE BLESSED—THE FOUR
GIFTS OF THE GLORIOUS BODY: IMMORTALITY
IMPASSIBILITY, AGILITY AND BEAUTY

65. In that eternal beatitude and perfection we enjoy God
in three ways: seeing him in all creatures, having him in ourselves, and what will be more joyous and blessed than all,
knowing the Trinity itself and comtemplating with the pure
eyes of the heart that glory without any shadow. This is life,
eternal and perfect, that we should know the Father and the
Son[199] with the Holy Spirit and see God as he is,[200] that is,
not in the way he is in us or in creatures, but as he is in
himself. How great is that blessedness, how hidden from our
eyes. Eye has not seen, nor ear heard, nor has it entered into
the heart of man, how great a charity, sweetness and joy
awaits us in the knowledge.[201] The peace of God in this surpasses all knowledge and understanding[202] and therefore how
much more beyond all our words? What it has been given to
none to experience, no one can try to explain. The Lord
says: "He will give good gifts without measure into your
bosoms, conferred (upon the inner man), shaken together (in
the outer man) and running over (in God himself)."[203] There
is the peak of happiness, there is the high point of glory,
there is overflowing blessedness. How this is to be seen in
creatures and to be possessed by us, we can conjecture in
part, in that we have already received the first fruits of the
Spirit.[204]

Knowledge as it is in God is unknown to us here, it is a
wonder and a strength of which we are not yet capable.[205]
Insofar as it is to be seen in what is created, we can in some
way know it when and in the way it is seen in them. Whence
the Apostle testifies: "The invisible things of God have been
perceived in the things that have been made."[206] However far a
man progresses in understanding the power, goodness and

199. Jn 17:3
200. 1 Jn 3:2
201. Cf. 1 Cor 2:9
202. Phil 4:7
203. Lk 6:38

204. Rom 8:23
205. Ps 143:6.
206. Rom 1:20.

prudence of the eternal Majesty who has made all things and rules and orders all things, yet he understands only a little about him. The time will come when by vision and contemplation and ineffable joy we will follow the Lamb wherever he goes, and will follow him in all creatures, that we may rejoice in them all.[207] We will rejoice for the sake of no one but God, just as he does not find his enjoyment in any other than himself. Insofar as this may be in us, we are able to know now in part.

There is a threefold nature in the soul. The wise men of the world have handed on to us that there are in the human soul reason, positive appetite and negative appetite. We learn by nature itself and by daily experience about this triple power of the soul. Along with reason go knowledge and ignorance, as a habit or a privation. With the positive appetite are longing or contempt and with the negative appetite are joy or wrath. The Lord will fill our reason with the light of wisdom, so that "there will not be lacking in us any knowledge."[208] He will fill our positive appetite from the fount of justice so that we will desire it alone and we shall be filled with it as Scripture says: "Blessed are they who hunger and thirst after righteousness for they shall be filled."[209] No other thing can fulfill the longing of the soul, nothing else save righteousness can make the soul blessed. When God fills our positive appetite with righteousness whatever the soul ought to cast off it will cast off, whatever it ought to desire it will desire, and among all these it will desire the more what is to be the more desired. Rightly then we attribute righteousness to our positive appetite, by which we shall be regarded as just or unjust. When God fills that in us which is called the negative appetite, it will become in us tranquility and we shall be filled with the peace of God in the height of joy and rejoicing. See how in these three there is perfect happiness as far as the soul is concerned, when knowledge already does not puff up[210]

207. Cf. Rev 14:4
208. 1 Cor 1:7
209. Mt 5:6
210. Cf. 1 Cor 13:4

because of righteousness, does not sadden because of joy. So
the proverb ceases to be true that "he who increases in
knowledge increases in sorrow,"[211] when righteousness will
not be indiscreet because of knowledge, nor burdensome
because of joy, when joy will not be suspect because of
knowledge, nor impure because of righteousness.

But in all this our external man receives nothing. For him
therefore, "so that glory may dwell in our land,"[212] and according to the Prophet, "the whole earth may be filled with
the majesty of the Lord,"[213] four things must be sought, as is
certain from the four elements of which he is made up. Do
not wonder that many seem in need, for this is a place of
need. As the Prophet says in the Psalm, "My soul thirsts for
you, my flesh longs after you."[214] Our earth will have immortality, it need not fear that it will return to the dust. Our
body will rise again, now to die no more, for death will have
no more dominion over it.[215] Of what use is it[216] if it comes
to pass that the body lives with miseries and the wretchedness of the ability to suffer by which this incorruptible part
too incessantly afflicts it; if it dies not once and for all, but is
always dying? From God it will have incorruptibility in
every way, for its disordered humors come from the passions,
as they say. In so far as our body is partly made of air, it
desires lightness, not to be weighed down with trouble. We
believe that the future lightness and agility of the bodies of
good men will be so great that they will be able to follow
without delay or difficulty the very speed of our thoughts in
all things. What else is lacking to the body's perfect beatitude? Only beauty. We will have this in perfection, and we
attribute it to that part of us that is fire. For as the Apostle
says: "We look for a Savior who will change the body of our
humiliation making it like to his glorious body, as it is prom-

211. Eccles 1:18
212. Ps 84:10
213. Ps 71:19
214. Ps 62:2
215. Rom 6:9
216. Reading *quid proderit* as the note in the PL edition suggests, rather than
the *sed prodiderit* as in the text.

ised."[217] And "the just shall shine as the sun in the kingdom of the Father."[218]

God will fill our souls with perfect knowledge, righteousness and joy; and his Majesty will fill all our earth when he makes the body immortal, impassible, agile and like unto his glorious body. And then indeed it can be said with a certain poet: "thrice and four times blessed."[219] No one can really think how great that joy and glory will be when we see God present everywhere, and governing the universe. And so he will be known and clear to us, so that he may be seen by the spirit of each, may be seen by the one in the other, may be seen in himself, and may be seen in the new heaven and new earth[220] and in everything which has now been created. Free from all ill and filled with perfect good, we shall rest and we shall see what God is,[221] and we shall be filled when he is all in all.[222] He will be the end of our desiring when we shall see him without end, love him without wearying, praise him without tiring. For whom is such pleasure in store? Without doubt those who are found faithful in the care of the little they have received in this time of service, that is, faithful in the care of the senses, the actions and the desires which they have received to control, so that they are shown to be faithful to their Lord.[223] The servant of Christ knows how to possess his vessel in sanctification and honor,[224] and he glorifies and bears about God in his body[225] and he follows after peace.[226] Amen.

217. Phil 3:20-21
218. Mt 13:44
219. Virgil, *Aeneid* 1:98
220. Rev 21:1
221. Ps 45:11
222. 1 Cor 15:28
223. Cf. Mt 25:21
224. 1 Thess 4:4
225. 1 Cor 6:20
226. Heb 12:14.

INDEX

References are the page numbers.
For Latin equivalents of the English terms used here, see 'A Note on the Translation', pp. 94–100.

CISTERCIAN
PUBLICATIONS

Titles Listing

1977

THE CISTERCIAN FATHERS SERIES

THE WORKS OF BERNARD OF CLAIRVAUX

Treatises I (*Apologia* to Abbot William, On Precept and Dispensation)   CF 1

On the Song of Songs I   CF 4

On the Song of Songs II   CF 7

Treatises II (The Steps of Humility, On Loving God)   CF 13

Five Books on Consideration   CF 37

THE WORKS OF WILLIAM OF ST THIÉRRY

On Contemplating God, Prayer, Meditations   CF 3

Exposition on the Song of Songs   CF 6

The Enigma of Faith   CF 9

The Golden Epistle   CF 12

THE WORKS OF AELRED OF RIEVAULX

Treatises I (On Jesus at the Age of Twelve, Rule for a Recluse, The Pastoral Prayer)   CF 2

Spiritual Friendship   CF 5

THE WORKS OF GUERRIC OF IGNY

Liturgical Sermons
two volumes   CF 8, CF 32

OTHER WRITERS

The Letters of Adam of Perseigne   CF 21

The Way of Love   CF 16

John of Ford, *Sermons on The Song of Songs*   CF 29

THE CISTERCIAN STUDIES SERIES

CISTERCIAN STUDIES

The Cistercian Spirit: A Symposium in Memory of Thomas Merton   CS 3·

The Eleventh-century Background of Citeaux by Bede Lackner   CS 8

Studies in Medieval Cistercian History, edited Joseph F. O'Callahan   CS 13

Contemplative Community edited M. Basil Pennington   CS 21

Bernard of Clairvaux: Studies Presented to Dom Jean Leclercq   CS 23

William of St Thierry: The Man and His Work by J. M. Dechanet   CS 10

Thomas Merton: The Man and His Work by Dennis Q. McInerny   CS 27

Cistercian Sign Language by Robert Barakat   CS 11

Studies in Medieval Cistercian History, II ed. John R. Sommerfeldt   CS 24

Bernard of Clairvaux and the Cistercian Spirit by Jean Leclercq   CS 16

MONASTIC TEXTS AND STUDIES

The Climate of Monastic Prayer by Thomas Merton   CS 1

Evagrius Ponticus: Praktikos and Chapters on Prayer   CS 4

The Abbot in Monastic Tradition by Pierre Salmon   CS 14

Why Monks? by Francois Vandenbroucke   CS 17

Silence: Silence in the Rule of St Benedict by Ambrose Wathen   CS 22

The Sayings of the Desert Fathers tr Benedicta Ward   CS 59

One Yet Two: Monastic Tradition East and West   CS 29

The Spirituality of Western Christendom ed. E. R. Elder   CS 30

Russian Mystics by Sergius Bolshakoff   CS 26

In Quest of The Absolute by Joseph Weber   CS 51